FOR THEM
THE WAR WAS NOT OVER

THE ROYAL NAVY IN RUSSIA 1918–1920

FOR THEM

THE WAR WAS NOT OVER

THE ROYAL NAVY IN RUSSIA 1918–1920

MICHAEL WILSON

The
History
Press

For my beloved wife,
Yvonne,
with all my love
for ever —
'To infinity and beyond'

First published 2010

The History Press
The Mill, Brimscombe Port
Stroud, Gloucestershire, GL5 2QG
www.thehistorypress.co.uk

© Michael Wilson, 2010

British Library Cataloguing in Publication Data.
A catalogue record for this book is available from the British Library.

ISBN 978 0 7524 4699 8

Typesetting and origination by The History Press
Printed in Great Britain

CONTENTS

ACKNOWLEDGEMENTS

I would like to express my gratitude to all those who have helped me with their time, knowledge and for sharing information held by them, which has played a large part in my attempt in telling the story of the Royal Navy in this little known War of Intervention in Russia. Their help has also been vital in helping to unravel the complex diplomatic and political aspects of this episode of history.

I wish to thank Commander W.J. ('Jock') Gardner RN, a former colleague at the Naval Historical Branch in London and Mr David Brown the one-time Head of Branch; Mr Philip Brace, of the MOD Information Centre; Mr Jerry Shore, of the Fleet Air Arm Museum at Yeovilton; Mr M.G. Little and Major A. Donald RM, of the Royal Marines Museum in Portsmouth; Mr Paul Evans, of the Royal Artillery Museum at Woolwich; Mr Guy Revell, of the RAF Museum at Hendon; Captain M. Gordon-Lennox RN, of the Coastal Forces Museum at Portsmouth and Dr John Montgomery, librarian at the Royal United Services Institute.

I also thank Colonel D. de Cock of the Belgian Embassy in London; Dr Richard Boijen, Head of the Documentation Centre of the Royal Army Museum in Brussels; and Mr Iben Bjørnsson of the Royal Danish Embassy in London. I am also indebted to the staff of the Stato Maggiore della Marina in Rome.

I am grateful to Mr Eryl Humphrey-Jones of Constable & Robinson Ltd for permission to quote the passage from *Nurse at the Russian Front* by Florence Farmborough, which appears in Chapter 5. In addition I would like to thank Mr Rodney Bennett, author of *Freeing the Baltic*, Mr Nik Cornish, author of *The Russian Army and the First World War*, and Major General Clifford Kinvig, author of *Churchill's Crusade*, for their kindness and help while writing this history.

My thanks also go to Ms Jennie Norberry of the Australian War Memorial, Canberra; to Ms Keeley Gibson of the British Library; to Ms Katie Simpson and Ms Marcelle Adamson of the Illustrated London News Picture Library; to Mr Antony Staunton, the Editor of *Sabretache* (the journal of the Military History Society of Australia); to Mr Allan Harris of the International Naval Research Organisation and Editor of their journal, *Warship International*; and also to Mr Brian Head and Commander John Guard.

Finally, no words can adequately express my thanks to my darling wife, Yvonne, for her love, help, endless patience, rock-steady support and constant encouragement while I have been writing this book. Her boundless enthusiasm for this project has become apparent on every page.

'If men could learn from history, what lessons might it teach us!
But passion and party blind our eyes, and the light which experience
gives is a lantern on the stern, which shines only on the waves behind us.'

Samuel Taylor Coleridge,
18 December 1831

INTRODUCTION

'There is no British policy, unless seven policies at once could be called a policy.' This remark is attributed to Bruce Lockhart, the one-time British Consul-General in Moscow, referring to how the Government in London seemed to regard the period from the outbreak of the Revolution in 1917 to the final withdrawal of British forces from Russia in 1920.

Intervention by Allied and American forces in Russia developed on an *ad hoc* basis in four different arenas at four different times even before the war with Germany was over. British forces became involved in North Russia around the ports of Murmansk and Archangel, in the Caucasus and Caspian Sea, and in the Far East, eventually stretching thousands of miles along the railway from the port of Vladivostok across the Urals and into European Russia. In the Black Sea area, intervention had to wait until the defeat of Turkey gave access through the Dardanelles. Since 1914 there had been a British Submarine Flotilla in the Baltic working with the Russians; the boats were scuttled in 1918 and further operations by the British in that area had to wait for the Armistice with Germany. In 1919 the Baltic became the most important theatre of British operations – and the most beneficial, both militarily and politically. Intervention here was a special and unique event.

Each area became involved for different reasons and each saw the introduction of forces from one or more of the Allied Powers at different times. Only one factor was common – the Royal Navy was present in every case.

Within twelve months of the end of the war with Germany, Allied intervention in Russia had developed into a fiasco. Most of the original reasons for an Allied presence no longer applied and the White Russian forces, who had been expected to crush the Bolshevik revolution, were in retreat. The British Government – arguably at one time the most fervent supporter of the idea of intervention – was coming to realise that the price in men and material was too high. The British forces, the Americans and the other Allied Powers involved were gradually withdrawn, leaving the Bolsheviks to defeat their fellow Russians and take full control.

The Bolsheviks were the major force in Russian politics at the time of the Revolution. They had split away from the Russian Social Democratic Labour Party in 1903; two factions were formed, the Bolsheviks and Mensheviks. The latter were in the minority and were considered to be the party of the socialist intellectuals and middle class. The Bolsheviks later became the Communists, emphasising their complete separation from any moderate or parliamentary socialism. At first there were many other parties with varying shades of revolutionary fervour, but gradually all were either disbanded, their members drifted away or were killed, or absorbed by the Bolsheviks.

The term Bolsheviks has been used extensively in this narrative, for that is how they were known initially, and the change to Communists was not universal by the time the Intervention forces withdrew from Russia. British troops frequently used the term 'Bolos' to refer to the enemy soldiers.

The Russian word *soviet* means council. After the Revolution the word became associated specifically with a council elected by members of working-class economic organisations or of deputies representing soldiers or sailors. Eventually, it became the term for the Government of post-revolutionary Communist Russia.

Finally, the Russian troops of those forces fighting to restore a form of Government in Russia similar to that in power before 1917 were known as 'Whites'. This was to contrast with the 'Reds' or Bolshevik forces, who fought under the revolutionary Red Flag.

ONE

THE PATH TO REVOLUTION

Since the time of the earliest Tsars their successors had followed a policy of ensuring that all political power was kept in their hands. The nobles, for their part, held virtually autocratic rule over the serfs, who lived in a state closer to slavery than peasantry. By the nineteenth century both relationships were under attack. In 1825 a group of junior military officers, seeking to force the adoption of a constitutional monarchy, tried to prevent the accession of Tsar Nicholas I. They failed – and their ideals were brutally suppressed.

For the remainder of the nineteenth century, Russia was torn by periods of dissent against the regime and shorter periods of very gentle and slow reform. During the reign of Nicholas I there were over 500 peasant uprisings. Among reforms instituted by Alexander II, Nicholas I's liberally minded son, serfdom was abolished in 1861, but the progress of reform came to an end after an assassination attempt on the Tsar in 1866. Both Alexander III and Nicholas II, who succeeded him, were autocratic by nature and determined to prevent the spread of reform or democracy.

At the time of his accession Nicholas was presented with a loyal address by some local elders. It included a wish for greater local government. In his reply he stated: 'Let every man know that while devoting all my strength to the well-being of my people I shall uphold the principle of autocracy as firmly and as undeviatingly as did my late father.' On the day of his coronation in Moscow a crowd of enthusiastic spectators stampeded and 2,000 people were killed. It was generally expected that a ceremonial ball to be held that evening would be cancelled as a mark of respect for the dead. However, the ball took place as if nothing had happened, and the Tsar and Tsarina opened the dancing. Nicholas remained remote from his subjects for all of his reign.

In 1897 the Russians leased Port Arthur from the Chinese, which gave them a vital Pacific Ocean base and port which was ice-free throughout the year. In the next few years the Russians set about extending their influence in Manchuria and Korea, leading the Japanese to fear that their own aims in this area would be totally negated. On 8 February 1904 the Japanese struck without warning at Port Arthur, leaving one Russian battleship sunk and two badly damaged. The Russian Far East Fleet became effectively blockaded in Port Arthur, as in successive sorties the fleet failed to break out, suffered further casualties and became increasingly demoralised.

On 1 May a Russian army was defeated on the Yalu River, the border between Korea and Manchuria. For the first time since the fourteenth century a European army had been beaten by an Oriental one; the significance of the battle reverberated far and wide. More immediately, the Russian armies were forced north into Manchuria and could give less support to their forces besieged in Port Arthur.

In June 1904 it was decided to send naval reinforcements to the Far East from the Baltic. Basically, the Russians had to send a fleet of over forty miscellaneous vessels, including supply and hospital ships, over 18,000 miles around the Cape of Good Hope to link up with the ships in Port Arthur and then destroy the Japanese. The fleet included four new battleships but were otherwise a motley collection of ships of varying ages and efficiency. All were from the Baltic Fleet. The ships, the Second Pacific Squadron as they were known, finally sailed in October under the command of Rear Admiral Zinovy Rozhestvensky.

Almost from the start events did not go well for Rozhestvensky. As the squadron entered the North Sea on the evening of 21 October, the captain of the supply ship *Kamchatka* – some accounts say that he was drunk at the time – reported that he was being attacked by a passing Japanese warship. The ship was in fact a Swedish merchant ship and, of course, there was no attack. Later that night officers on duty in some of the ships reported the presence of Japanese torpedo boats. There were no Japanese ships, only thirty British fishing vessels. One British trawler was sunk and others damaged as the Russians opened fire on 'the enemy'. Two men were killed and six wounded. In the ensuing panic some Russian ships, including the cruiser *Aurora* which was rejoining, were hit.

The incident led to a serious diplomatic war of words between the two Governments. Hawkish British newspapers demanded retaliatory action by the Royal Navy. It was a particularly dangerous situation for the Russians, as the British had an alliance with the Japanese. Meanwhile, the Royal Navy shadowed the Russian Fleet as it continued on its way through the Channel to the Spanish port of Vigo, where it was scheduled to take on coal. Before its fleet sailed again, the Russian Government agreed to investigate the incident thoroughly and pay £65,000 compensation to the fishermen.

The whole Dogger Bank Incident, as it came to be known, could only have added to Rozhestvensky's worries. It highlighted not only the complete naivety of some Russian officers in believing that a Japanese fleet could be present so far from home, but also the lack of professionalism and discipline in the Russian ships.

A second group of naval reinforcements left the Baltic in December. The ships of the Third Pacific Squadron were even more aged and less reliable or efficient than those of the Second. They had the advantage of being allowed to pass through the Suez Canal and were to meet up with the other ships off French Indo-China (now Vietnam). Despite their old age, there was no chance of refitting or overhauling the ships before they sailed; the dockyard workmen in Libau and elsewhere were seething with unrest and strikes were commonplace.

On 2 January 1905 the Russians scuttled the remaining ships of their Far East Fleet and blew up the defences; Port Arthur surrendered. The siege had lasted 148 days and cost the Japanese 60,000 casualties – more than double those suffered by the Russians.

By the time the two squadrons of reinforcements had reached the Far East and were united the fortress of Port Arthur had fallen; they could only go on to Vladivostok. They took the shortest route, passing between Japan and Korea through the Tsushima Straits. On the morning of 27 May 1906 this incredible collection of ships – hardly a fleet – met the Japanese. By the time the battle was over the Russian squadrons had been annihilated. Six battleships were captured, later to be refitted and incorporated into the Japanese Navy. Only one light cruiser and two destroyers reached Vladivostok. Another cruiser[1] and some transports were interned in Shanghai, and three cruisers[2] were interned by the Americans in Manila.

Meanwhile, the Russian Army had been humiliated further in several battles in Manchuria after surrendering Port Arthur. Peace was brokered by the American President Theodore Roosevelt and signed in Portsmouth, New Hampshire, in September 1905, leaving the Tsar's Asiatic ambitions in ruins. The Russians then had the task of not only rebuilding their fleet but of restoring the shattered morale of both army and navy. During the war the Russian infantryman had fought stoically but they had been let down by sheer incompetence of command, administrative inefficiency and corruption, as well as the general lack of unity of the nation. It was these lessons of the war that had to be learned and rectified before 1914. They were not.

While the war was being fought in the East, European Russia was suffering once again from widespread dissatisfaction. The Russian capital, St Petersburg[3], was in the grip of industrial unrest. Strikes, which had begun with a demand for a minimum wage and an eight-hour day in a munitions factory, soon spread to the shipbuilding yards and to most of the factories throughout the city, crossing the enormous gulf that existed between the classes in Tsarist Russia. The situation began peacefully enough but ended in bloodshed because of the total misjudgment of the situation by the Tsar himself and his advisers.

The strikers planned a peaceful march to the Winter Palace to present a petition to the Tsar. Unbeknown to the marchers, Nicholas and his family were not in residence but had left the capital for Christmas and were at the Alexander Palace at Tsarskoe Selo, about 15 miles away. No one thought it necessary to inform the organisers of the march of this fact, nor did the authorities think to inform the Tsar that a mass demonstration was to take place with the ultimate aim of presenting him with a petition.

On 9 January 1905 (by the Russian calendar)[4] a great crowd of workers, with their wives and children and accompanied by numerous priests, set out through the icy windswept streets of the capital for the Winter Palace. Nearing the palace, they found further progress blocked by the police and Cossack cavalry. The demonstration was broken up with the loss of over 100 lives and with many more wounded.

In the following months the story of unrest and industrial disorder was repeated elsewhere throughout European Russia. Even the Black Sea Fleet, the only major part of the navy not affected by the disasters in the Far East at the hands of the Japanese, became involved with revolutionary fervour. Throughout the fleet political agitators were at work, spreading their own brand of disaffection and inciting the crews of the ships to join the workers ashore in their protests against the Government.

In this volatile atmosphere the new battleship *Kniaz Potemkin Tavrichesky*[5] was known to be amongst the most loyal of the Commander-in-Chief's ships. On 27 June 1905 this changed, with fatal consequences. The clash with authority began with a protest over maggoty meat, which had been pronounced as fit to eat by the ship's doctor. The ensuing events were handled badly by the ship's senior officers and soon escalated into open mutiny. Seven officers, including the captain, were killed in thirty minutes of pitiless violence.

The crew of the torpedo boat N267, in company with the battleship, was persuaded to join the mutiny and for several days the two ships roamed the Black Sea, defying the Government and the rest of the fleet, their crews unsure what to do next. Their actions off the port of Odessa were to bring them legendary fame with the release in the 1920s of the film *The Battleship Potemkin*. They eventually sought refuge in the Romanian port of Constanza, where the crew was allowed to stay after scuttling their ship. The battleship was subsequently raised and taken back to Sevastopol, where it was refitted and renamed *Panteleimon*.

In November 1905 there was fresh trouble in Sevastopol. A regiment of infantry mutinied and among those released from prison was a naval lieutenant named Petr Schmidt, who was serving a sentence for subversive activities. He soon managed to persuade the crews of a cruiser and four destroyers to join the mutiny. The uprising was quelled by loyal troops and Schmidt was recaptured. He was executed in March 1906 along with three sailors; their bodies were buried at sea to prevent a pilgrimage to the graves.

Not even the rump of the Baltic Fleet, those ships which had not been sent to destruction in the Far East, was immune from trouble. The old cruiser *Pamiat Azova* was the centre of further unrest. As a result the ship lost the right to fly a special ensign, a distinction given in recognition of the services of a previous ship, the flagship *Azova*, at the Battle of Navorino in 1827. The cruiser's name was changed to *Dvina* on the orders of the Tsar.

The country gradually returned to a sort of peace. The price of what Lenin was later to call a 'dress rehearsal' for 1917 was high for Nicholas. This ultra-reactionary Tsar, weak-willed, obstinate and suspicious of all advice, was forced to summon the Duma, or Parliament. Immediately there was a clash of wills; while Nicholas wanted a reconstruction programme for the navy to begin without delay, the Duma would not vote the necessary money until an inquiry had been held into its shortcomings in the war against Japan. This led to a delay of two years out of the all too short time before war broke out again. It was the spring of 1908 before the Minister of the Navy was given money for four new battleships, three submarines and a depot ship for the Baltic Fleet and similar construction for the Black Sea Fleet.

Finland provided different problems for the Tsar. From the twelfth century until the eighteenth the people were vassals of the Swedes, after which the country became a Russian Grand Duchy. Alexander I had allowed the Finns to keep their elected Parliament, or Diet, and their Swedish-based constitution. However, Nicholas II had other ideas. In 1899 he abolished the right of the Diet to enact its own legislation and gave a Russian Governor-General dictatorial powers. Unsurprisingly, this gave rise to considerable discontent and led to a general strike and the assassination of the Governor-General in 1904. Anti-Russian feelings were widespread and the clash with authority was bloody and brutal. The all-embracing extent of the trouble surprised the Tsar and he found that he had to restore the situation to that which prevailed before 1899.

The desire of the Tsar to bring these independently minded subjects more fully under his rule brought about further clashes with authority in the years up to 1914, as Nicholas imposed ever more restrictive measures.

Across the Gulf of Finland lay Estonia and further south Latvia and Lithuania. All three formed part of the Russian Empire. The greater cause for unrest in these areas was the influence of the Baltic Barons, the nineteenth-century version of the largely German Teutonic Knights. The German influence of these Barons was to play a large part in the troubled area in the years immediately after the end of the war in 1918.

By 1914 Russia was a seething cauldron of discontent. The Tsar regained some popularity at the time of the outbreak of war, when the people felt a pride in their army and believed that it would easily smash the Germans in Prussia. This feeling soon changed as the casualties were counted in hundreds of thousands and people became aware of the lack of equipment for the troops, the blatant corruption of officials and the poor direction of the war. It was not a question of 'if' but 'when' a revolution would occur.

TWO

THE END OF THE BEGINNING

In September 1914 two British 'E' class submarines entered the Baltic through the Kattegat and began operations against the Germans. Despite the fact that the Russians were not informed of this deployment before the submarines arrived, the intention was that they should work with the Russian Submarine Flotilla; it was a way of showing support. They were to be based in Revel (now Tallinn) in Estonia. Eventually, the flotilla was reinforced to a strength of five 'E' class submarines, of which one subsequently was sunk while on patrol. Two other submarines failed to enter the Baltic; one returned to base, the other stranded in shallow water off Denmark and was shelled by the Germans before being scuttled. In 1916 four 'C' class submarines were added to the flotilla; they were towed to Archangel and then ingeniously carried on barges down the rivers and canals to Petrograd[1].

In late December 1915 the Armoured Car Division of the Royal Naval Air Service, raised and commanded by Commander Oliver Locker Lamson RNVR, arrived in Murmansk. With the arrival of better weather in the spring of 1916 the cars began a remarkable saga of distinguished service on different fronts in Russia, including the Caucasus, Galicia and Romania[2].

The British submariners, wintering in their base at Revel, were very much aware of the mood of intense dissatisfaction that prevailed among the Russian middle and working classes as 1916 gave way to 1917. The ruling class in Russia continued to act as before and either ignored all the signs or deluded themselves into believing that events would not get any worse.

On 26 February 1917 (by the Russian calendar) small-scale disturbances broke out in Petrograd, where a high proportion of the Russian war industry was located and where as many as one-fifth of all the 250,000 workers were employed in only five factories. On that day crowds of up to 500 people gathered to march through the streets. They sang the revolutionary *Marseillaise*, shouted slogans and, inevitably, smashed a few windows. As the days went by the crowds grew larger as more and more workers went on strike. In those last days of February it was significant that the problems of daily life – poor pay and shortages of food – were foremost in driving the people to action, rather than any political agenda.

One account of the time records an unusually quiet city with no trams running and the streets almost deserted. Then, at a major junction, groups of women began assembling, with mounted police riding into the crowds and using the flat of their swords to try and disperse the throng. Cursing their heavy-handed attackers, the protesters parted to avoid the horses, only to re-assemble after the police had ridden on.

By 8 March the shortage of food in the capital led to the outbreak of serious rioting, with several bakeries and food stores being broken into and looted. The Cossacks, normally stalwart bastions of authority, were called in to help the police control the crowds but they carried out their duties with less than their customary zeal. On the 10th the Tsar ordered General Khabalov, the Garrison Commander, to suppress the demonstrations with all the force at his command.

However, Khabalov could no longer rely on the discipline of his troops. The army as a whole had already lost millions of men either as casualties or prisoners of war; the remaining units were too diluted by wartime conscripts who only wanted an end to the war and feared being sent to the front with poor, or even no, equipment. Regiment after regiment of the garrison mutinied, slaughtered many of their officers and joined the crowds on the streets.

12 March 1917 is the day regarded as the start of the Russian Revolution. The temperature had dropped below zero degrees Fahrenheit, there was no bread, little fuel for heating and no transport in the capital. The police were unable to restore order and most of the troops had mutinied.

Russian sailors of the Baltic Fleet soon followed suit. Men in shore establishments around the capital, having little to do over the winter months and with their officers more concerned with their own welfare than that of their men, travelled to the city and joined the rioters and mutinous soldiers. The captain of the cruiser *Aurora*, which was refitting in a nearby shipyard, was shot and killed while remonstrating with a mob who had boarded his ship.

At the great naval base at Kronstadt on Kotlin Island there were thousands of sailors in various stages of recruit training or undergoing courses. There were also a number of prison hulks and detention centres, full of offenders who would be undesirable in any ship but who could not be discharged because of the war. In these circumstances the base – only 20 miles across the water from the capital – was ripe for trouble.

When the Revolution broke out Commander Francis Cromie, the Commanding Officer of the British Submarine Flotilla, was in Petrograd for a few days of well-earned leave. He stayed in the Hotel Astoria, a military hotel catering for foreign officers as well as Russians on leave with their families. Coincidentally, also a guest in the hotel at the same time was Commander Oliver Locker Lamson. Both Cromie and Locker Lamson recorded their impressions of the outbreak of the Revolution in letters, both of them stressing that in their opinion it was something affecting the Russians only, and at that stage foreigners – particularly the British – were not maltreated.

Cromie had arrived in Petrograd on 12 March and was taken by Colonel Alfred Knox, the Military Attaché, to stay at the Astoria. Knox told Cromie that he considered the disorders as quite minor affairs – arguably the understatement of the period! That morning a crowd had gone to the Duma and asked the Minister of the Interior to meet their delegates. He refused. The Minister reported the situation to the Tsar, who responded by suspending the Duma. The members expressed their regrets and ended proceedings immediately, meeting again elsewhere in the name of the people to restore order in the city

Troops who were ordered to fire on the crowds immediately sided with the people, disarming their officers; any resistance meant death. Sporadic firing broke out all over the city, two of the worst areas being around the Duma and the Arsenal. That afternoon the mob burnt the Regional Assize Court – with much of its necessary paperwork – and many of the prisons, freeing all the inmates, criminal as well as political. The Government could rely on only two regiments and the police, who still held a few areas of the city in fairly good order. However, during the course of the day there were many casualties on both sides.

At about one o'clock the following morning trouble began around the Astoria. Commander Eady, the Assistant British Naval Attaché, went down to see what was happening and was met by a Russian officer who wept on his neck, beseeching Eady to save him. Eady arranged for all the foreign officers, led by Major General Poole, Head of the British Military Supply Mission, to assemble in the vestibule. The Russian officers were sent upstairs and told to stay quietly out of the way. When the yelling mob entered the hotel they were surprised to find only foreign officers gathered to meet them. They quietened and began to listen to reason. After searching one or two rooms, they left the building.

Later that morning a policeman started to fire on the mob from the roof of the hotel. Instantly, the crowd burst back into the building, shouting and firing indiscriminately. One Russian general was killed, as was a woman who was shot in the neck. Lieutenant Colonel Thornhill, the Assistant Military Attaché, saved another general's life by snatching a hooligan's rifle as he was about to fire – many of the soldiers had laid aside their rifles when they got tired and these had been picked up by any civilian who wanted one. Commander Locker Lamson found himself comforting a Russian lady; the fact that she was young, beautiful and a princess was surely coincidental.

All the Russian officers were made to give up their swords, insignia of their rank and any firearms; those that resisted were killed. Some who gave up these symbols of their status later killed themselves, such was their shame. Russian sailors then took charge and posted sentries on every floor of the hotel, keeping out anybody who did not have room keys. By contrast, the British officers were well treated and if their swords were confiscated by mistake they were immediately returned. They found themselves caught up in a situation that was quite unlike any other, but it was one they were to meet time and again as long as they remained in Russia.

Cromie realised that he had to get back to Revel if at all possible to be with his men and their boats. Conditions in Petrograd were chaotic; few trains were running and those that did were not conforming to any timetable. Cromie collected together a small party including Count Keller[3], who commanded the Russian Submarine Flotilla, and walked the 2 miles to the station. They had to avoid indiscriminate machine-gun fire and aimless mobs along the way. Once there, they had to push their way through crowds of sailors from Kronstadt who were arriving to join the revolution. Cromie found that the men were surprisingly good-natured in spite of their recent violence at the base, where most Russian officers had been brutally murdered or imprisoned.

In the midst of all the anarchy a small group of British submariners arrived in Petrograd on their way to join the flotilla at Revel. The men had travelled by steamer from Liverpool to Murmansk and then down the railway to the capital. A young able seaman, who was one of the party, recorded his impressions of their arrival in the city:

Snowing fairly heavily. We made some tea while waiting for our baggage to be taken away, and had to go underneath the station to get the water. What a sight! Everything was smashed up, evidently there had been a large food store there. We loaded our gear into motor lorries, and were driven to the British Embassy. Our lorries were stopped by the crowd, and didn't they cheer when they knew who we were. It made one proud that we were British. We had only a few hours to wait in Petrograd, I should have liked to stop longer, but in the circumstances this was not advisable. All the shops were closed except the bakers, outside of which people were formed in long queues. Occasional shots were still being fired. We left the Embassy and were driven to the Baltic Station, where we waited for four hours, being the centre of attraction the whole time. Just before our train left some excitement was caused by several machine guns opening fire just outside the station, as did also hundreds of soldiers who were entraining. It appears that a police spy was seen on the roof of a house, and they meant to make sure of him, anyhow. During the action the belt of one of the machine guns jammed, and there was not one soldier there who knew what was the matter with it.

The young man concluded the story with obvious pride: 'One of our Petty Officers set it going again.'[4]

Meanwhile the Duma, having been prorogued by the Tsar on 12 March, had continued to meet elsewhere in the capital. Its first task was to approve the establishment of a Provisional Government under Prince Lvov in an attempt to restore order. On the 13th Nicholas decided to return to his capital from Imperial General Headquarters (the STAVKA) at Mogilev, where he had been directing the war. His train was intercepted at Pskov, where it was boarded by two delegates from the Duma. At first Nicholas believed that he could still grant some minor constitutional reforms which would save the day – but it was too little, too late. He was told that he no longer possessed any support in the country as a whole and that only his abdication would suffice. At 11.40 p.m. on 15 March he then formally abdicated in favour of his brother the Grand Duke Mikhail. Wisely, Mikhail renounced his claim the following day, although he added that he would resume the crown if it were offered him by a properly elected Constituent Assembly.

As soon as King George V heard of the Tsar's abdication and the subsequent events he sent Nicholas a telegram saying he was concerned for the safety of his cousin and his family and would be happy to see him in England. He even offered to send a cruiser to Murmansk for their journey. Through the auspices of the Swedish Government an agreement was made with the Germans that the cruiser carrying the Imperial family would not be attacked.

It was not the intention of the Provisional Government that harm should come to Nicholas and his family, nor that they should remain in close proximity to the capital where disorder was rampant. The British offer appeared as an attractive solution, but Prince Lvov and his Ministers took too long to reach a decision. By then, second thoughts had prevailed in London and the offer was controversially withdrawn. There is uncertainty as to whether this was as a direct result of fears by the British Prime Minister for stability within the country, or if the King himself became concerned that the presence of the Romanov family would compromise his own position. Existing records indicate that there are many missing documents. Nevertheless, despite whoever was responsible for this change of attitude, the Foreign Office sent a telegram to the Ambassador in Petrograd on 13 April ordering him to cancel the King's invitation to the Tsar.

The Tsar and his family, together with a small retinue, became prisoners in their own palace at Tsarskoe Selo, a few miles south of the capital. Apart from restrictions on their liberty, life for the Imperial family was not unpleasant. In August 1917 the family was moved to Tobolsk in Siberia, where they were installed in the Governor's house. Again, life at first was tolerable. After the 'October Revolution' brought the Bolsheviks to power the situation changed, and they became prisoners in fact as well as in essence. Eight months later they were moved again, to Ekaterinburg (later known as Sverdlosk).

At Ekaterinburg the family endured a harsh regime, strictly guarded and with little privacy, while the behaviour of the guards was designed to humiliate the prisoners. On the night of 17 July 1918, as anti-Bolshevik armies drew closer to the town, the whole family was shot in the basement of the house where they were imprisoned – or so the Bolsheviks stated at the time. The actual details of the fate of the Tsar and his family are outside the scope of this book. Suffice to say that myth and legend merge with so-called fact to produce many different versions: that the Tsarina and her daughters were taken away by train and were killed at a later date; that the youngest daughter, Anastasia, escaped and died much later in the United States of America; that another daughter, Tatiana, was rescued by a British Secret Service officer and died in the 1920s in Hampshire of tuberculosis – and others even more fanciful.

The Provisional Government under Prince Lvov tried to pursue a moderate policy, calling for a return to law and order and promising a reform of workers' rights. However, it refused to accede to the demands of the powerful Soviets – councils of workers and soldiers – to end the war with Germany and Austria. For the next seven months Lvov, and later Aleksandr Kerensky, tried to carry out these aims and establish the Government's authority over the country. They were increasingly thwarted by the Soviets, who had the backing of the Bolsheviks.

Meanwhile, the disorders spread to the Baltic Fleet in their winter base at Helsingfors (now Helsinki). Admiral Nepenin, the Commander-in-Chief, was unable to take the only course of action that might have staved off the trouble, winter ice preventing him from taking the fleet to sea. Instead, the crews of the battleships *Andrei Pervozvanni* and the *Imperator Pavel I*, who had seldom been to sea since the start of the war in 1914, led the slide into full-scale mutiny by butchering many of their officers and imprisoning the remainder. Other ships followed their example with differing degrees of ferocity and willingness. Nepenin himself was shot in the back and killed while on his way to meet some delegates from Petrograd; some say that German agents carried out this assassination, but more probably it was a single disgruntled sailor acting in the heat of the moment. This left the ships of the fleet being run by elected committees. In theory the new Commander-in-Chief was Admiral Maximoff, a weak self-serving officer and hardly the figure to begin to impose order on the rampant mutineers. He was soon relieved by Rear Admiral D.N. Verderevsky, who earlier had commanded the Russian Submarine Flotilla.

At Revel the situation was not nearly as explosive. The main trouble was on board the old cruiser *Dvina*, which had been at the centre of trouble in 1905 and had become the depot ship of the British Submarine Flotilla. Commander Cromie's actions in preventing trouble from getting out of hand are typical of everything he was to do in the months to come. He gave discreet help to those in trouble and refused to let the political situation or the revolutionaries interfere with the routine of the British sailors or their submarines. It required considerable tact and a lot of courage. He later wrote in an official report to the Admiralty:

> The men came aft, and would not permit any officer to leave or enter the ship until their Committee decided what to do with certain officers. I went over to the *Peter Valiki*, an old battleship being used by the Gunnery School, who had a better crowd of men, and they sent deputies who persuaded the *Dvina's* men to return the arms. [These had already been taken from the officers.] This was done and I then persuaded Captain Nikitin to once more give the arms to the men and place the onus of the officers' protection on the more sane of the sailors.
>
> Next morning I had some argument as to my rights to receive Russian officers on board. I obtained this on the understanding that they did not discuss current matters with the ship's officers[5].

Another crisis showed Cromie's determination not to be dictated to by the mutineers. The Ship's Committee arrested two Russian officers. They were Lieutenant Boris Miller and Sub-Lieutenant Makaroff, two of the Russian Liaison Officers with the submarines. Without hesitation Cromie faced the crowd of truculent armed Russian sailors and demanded their release. He said that the Russians were serving under his command and that he would deal with any complaints if they were made to him in writing. Taking advantage of the respite afforded, both the officers were sent on leave. Miller survived the revolution and emigrated to Australia. During the Second World War he served in the Royal Australian Air Force and in 1944 returned to Moscow, where he acted as an interpreter during one of Churchill's visits to Stalin. The fate of Makaroff is unknown.

Spring was late in 1917 and it was 19 May before the first four Allied submarines sailed from Revel to patrol against German shipping along the Swedish coast. Surprisingly, in view of the unsettled situation prevailing ashore, the boats were all Russian. One of these, the *Bars*, failed to return. The British 'E' class submarines were directed by the Russians to keep watch off the German-occupied port of Libau (now called Liepaja) or to seaward of the Irben Straits, as the main fear of the Russian naval staff was a German attack on the Gulf of Riga. The smaller British 'C' class boats were used to support the Russian defences inside the Gulf. It was a frustrating time for the British sailors, who wished to be taking a more aggressive part in the war; however, this was a policy that not even Cromie's powers of persuasion could change.

The actions of the Russian submarines *Gepard* and *Volk* illustrate how tenuous was the discipline that the Commanding Officers were able to enforce. The *Gepard* attacked a small German convoy approaching the Swedish coast; three torpedoes were fired. The two wing torpedoes passed ahead and astern of the target, while the centre torpedo misfired and did not leave the tube. The submarine was then heavily counter-attacked for four hours but suffered no real damage. Nevertheless, the crew decided that they had suffered enough and forced the Commanding Officer to return to their base. The *Volk* was ordered out on patrol as a replacement, but after proceeding for only about 20 miles the submarine returned with a defective main bearing. The Commanding Officer was convinced that the damage was deliberate following the experience of the *Gepard*.

Lenin was in Switzerland when the Tsar was deposed and Prince Lvov formed his Provisional Government. He returned to Russia with the help and connivance of the German Government. who provided him with a sealed train to take him to Sweden. They had no wish to risk his fiery oratory spreading dissension in Germany but hoped that he might promote further unrest in Russia, gain power and bring about his idea of a separate peace. In Petrograd Lenin was joined by Josef Stalin and Leon Trotsky, the latter arriving from the United States of America.

There were two more attempted revolutionary coups during the summer to disturb the doubtful efficiency and low morale of the Russian Army and Navy. In July the Bolsheviks tried to seize power. They failed – but only just. The Provisional Government instructed the Commander-in-Chief of the Baltic Fleet, Rear Admiral Verderevsky, to send some trustworthy destroyers to the capital to provide support for the Government. He acceded to the request, but with some delay. The Minister of War, Alexandr Kerensky, considered that some of Verderevsky's actions were suspect and he was arrested and imprisoned. For three days the situation was very tense and volatile before the Bolsheviks surrendered. Lenin fled, Prince Lvov resigned and Kerensky took over the Government. Verderevsky was then released from prison to become Minister of Marine and was promoted to vice admiral.

In September an uprising against the Government was led by General Lavr Kornilov, a Siberian Cossack who had risen through the ranks through sheer military ability and courage – no mean feat in the Tsarist Army[6]. His political acumen did not match his military prowess for he had misjudged the situation entirely. His support melted away and the revolt was suppressed without a shot being fired. Kornilov was jailed briefly but was released by sympathisers. He was killed in 1918 during fighting in the South against the Red Army in the Civil War.

Conditions throughout Russia became daily more chaotic. Soldiers were deserting their regiments in their thousands and moving in an aimless surge over the countryside, looking for work, food and somewhere to settle. Huge strikes and lockouts paralysed many of the large cities and the important coal mines of the Don Valley. Transport came to a halt and the army starved. Kerensky's Government was split between democratic and revolutionary factions and could do nothing. The generals and admirals demanded harsh measures to restore discipline throughout the armed forces. Admiral Verderevsky sought in vain to impose a new voluntary and democratic code of discipline based on co-operation with the Soldiers' and Sailors' Committees, which would save the army and navy. His recommendations were ignored.

Reactions to Kornilov's attempted revolt had spread to the Baltic Fleet, where it was taken as an instance of the officers trying to reassert the old ideals. The Sailors' Committees decided that all officers had to sign a declaration that they would obey the orders of the Centrobalt – the main committee of sailors of the Baltic Fleet – rather than the Commander-in-Chief should there be any dispute. Four junior officers on board the battleship *Petropavlovsk* refused to sign, pointing out that the Commander-in-Chief was appointed by the Provisional Government and only acted as they directed him. The four were arrested, taken ashore and shot.

On board the old *Dvina* – or *Pamiat Azova*, as the ship had resumed its previous name – Commander Cromie had to confront the Centrobalt delegates when they came on board with the declaration for all the Russian officers to sign. He assured them that he would work in conjunction with the Centrobalt but pointed out that the Russian Liaison Officers on board the British submarines came under his authority as they were under British discipline. He insisted that politics would not be allowed to get in the way of ensuring that the British submarines were available for sea to fight their common enemy, the Germans. Charm, tact and unflinching determination won the day. Cromie got his way.

Following Kornilov's failed coup the Petrograd Soviet had established a Military Revolutionary Committee, composed mostly of Bolsheviks, to co-ordinate the defence of the capital. The Committee persuaded the garrison troops to obey it rather than the Provisional Government. Throughout September Lenin urged his followers that the time had come for another revolution. Lenin was initially in Finland, where he was defying an arrest warrant after his failed bid for power in July; he then went into hiding in Petrograd. Kerensky in fact provided the match that lit the fuse when he closed down two Bolshevik newspapers and arrested their editors and some staff on charges of anti-Government actions. Lenin's party members, the troops of the garrison and sailors from Kronstadt conducted a well-planned takeover of power. The Provisional Government was arrested on the night of 25-26 October[7] – with the notable exception of Kerensky, who fled the city. He later escaped from Russia disguised as a seaman and spent the remainder of his life in the United States. An election for a new Constituent Assembly was held in November and Lenin promised to abide by the result. In the event, the Bolsheviks polled less than a quarter of the vote, but when the Assembly met on 18 January 1918 the non-Bolshevik members were overwhelmed by noisy elements supporting Lenin. The session had to be abandoned in utter confusion and the following day the Assembly was dissolved. Lenin had achieved his goal: Russia had seen the last democratic election to take place there for over seventy years. The outcome of this takeover was to have serious consequences for the Allies.

In the early hours of 1 September 1917 the Germans had begun their offensive to capture Riga. By the 4th they had captured the city, but the Russians had started to fight back and were able to stabilise the situation. At the same time German naval forces became increasingly contemptuous of the Russians. Their minesweepers started clearing the minefields protecting the Irben Straits and the nearby islands of Dagö and Ösel, which covered the Russian ships in the Gulf of Riga and their base in Moon Sound. A massive German attack was launched on 12 October with the aim of capturing the islands and denying use of the area to the Russian Navy. German forces were overwhelming: the battlecruiser *Moltke*, ten older battleships, eight small cruisers, fifty-five destroyers, six submarines and numerous other small craft and support ships. Six Zeppelins and over 100 aircraft gave air support to a landing force of 23,000 men. The Russians could counter this only with a nominal strength of 14,000 men, though many had deserted or were absent. Two old Russian battleships, the *Slava* and the *Grazhdanin* (formerly the *Tsarevitch*), provided their main defence, with the British 'C' class submarines also being present at the time of the attack.

The fighting on land was soon over, leaving the Germans in control of the islands. The *Grazhdanin* was twice hit by gunfire from the German battleship *Kronprinz* but escaped and took no further part in the battle. The *Slava* was also hit and had to be scuttled before the Russians withdrew from the Gulf; the Germans controlled the Irben Straits to the south and escape northwards through Moon Sound was impossible as it was too shallow.

This attack on the islands had been expected all summer; indeed, the anticipation of this move had been the main reason that the British 'E' class submarines had not been sent out to intercept the Swedish iron ore trade with Germany or to attack German warships. Nevertheless, the actual assault seemed to have caught the Russians by surprise; none of the 'E' class submarines were on patrol. The C26 (Lieutenant Basil Downie) forced a way into the Gulf through the Irben Straits but then, while attacking an enemy group of two battleships and three cruisers, the submarine went aground in shallow water. In breaking free the submarine bobbed briefly to the surface and was hunted by the Germans until after dark. By the time the submarine was able to surface safely Lieutenant Downie was faced with a mounting number of defects. He had no option but to take his boat to the port of Pernau, hoping for time to make the C26 seaworthy again. The C27 (Lieutenant Douglas Sealy) fired two torpedoes at a battleship but missed, as the submarine was too close to the target and the torpedoes ran deep. In another attack Sealy fired a torpedo which sank a transport acting as a depot ship for minesweepers. While on the surface, the C32 (Lieutenant Christopher Satow) was attacked by gunfire from a U-boat, but was not hit. After two more attacks, in which a netlayer was sunk, Satow believed he was trapped in the Gulf and beached his submarine before destroying it.

As a result of the fighting the Germans captured Riga but failed to follow up their advantage, though they remained poised to advance further towards Revel and the Russian capital. The Germans also gained control of the Gulf and closed the Russian base in Moon Sound for minimal loss. The British and Russians had little to show for the summer's operations; six submarines had been lost: the C32 and five Russian boats.

Before the winter ice prevented any ship movements Commander Cromie wisely sailed the submarines and the Russian depot ship from Revel to Helsingfors, where they would not be threatened by any German advance from Riga towards Petrograd. However, Helsingfors had the disadvantage of the volatile revolutionary atmosphere which was rampant throughout the Russian Baltic Fleet based there. A Finnish Declaration of Independence, accompanied by a demand for the withdrawal of all Russian forces, increased the problems facing the British submariners. At this time the Admiralty decided that the majority of the crews were to be brought home, leaving just a care and maintenance party to look after the submarines: Lieutenant Downie, three other officers and twenty-two sailors. If the Russians were able to continue the war, then fresh crews could be sent out before the ice melted in 1918.

The main party of submariners themselves returned home via Mirmansk in January 1918, but first they had one last task to perform. Before the winter ice immobilised the Russian Fleet the Sailors' Committees decided they would sail for Kiel and fraternise with their 'German Brothers'. Whether they could have navigated safely through the many minefields which were strewn throughout the Baltic, or even if their unexpected arrival near Kiel would have gone unchallenged by the Germans, is debatable. Cromie decided to ensure that this would not happen; he could not risk the ships falling intact into German hands. If he learned that the sailing of the Russian ships was imminent Cromie planned to board the flagship, along with his engineer officer, and confront the Ship's Committee. Either they were to allow the ship's engines to be immobilised or, at a pre-arranged signal, the British submarines would torpedo the battleships one by one. Fortunately such desperate measures were not needed; the dire consequences which would have befallen the submariners can only be imagined.

Downie and his men faced an uncertain future as they settled in to pass the winter and await developments in the spring. After a battle in January 1918 the Finnish Whites were forced to leave the city; with their departure, control was left in the hands of militant Reds. Not only did Downie have to cope with an increasingly hostile crew of the *Pamiat Azova* but also there was a lack of money to pay his crew. It became virtually impossible to cash Navy Bills – essentially Admiralty cheques – leaving Downie no choice other than to trade on the black market. There were six months' stores in hand and, with the situation worsening all the time, he felt he might get the order to scuttle the submarines and return home at any minute. He took the risk of selling off much of the surplus clothing and tobacco – at a profit – enabling him to keep the crew paid and fed.

Downie was not alone in facing problems over money; Cromie too had his difficulties in this regard. He was offered the large sum of £50,000 by a group of Finnish businessmen for his assistance in preventing the Red sailors from landing while the White Finns staged a takeover in the city. Of course, he had to refuse. He was also offered £5 million for the purchase of the British submarines, although how useful they would have been to the Whites without trained crews to man them is open to doubt. Again, Cromie refused.

Lenin, following his assumption of power in November 1917, was seeking to make peace with the Germans. The Russian Army, and the people as a whole, lacked the will and the resources to fight on, while the Bolsheviks wanted to be able to devote all their efforts into consolidating the success of the Revolution. Peace moves were inevitable, although not necessarily acceptable to the other Allied Powers. A Russian admiral who was a representative at the negotiations told Cromie that the Germans had refused to begin talks on naval matters unless they were assured that the English (*sic*) submarines had ceased hostilities.

The armoured car crews had already returned home via Murmansk. Their final actions had been in support of the Russians in the south-west. Over one period of ten days the cars had covered a massive twenty-five-mile gap in the lines, where the Russian regiments had abandoned their trenches and 'gone home'. They repeatedly balked the Austro-German advance and bought time for the Russian commanders to find some troops who would at least attempt to defend their country; offensive operations were out of the question. Their departure was not without drama. In Murmansk a message was received from Trotsky saying that if any of the men had passports which had not been issued and signed by him, they were to be sent back to Petrograd under guard. This applied to most, if not all, of the men. The reason for this strange order was probably Trotsky's wish to show the Germans at the Brest-Litovsk Peace Conference that he was trying to comply with their demands to restrict the movements of Allied forces in Russia. Fortunately many of the men of the armoured car unit had already left; the remainder were hastily, if uncomfortably, evacuated in trawlers.

A small party was left behind at Kursk over the winter to look after the vehicles and 500 tons of supplies and spare parts, which had been accumulated for operations in 1918. These men too were withdrawn in January after a series of difficult confrontations with Bolshevik Commissars – their equipment and stores all had to be left behind.

On 3 April 1918 the remaining submariners in Helsingfors heard that the Germans had landed in Finland to give support to the Whites and were advancing on the capital. With the help of a few loyal Russian officers the submarines were taken out into the bay and scuttled, while the stock of torpedoes was blown up. The remaining sailors left for Murmansk, from where they too returned home. Left behind was Francis Cromie, now an acting captain, who had been appointed to be the Naval Attaché at the embassy in Petrograd. In the absence of the Ambassador and most of the staff, who had left for England, Cromie virtually ran the Embassy until his untimely death on the last day of August 1918.

Much of Cromie's activities until then remain shrouded in mystery. In this narrative it is sufficient to say that he worked closely with Commander Le Page, who had been Liaison Officer with the Black Sea Fleet at the beginning of the war and had moved to Petrograd in June 1917. He also worked with Bruce Lockhart, the British Consul-General in Moscow who had gained the trust, if not the actual friendship, of both Lenin and Trotsky.

The Germans occupied Revel on 26 February and Helsingfors on 13 April. The Russians had managed to evacuate most of their ships from these ports, forcing their way through the ice to Kronstadt. The Admiralty in London was concerned to ensure that should the German advance continue and Petrograd be occupied, the Russians would scuttle the more important ships to avoid their capture. Bruce Lockhart had earlier reported that he had been assured by Trotsky that ships of both the Baltic and Black Sea Fleets would not fall into German hands. Nevertheless, the War Cabinet remained worried; the Germans were indeed advancing and yet the Russians appeared to lack any inclination to make preparations for the scuttling of their ships.

On 10 May the War Cabinet considered an audacious plan for the destruction of the Baltic Fleet which had been suggested by Captain Cromie. This involved blocking the main basin at Kronstadt by sinking three British merchant ships – which had been trapped in the Baltic since August 1914 – in the approaches. Subsequently, several teams of Russians, which Cromie had recruited, would blow up four of the battleships and as many as possible of the new Norvik class destroyers. The Russians were to be paid £300,000 for carrying this out, of which 85 per cent would be paid only in the event of a positive outcome. The main worry for the Cabinet was the risk of antagonising the Russian Government and potentially driving them into the German camp. British involvement in this plan would soon become known, or assumed, once it was attempted. It was a similar situation to that faced by Churchill in 1940 when deciding what action to take against the French Fleet at Mers-el-Kebir.

The Cabinet did not make a final decision and Cromie was permitted only to continue planning and to pay out any initial expenses. Later, on 27 May, he was authorised to 'take whatever steps he thought necessary' to avoid the ships falling into German hands. In fact the Germans halted their advance and once again Cromie was not required to take any action[8].

On 30 August a young Russian officer cadet murdered Moisei Uritsky, the head of the notorious Cheka[9] and forerunner of the KGB. The following day a Jewish girl, Dora Caplan, attempted the murder of Lenin, leaving him seriously wounded. Both events led to a series of bloody reprisals and scores of arrests. In this atmosphere the Cheka raided the British Embassy, where Cromie was killed. There are several different versions of his death, the most bizarre stating that he died bravely defending the Embassy against a mob trying to gain entry. More likely, it is probable that he recognised one or more of the Cheka agents that had entered the Embassy, and perhaps feared that they had come to arrest him. Whatever the reason he tried to avoid them, running down the imposing marble staircase towards the entrance. He was shot in the back and killed as he ran[10].

Commander Le Page and the other remaining members of the Embassy staff were rounded up and taken to the infamous Peter and Paul Fortress. For the next three months they were held in squalid conditions but were not otherwise unduly harshly treated. They were then released and allowed to return to London.

The British Government was affronted by the incident. Arthur Balfour, the Foreign Secretary, announced that 'unless full reparations were immediately made, the British Government would hold members of the Soviet Government individually responsible for the outrage and would make every effort to secure that they shall be treated as outlaws by the Governments of all civilised nations and that no place of refuge shall be open to them'. It was strong diplomatic language, especially when used to a Government that was, at least nominally, an ally. It had no effect; no one was ever held to account, there was no apology.

In this sad manner not only was a very gallant, determined and astute submariner killed but also the British wartime presence in Russia came to an end.

Meanwhile, the peace negotiations at Brest–Litovsk had dragged on, with the Russians endeavouring to prolong the proceedings as long as possible. On 2 March the patience of Germany and Austria had been exhausted and their armies resumed their march into Russia. Most of the old Imperial Russian Army had already melted away and the newly formed Red Army was incapable of offering a worthwhile resistance. Within a fortnight the Russians had capitulated and signed a peace treaty[11]. Large areas of the Ukraine and the Crimea, with their rich farmlands and half the industrial capacity of the country, were occupied by the Germans, as was the naval base at Sevastopol. Russian forces were to have been withdrawn from Finland, but Russian sailors and soldiers decided to stay and help their Finnish colleagues assume control of their Government. That unfortunate country then descended into civil war.

THREE

THE NORTHERN FRONT
TO THE END OF 1918

The Royal Navy first established a presence in North Russia in February 1915, when the old pre-dreadnought battleship HMS *Jupiter*[1] was sent from the 7th Battle Squadron, based on the Humber, to Murmansk. Her task was to act as an ice-breaker and try for as long as possible to keep an ice-free passage for ships proceeding to Archangel. At that time Murmansk was just a small fishing village on the Kola Inlet, with no railway communication to the south and only poor road tracks. Russia's only northern port capable of handling a constant supply of munitions and other war supplies was Archangel. However, it was usually ice-bound from December to the end of May each year. In 1915 the ice broke early, enabling the *Jupiter* to leave for the Humber on 1 May, her task completed.

Soon after the opening of navigation in the early summer of 1915, the Germans sent the auxiliary minelayer *Meteor* to operate in the approaches to the White Sea and 285 mines were laid. As a consequence, eight British minesweeping trawlers were sent to the area and they began to clear the minefields in early July. One of these ships, the *Lord Denman*, was sunk in October and the armed merchant cruiser HMS *Arlanza* struck a mine in November. She was badly holed forward and had to be towed to safety in the then relatively unknown harbour of Yukanskie, on the Kola Peninsular about 200 miles south-east of Murmansk. There the ship was abandoned for the winter, leaving only a skeleton crew on board. These men had a very unpleasant time as the harbour was constantly frozen over and gales raged almost continuously, though the ship rode safely at her anchors. The *Arlanza* was eventually taken into Murmansk the following April from where, after some temporary repairs, she returned to England.

At the end of the year the old cruiser *Iphigenia* arrived in Murmansk and Captain T.W. Kemp assumed the duties as Senior Naval Officer (SNO) in the area. Slowly, and almost inevitably, the strength of the British force in the White Sea area grew. The trawlers continued carrying out extensive minesweeping, as the Germans used their submarines to lay mines off the coast to try and catch the increasing number of ships sailing for Murmansk and Archangel with vital supplies for the Russians.

The Russians, for their part, began construction of port facilities at Murmansk in 1915, giving them an 'open-all-year' harbour, and by the end of 1916 they had completed a single-track railway 600 miles long to link it with Petrograd. That the task was completed in this time scale was largely due to the efforts of Captain Roschakoffsky and thousands of German and Austrian POWs. Roschakoffsky had left the Imperial Navy before the war and had been appointed to an obscure diplomatic post in Germany. Recalled for service with the navy on the outbreak of war, he had been sent to the north especially by the Tsar to organise transport south for all the stores and munitions arriving by sea. He was a notorious eccentric and appeared to be the very model of what many believed a typical Russian to be: tall, stately, bearded and smothered in medals. He had a booming voice and a choice of language hardly suited for diplomacy; he was feared by most of his subordinates and thoroughly disliked by higher officials. His boundless energy was devoted to the unglamorous but essential task he had been given. There was no port, so he built one. There was no railway, so he built one. In the meantime, he used thousands of reindeer and horses to take stores southwards. Despite his efforts, mountains of vital stores continued to accumulate in Murmansk and the surrounding area.

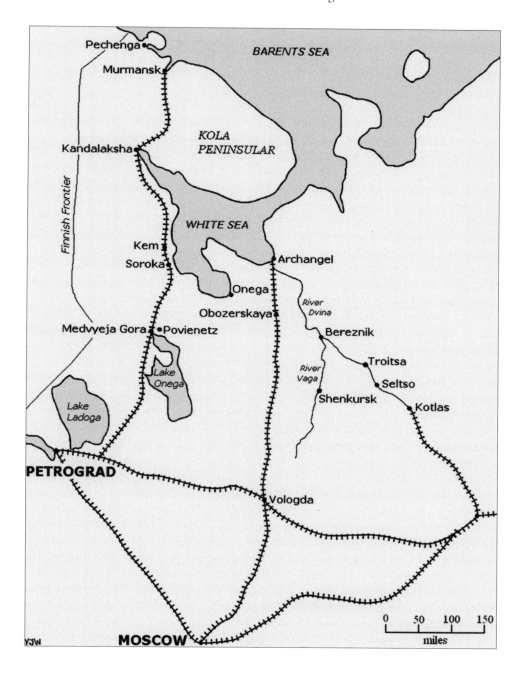

The dangers of navigation in the ice are graphically illustrated by the story of the British supply ship *Sappho*, which became locked in the ice with only three weeks' provisions on board. The crew decided to abandon ship and try to reach another which was in sight about 10 miles away. They set off to walk across the ice but were frozen to death one by one; only four men reached the other vessel, which proved to be a deserted wreck. Two more men died while on board the wreck and the last two struggled ashore, where they fell in with a party of Lapps who took them to safety. One more man died on the journey and the sole survivor was taken on board the *Arlanza*.

As soon as the ice permitted, the minesweepers began the task of checking that the northern coast was free of mines. Shipping started to gather at Yukanskie and in the Kola Inlet at the beginning of May 1916, waiting for the ice to clear for their passage to Archangel. During the first week of June about 100 ships with coal, munitions and other military stores were able to complete their voyage.

The amount of traffic can be gauged by the fact that during 1916 over 1,200 ships passed along the northern coast heading for either Murmansk or Archangel. Between them they carried a vast tonnage of coal and other supplies as well as about 4¼ million tons of ammunition. Inevitably, this attracted the attention of the German U-boats. More importantly, the facilities were insufficient to cope with the large volume of cargo that arrived, which had to be unloaded and then transported south; large stockpiles grew up around both ports.

British submarine counter-measures included the sending of Q-ships[2] to the area, but their operations were without success. During 1916 three 'G' class and in 1917 two 'E' class submarines were based in Murmansk, but they too failed to sink any of their German opposite numbers. The elderly Russian submarine *Delfin*, which had been built in 1903 and had been brought to Archangel from Vladivostok in 1916, proved to be hopelessly inadequate for this type of operation. Russian sources indicate that in 1917 the submarine was transferred to the Baltic, using the intricate system of inland waterways; other records show that the boat was abandoned and hulked in Murmansk. In either case, the submarine paid no further part in the war. In November 1916 the Russian minesweeper the *Groznyi*, part of the escort of a small convoy, encountered the U56 on the surface. The submarine was badly damaged by shellfire and sank. In January 1917 a Russian trawler rammed the U76 near the North Cape; the boat was damaged but did not sink. The next day the submarine's engines broke down and she was unable to submerge, as the batteries could not be charged. Her crew were rescued by a Norwegian fishing boat. The most striking loss of a U-boat occurred in September 1917, when the U28 was sunk. After torpedoing and stopping the British merchant ship *Olive Branch*, which was bound for Archangel, the submarine surfaced and approached to about 250 yards before opening fire with the deck gun. The second shot exploded a quantity of ammunition in the holds of the British ship. So violent was the explosion that a motor lorry carried on the upper deck of the steamer was blown onto the submarine. Ironically, this caused such extensive damage to the U28 that she began to sink. As the survivors of the *Olive Branch* pulled away from their stricken vessel in the only undamaged lifeboat they saw some of the submarine's crew in the water, whilst others remained on deck, waving for help. The merchant seamen felt no sympathy for the Germans and no survivors were picked up.

The Revolution of March 1917, which saw the abdication of the Tsar, passed without any essential changes in the functions of the British squadron in Murmansk and the White Sea. Allied ships continued to pour supplies of all kinds into the two North Russian ports. The battleship HMS *Glory* was now the flagship of the squadron and Captain Kemp, the original SNO, had been promoted to rear admiral. The real trouble began in November, following Lenin's successful coup in Petrograd and his openly stated desire to take Russia out of the war.

The Russians had not maintained a very large or powerful fleet in northern waters before the war and this force had not been substantially reinforced prior to 1917. The main unit was the pre-dreadnought battleship *Chesma*, which had suffered a chequered career. In 1904 the ship, then called *Poltava*, had been sunk in shallow water during the initial Japanese attack on Port Arthur. She was salvaged by the Japanese in 1905, refitted and commissioned into the fleet as the *Tango*. In 1916 the battleship was sold back to the Russians at Vladivostok and became the *Chesma*. She transferred to the Arctic Flotilla via the Indian Ocean and the Suez Canal, reaching northern waters on 3 February 1917. Although neither very efficient nor modern, the guns of the old battleship were, in theory, an effective force against any German attack.

In April 1917 eight Russian minesweeping trawlers, which had wintered at Murmansk, were placed under the orders of Captain Burt, who had arrived from England with twelve British minesweepers. In June and July a further sixteen Russian vessels were added to the trawler force. Although the crews were clothed and fed – and in some cases paid – by the Royal Navy, the failure in morale which followed the break up of the Imperial Navy greatly reduced their value. Despite every possible attempt being made to induce them to work, their usefulness steadily decreased. Originally, as many as sixteen were working at the same time; by October the number had dwindled to ten or less, and by November all work had ceased.

Four Russian destroyers[3] had arrived from the Far East in October. They worked well for the first few months until the arrival of the winter ice. They were then sent to Murmansk, where the crews rapidly succumbed to Bolshevik influence. The most interesting arrival in 1917 was the cruiser *Askold*[4], a survivor of the debacle at Port Arthur earlier in the century. In 1915, under the command of Captain Sergei Ivanov, the *Askold* was sent from the Far East to provide a Russian presence at Gallipoli, where the Tsar hoped that some of the glory of a great victory would accrue to the Russians. During this period of service in the Mediterranean the ship acquired from the British sailors the nickname of 'the packet of Woodbines' from her distinctive five funnels.

When that dream faded the cruiser was sent to the French naval base at Toulon for a refit, where the crew came under the influence of the many Russian subversives living in exile in France. In February 1917 the cruiser sailed for Devonport to finish the refit and was there when the Revolution broke out in March. The crew instantly formed a committee and sent two delegates to London to meet Ivan Maisky, then one of the *émigré* leaders in London and later the Soviet Ambassador to Britain. Maisky introduced the two seamen to Ramsay MacDonald, the Leader of the Labour Party, who gave them lunch in the House of Commons. Maisky went to Devonport, where he persuaded the crew not to mutiny at that time, as he feared British reaction if such an event took place in a Royal Navy Dockyard. The *Askold* sailed for Murmansk where, on arrival, the crew finally did mutiny and Captain Ivanov was taken ashore and shot. The same fate eventually befell most of the other officers.

Despite the two Revolutions in 1917, the Royal Navy ships in North Russian waters continued to carry out their tasks as before. Merchant ships arrived at Murmansk and Archangel with their cargoes of war materials and supplies. The Russian ships stayed in harbour. The crews had mutinied and then, having disposed of the officers in one way or another, were content to have endless meetings; they had no desire to fight either the Germans or the elements.

By early 1918 the White Finns – anti-Bolshevik – were co-operating with the Germans and there were fears that at German insistence they could advance on Murmansk and capture that port. This would provide an excellent new base for the U-boats, from where they could sail to attack Allied shipping not only in the North Atlantic but also on the routes bringing supplies to Russia.

On 2 March 1918 the Murmansk Soviet received a telegram from Trotsky which stated:

> Peace negotiations are apparently broken off. Danger threatens Petrograd. Measures are being taken to defend it to the last drop of blood. It is your duty to do everything for defence of the Murmansk line. Germans are advancing in small bodies. Opposition is possible and compulsory. Nothing must be left for the foe. You are ordered to co-operate with Allied Missions in everything and to put all obstacles in the way of advance of Germans.

This was strong language from the Bolshevik leadership, which remained firmly in favour of taking Russia out of the war and making peace with the Germans, but only on their own terms. Consequently, on 6 March 1918, at the request of the Murmansk Soviet, a company of Royal Marines was landed from HMS *Glory*. It marked the start of Allied intervention in the affairs of post-Revolution Russia, and it is deeply ironic in the light of events that followed that it was at the request of the Bolsheviks to aid them in their defence against a possible advance by White Finns and Germans.

It was an uneasy alliance. Trotsky soon changed his mind and forbade the Murmansk Soviet from any form of co-operation with the Allies. The Russians in Murmansk were, however, more pragmatic and far more concerned about a possible advance from over the border in Finland than they were of any repercussions from disregarding instructions from Petrograd. The Royal Marines stayed ashore. However, the situation was tense; mutinous sailors from the Russian Northern Squadron roamed the streets of Murmansk and, as had been the case in Petrograd, they were firmly and violently committed to the Revolution. In the background were the 12in guns of the battleship *Chesma* and the 6in guns of the *Askold* – though rusty and poorly maintained, they could still theoretically be brought into action against either Germans or British.

Rear Admiral Kemp informed the Admiralty of the tenuous position of his forces and urgently sought reinforcements. Troops were out of the question; they were all needed in France, where a German offensive was awaited. On 1 March the transport *Porto* had left Liverpool for Murmansk, carrying a number of Russians for repatriation. Also on board was a guard of thirty marines and Admiral Kemp was told that he could retain them in Murmansk. Another transport, the *Huntsend*, arrived with a detachment of twenty-one Royal Engineers, in case it became necessary to destroy portions of the railway line to hinder any German advance. The ship returned to England with a large number of Allied refugees who had gathered in Murmansk and also the final group of British submariners.

The cruiser HMS *Cochrane*[5] was also detailed for service at Murmansk, arriving there on 7 March. The French Government sent another cruiser, the *Amiral Aube*[6], which arrived on the 19th. A similar request to the American Government was supported by Admiral Sims, Commander of the US Naval forces in Europe, but turned down by the State Department. The Americans had no wish to be dragged into the affairs of revolutionary Russia and feared any intervention would mean an ever-increasing diversion of resources from the war against Germany. However, in April the Americans reluctantly agreed to send a cruiser, but the famous old *Olympia*[7] did not arrive until 24 May.

The first incident took place in the middle of April. At the request of the Murmansk Soviet, a detachment of marines from HMS *Cochrane* went into action south of Murmansk to aid a party of Red Finns, who were being harried by some Whites along the line of the railway. A few days later the marines joined forces with troops of the French Military Mission to Romania, who had arrived in Murmansk expecting to be evacuated back to France. The combined force set out by armoured train for the village of Kandalaksha, about 130 miles south and nestling on an inlet of the White Sea. Flat cars carried several 3-pounder guns and machine guns, all protected by sandbags. The wood-burning engine took them at a sedate pace down the line; they found no Finns of either colour and returned at the same steady speed to Murmansk. About another 150 miles further south on the railway the White Finns captured the seaside town of Kem but were soon evicted by some Russian Red Guards.

On 2 May the local Soviet informed Admiral Kemp that they had been told that White Finns and Germans had reached Pechenga (later known as Petsamo). It was a small fishing village with no wharves or communications. There were acres of mud flats at low tide but it was potentially a useful submarine base with a fine landlocked harbour. HMS *Cochrane* was ordered to re-embark her marines and sail for Pechenga, only 50 miles to the west. Forty marines and forty Red Guards were landed, along with 100 seamen from the cruiser. The first exchange of shots in a series of brisk engagements forced the marines to retreat back towards the village. On the 6th they were reinforced by thirty-five marines from the *Glory*, who brought with them five Lewis guns and a naval 12-pounder. Over the next few days the marines and sailors established control of the area and beat off determined attacks by over 150 Finns. The fighting was little more than a skirmish prolonged over several days, but it was significant in that these were the first shots fired by the British in this new war.

While on passage from America the *Olympia* called in at Scapa Flow and embarked Major General Frederick Poole[8], who was to be the Commander of British Land Forces in North Russia. In the following months the number of troops sent to the area gradually increased. It was a measure of the critical state of the front in France that these reinforcements were multinational and often either untrained or of poor quality. Besides British and French troops there were units from America, Italy and Serbia. Major General Charles Maynard was appointed to command at Murmansk, leaving General Poole in overall command and able to concentrate on operations at Archangel.

In mid-July the light cruiser HMS *Attentive* (Acting Captain E. Altham) was anchored off the small White Sea port of Saroka, which also lay on the railway line running south. Some of the crew who were working ashore met with about 400 disaffected Russian sailors from Murmansk, who were walking to Petrograd, including many from the *Chesma* and the *Askold*. The Russians were refused shelter in the town and had to continue their walk. As one petty officer recorded in his diary: 'Only another 157 miles to go! Hope they enjoy it.'

The British and Allied forces in Murmansk were firmly in control of the town in the summer of 1918, but there remained the threat posed by the Russian ships which lay anchored in the port in the rear of the forces ashore. The ships themselves were in poor condition but the crews who remained on board, like many Russian sailors of the time, were strongly in favour of the Revolution. Many had gone south along the railway to join their comrades in Petrograd; those that had stayed might be expected to give trouble at any time. Accordingly, at the beginning of August 1918 it was decided to take over the ships. This was done on the 3rd with little opposition. The *Askold*'s mutinous sailors had become the centre of resistance to the unlikely collaboration between the Murmansk Soviet and the Allies and consequently a strong force was gathered to ensure that the capture of the ship was completed quickly and with minimum casualties. One hundred and fifty marines from the *Glory*, the *Olympia* and the *Amiral Aube*, supported by a British Army machine-gun detachment, carried out the task and the crew were soon under lock and key. The *Chesma* was aground and the hulk was left until later when there was a need for a prison ship. The *Askold* was commissioned with a British crew as HMS *Glory IV* and became the guardship at Petchanga in October before sailing for the Clyde to be laid up. The cruiser remained in the Holy Loch until 1922; the Soviet Government refused to accept her back as being uneconomic to refit and she was scrapped.

This also marked the virtual end of naval operations at Murmansk in 1918. Until the end of the year the navy's main task was to ensure that ships could sail safely on to Archangel, as long as the port was free of ice. The navy also had to secure the safe passage of ships passing along the Murman coast back to Britain. Operations inland and down the railway towards Petrograd were left to the army, under the command of Major General Maynard.

Maynard had to prepare for any attack by Finns and Germans, either directly on Murmansk or on the more westerly anchorage at Pechenga. He tentatively sent troops down the railway to Kem and Soroka, where they set up defensive positions. The small port of Onega on the gulf of the same name, an inlet of the White Sea, was also occupied. This gave the Allies control over a precarious and limited land route between Murmansk and Archangel which could be used in winter.

Allied intervention in Murmansk had originally taken place when the local Soviet requested help in dealing with the Finns and preventing them from capturing the vital railway from the new port southwards. The Germans brought increasing pressure to bear on the Government in Moscow to compel British and Allied forces to make a complete withdrawal from Murmansk and the surrounding area. The Murmansk Soviet received a series of telegrams from Tchicherin, the Commissar for Foreign Affairs, stating that accepting help from the British was totally inadmissible and must be stopped.

On 1 July 1918 Admiral Kemp reported this to the Admiralty and added that the Murmansk Soviet had been threatened for their continued acceptance of help from the British. The local authorities had in fact passed a resolution that orders from the Central Government should be opposed and asking that the Allies continue to protect the province. This led to an agreement being signed on 6 July, between Great Britain, France and the United States on the one hand and the Murmansk Regional Council on the other, which permitted Allied forces to remain in the area and allowed for Russian forces to be under Russian authority. It also stated that the Allies would not interfere in the internal affairs of the region but would supply the Russians with food, equipment and supplies of all kinds.

At Archangel the situation was different. The local Soviet was very subservient to Lenin and his Commissars and as such was unwilling to give any assistance to the Allies. The fact that the port was ice-bound until late in April 1918 meant that the Allies had not been able to take any action there since the 'October Revolution' and vast amounts of stores lay unguarded. The British ice-breaker HMS *Alexander*[9] (Captain H. Hurt), with two food ships in company, had been able to reach Archangel in April. The intention was that the food could be unloaded and in return some of the military stores already in the port could be back-loaded. In the event the plan misfired, as the local authorities would not allow any stores to be embarked in return until permission had come from Moscow[10]. This was not forthcoming.

The local Bolsheviks received a series of orders from Lenin to move all metals and munitions away from Archangel and a Special Commission arrived in the city from Moscow to oversee this task. Gangs of men were enlisted to work night and day on the removal of such stores, but the chaotic state of the railways meant that they were not able to achieve as much success as was hoped. Nevertheless, millions of pounds worth of material sent from Britain, France and America was taken away. Some was damaged by the unskilled handling, and some was to be destroyed; comparatively little could be used. The Special Commissioners ordered that the ammunition dumps be prepared for destruction, an action that might well have obliterated Archangel if carried out. Fortunately, the engineers assigned to this task were unskilled in explosive demolition.

On 22 June a note was handed to the Allied Consuls demanding the immediate withdrawal of Allied ships from Russian waters, adding that the appearance off Archangel of any other Allied warships would be a signal to detonate the ammunition dumps. The *Alexander* was the only warship present, though hardly a powerful one. The Consuls replied saying that the Russian note was being sent to London for consideration and that meanwhile they could not take any action as requested by the Russians.

The situation was deadlocked. Nothing further took place until 2 July, when Admiral Kemp, with political and economic advisers, left Murmansk for Archangel in the yacht *Salvator*. Kemp found that food, especially bread, was very scarce in Archangel and that the supplies in the two cargo ships were urgently needed by the local population. Kemp knew that there were plans for the Allies to occupy the town and he believed that it would be beneficial for the Allies, when that time arrived, if the people were not starving. He was also concerned to evacuate some 700 Allied refugees, who had reached the town during the winter. While no military stores could be back-loaded Kemp felt that he had reached a satisfactory deal and the ships, escorted again by the *Alexander*, returned to Murmansk.

While forced to wait at Archangel for a decision to be made regarding the two food ships, the *Alexander* was involved in two interesting incidents. In the more sinister, the ice-breaker was at the centre of a confrontation with Russian (Red) warships. At the end of June Captain Hurt received a strange message from an unknown person ashore stating that at noon that day an attempt would be made to seize the ship. There was no way of knowing if the message was valid or how serious the threat was, but Captain Hurt had to take all possible precautions; the cable was prepared for slipping, steam was raised on the engines and the very limited armament was readied.

Sure enough, at about 9.30 a.m. an armed yacht, with two 4in guns, was observed to leave the dockyard. As she approached it was seen that the guns were manned and trained on the British ship. The British guns were also ready for instant action, although still trained fore and aft, but with their crews lying down and hidden from sight; to the Russians it appeared that the British were totally unconcerned. Eventually, the Russian yacht anchored about 400 yards away on the bow of the *Alexander*. Next to arrive on the scene were four Russian trawlers, each armed with a single 12-pounder gun; they too anchored around the British ship. Then the ice-breaker *Sviatogor*, with two 5in and two 12-pounder guns, anchored half a mile astern. Finally, a merchant ship lying alongside a nearby jetty loaded her solitary anti-submarine gun and trained it on the *Alexander*. It was a potentially dangerous situation, where one false move could have triggered a tragedy.

Noon came and went; nothing further happened. At 1.30 p.m. the Russians still had not made any further moves against the British ship and Captain Hurt decided to go ashore, where he met the British Consul, Douglas Young, and the Consuls of all the other Allied Powers present in the town. It was considered that it would be best to seek a meeting with the local Soviet and request an explanation. This was speedily arranged.

Mr Young and Captain Hurt were surprised to find that they were greeted cordially by the Russians. The Consul explained the situation to the Russians, who were told of the hostile actions of their ships. The awful consequence of attacking one of His Majesty's Ships was explained and it was hinted that a large force of British cruisers was not far distant. Finally, the Consul told the Russians that it was essential that the Russian ships withdraw before sunset. In reply the President of the Soviet, in an obviously conciliatory manner, expressed surprise that the movements of the Russian ships had been misconstrued and stated that they had been sent purely as a precautionary measure. This was because it had been decided that sixty Serbs in Archangel were to be disarmed before repatriation, and it was believed that the British ship would try and prevent this by opening fire on the town. The explanation was obviously spurious, but it was accepted by Mr Young. The meeting was terminated by the Russians, asking that the misunderstanding be overlooked. That evening the Russians ships returned to their normal berths alongside the dockyard wall; the incident was at an end. A Russian officer later informed Captain Hurt that the local authorities had informed the Central Government in Moscow that the *Alexander* had in fact been seized and disarmed 'in accordance with your instructions'. Whether this message was sent cannot be verified, but if true it does add some credence to the day's events.

The other incident concerned four American civilians, who had arrived in Archangel from Moscow. The American Consul asked Captain Hurt if they could be taken on board the *Alexander* as a matter of urgency for their safety as he had received a signal from Washington requesting that 'immediate and extraordinary measures be taken to remove these men to a place of safety'. The men were embarked secretly and temporarily entered on to the ship's books. They were on board for a number of weeks before being transferred – again secretly – to a merchant ship sailing for Murmansk. It was a successful ending to a strange and seemingly 'cloak and dagger' operation, the nature of which remains a mystery to this day.

A welcome reinforcement was the arrival on station of the seaplane carrier HMS *Nairana* (Commander Charles Cowan) at the beginning of July. The terrain around Murmansk was either frozen hard in winter or marshy once the thaw had set in, making it difficult to construct suitable landing grounds for aircraft. However, the large number of lakes in the area provided admirable bases for seaplanes. The *Nairana* had been converted from a merchant ship that was being built on the Clyde for an Australian company. The conversion allowed for landplanes to be accommodated forward, where a basic flight deck 95ft long was added. The seaplanes were carried aft and had to be hoisted in and out by crane. For operations off the coast of Northern Russia the complement of aircraft was two Sopwith Camels and five Fairey Campania seaplanes. The ship's armament consisted of four 12-pounder guns, two of which could be used in an anti-aircraft role. The Royal Naval Air Service and Royal Flying Corps had been amalgamated on 1 April 1918 into the new Royal Air Force. On board the *Nairana* all the aircrew were therefore nominally from the new service, though many still wore their old RNAS uniforms and carried their old-style ranks.

It was an open secret that General Poole planned the capture of Archangel; the only aspect that was not widely known was when this was to take place. A Russian officer of the former Imperial Navy – with the English-sounding name of Georgi Chaplin – had arranged for a coup to take place in the city on 1 August. He badly needed support from the Allies to ensure that, after he had succeeded, the Bolsheviks were not able to turn the tables. Poole had just 1,500 men available: 100 Royal Marines, some British infantry and machine-gunners, the newly arrived French 21st Colonial Infantry Regiment, some Poles recruited in Murmansk and a detachment of American marines. Not all could be taken to Archangel in warships for the landing; the remainder would follow in merchant ships.

The force sailed for Archangel in the light cruiser *Attentive*, the seaplane carrier *Nairana*, the French cruiser *Amiral Aube*, some minesweeping trawlers, Admiral Kemp's yacht *Salvator*, and two Russian destroyers manned by Royal Navy crews. The *Amiral Aube* became separated from the other ships in fog and then reported that she had gone aground; it was later found that she had merely struck a sunken wreck and was not badly damaged. The first objective of the Allies was Modyugski Island at the mouth of the River Dvina. The *Attentive* and *Nairana* reached a rendezvous off the lightship marking the entrance to the river, where the cruiser anchored and the carrier hoisted out three of the seaplanes. The lightship was connected by telephone to the fort on the island and an ultimatum was passed that unless the fort surrendered it would be bombarded.

Initially, the Russian Bolshevik commander agreed to this but then sent out a tug with a message cancelling the surrender, probably as a result of pressure from the Soviet in Archangel. The *Attentive* opened fire on the fort at a range of 5,000 yards and the seaplanes bombed the battery. The Russians returned fire and a shell hit the base of the forward funnel of the cruiser, putting two boilers out of action but otherwise doing no real damage. Ten minutes later the eight 6in guns of the fort ceased fire and the troops were landed. Only light resistance was encountered as the majority of the Russian garrison had escaped to the mainland. The only Allied casualties were two lightly wounded French soldiers. The *Amiral Aube* rejoined the force that evening.

The following morning the French cruiser was ordered to remain off Modyugski Island to guard the approaches to the Dvina while Captain Altham led the remaining ships 30 miles upriver to Archangel. No opposition was encountered; the two ice-breakers[11] which had been scuttled in the fairway posed no difficulty and the force easily navigated around them.

The ships anchored off Archangel in the afternoon, troops were landed and the city was occupied. The Allied commanders were greeted with apparent enthusiasm when they went ashore, although one report states that the crowds were predominately middle class, with scarcely a workman to be seen. The erstwhile Bolshevik rulers had fled southward. The only resistance came from the armed yacht *Gorislavna*, which briefly opened fire on the town with a single 100mm gun. The *Attentive*[12] was soon under way. She was laid alongside the Bolshevik vessel, subsequently taking it back as a prize to Archangel.

The town of Bakharitza, on the opposite bank of the Dvina, was not occupied until the following day, when news was received that Red troops were advancing up the railway towards the town. Their progress was halted after the guns of the *Attentive* had shelled the enemy troops and they had been bombed by seaplanes from the *Nairana*. The rest of the Allied troops arrived from Murmansk on 3 August. An advance was begun southwards on both banks of the river, led by a small force of French marines landed from the cruiser *Amiral Aube* and embarked in two river steamers, which were lightly armed with a mountain gun apiece.

For the first time the RAF had been involved in a combined operation. Successful though that had been, it had changed the status of Allied intervention. Forces at Murmansk were present, nominally at least, at the request of the local Soviet. At Archangel, Russia had been invaded and the Bolsheviks ousted.

Bruce Lockhart in Moscow was dismayed when he heard the news: 'We have committed the unbelievable folly of landing in Archangel with fewer than twelve hundred men (*sic*). It was a blunder comparable with the worst mistakes of the Crimean War.'

Captain Georgi Chaplin's coup had been successful and he was in virtual control of Archangel even before the arrival of Captain Altham's ships. Chaplin gave himself the title of Commander of the Armed Forces of the Supreme Government of the Northern Region. General Poole installed a veteran socialist leader, Nicholas Tchaikovsky, as the leader of the pro-Allies, anti-Bolshevik Northern Provisional Government. Tchaikovsky, who had spent over thirty years in exile in England and the United States, had no love for the many Tsarist ex-officers, including Captain Chaplin, who had gathered in Archangel and in September the resulting friction led to another *coup d'état*. At midnight on 5 September Chaplin ordered a detachment of Russian troops to surround the building where Tchaikovsky and his Ministers were staying and arrest them. They were then taken on board a steamer to the island of Solovetsky in the White Sea, where they were imprisoned in an old monastery. The extent to which General Poole was an accomplice in this piece of political chicanery is open to question but at the very least there seems little doubt that he knew something was in the wind and took no steps to stop it. The reaction of many Russians in the city can be gauged by the fact that the workers all went on strike.

The American Ambassador, David Francis, was furious over Chaplin's actions although, as the latter correctly pointed out, he was a Russian officer on Russian soil and not an underling of President Wilson. Francis persuaded Poole and the other Ambassadors and Consuls that Tchaikovsky and his Ministers should be reinstated and they were to be brought back from their monastic prison. Chaplin's protestations notwithstanding, this was done. Chaplin decided to take refuge in a British ship for his own safety until he felt able to move around freely in Archangel again.

As General Poole's troops began their advance upriver, Captain Altham of the *Attentive* organised a naval flotilla to support the army's operations. The flotilla was manned by both British and Russian personnel and consisted of the two monitors M23 (Lieutenant Commander St A.O. St John) and M25 (Lieutenant Commander Sebald Green), both newly arrived from England, four Russian armed river steamers[13], two Russian motor launches with Royal Navy crews and an armed Russian tug. The British monitors were powerful ships of only 540 tons and were armed with a single 7.5in gun, a 12-pounder and a 6-pounder. Diesel engines gave them a top speed of 11½ knots. Their draught of less than 7ft made them useful ships for working on the river.

Captain Altham organised two river steamers to be fitted out with 12-pounder guns and pompoms, manned by crews from the *Attentive* and sent upriver. The Russians fitted out two more flat-bottomed river steamers, the *Opyt* and *Tolstoi*, bristling with captured Austrian field-guns. There was, however, a problem with arming the river steamers with too many guns. Their decks and frames were not strong enough to withstand the repeated shocks of firing the guns. It required great ingenuity and a lot of labour over the coming months to maintain them in active service.

By the beginning of September the troops had occupied the town of Bereznik, about 140 miles from Archangel, where the River Vaga joins the Dvina. At this point the Dvina is about a mile wide, meandering through a marshy countryside and dotted with many small islands. The troops moving south along the railway reached Obozerskaya, 75 miles from Archangel, at about the same time. Their advance was then halted by blown railway bridges. However, General Poole decided that, because of difficulties in the supply of food and winter clothing, he would not be able to capture the vital rail junction at Kotlas before the onset of winter. He planned to consolidate his position south of Bereznik.

The day after General Poole's forward troops had captured Bereznik the Americans at last landed at Archangel: 4,500 infantry, engineers and medical personnel. They had arrived after much pleading to President Wilson for reinforcements to be sent to North Russia. He had stipulated, however, that they could only be used to guard the stores and give 'such aid as may be acceptable to the Russians in the organisation of their self-defence'. The President made it quite plain that American soldiers were not to take part in offensive operations. However, immediately after they had landed, General Poole deliberately sent one battalion down the railway towards Vologda and another battalion downriver to Bereznik. He argued that if the fronts were to be held against the growing Bolshevik forces then the American troops had to be involved, whatever their President said. Many of the British troops were officially classified as unfit for active service, the French force was mostly colonial infantry unsuited to fighting in such northern latitudes, the Serbs were unfit and war-weary, the Slavo-British Legion too few in number and of doubtful reliability – but there were a handful of excellent Poles.

During the passage from England the American troops had suffered badly from influenza; many were still recovering when they landed in Russia and others were in the first stages of the illness, carrying their equipment with difficulty. Those going down the railway boarded a couple of troop trains, which were waiting in the dreary sidings by the station in Bakharitza. It was cold and raining – hardly an auspicious welcome to the country. At one stage as they moved slowly south through the pine forests they passed another train heading in the opposite direction with a cargo of Bolshevik prisoners – dirty, dispirited and dressed in a motley array of civilian clothing and uniform – guarded only by a few American sailors.

The battalion going south by river was transported in a string of barges, which made a slow and tedious passage to Bereznik as they were towed against the current at a stately 5 knots. The barges were woefully short of even the most basic elements of any comfort; if only they had known it, the troops on board the trains would have considered themselves in luxury by contrast. The barges had been used over the years for hauling a variety of cargoes, including coal and cattle, and the American soldiers shared their filthy leaking accommodation with a host of fleas. Several men died of the effects of influenza before they reached Bereznik.

The first operation carried out by Captain Altham's *ad hoc* riverine flotilla took place on 14 September. The ships were planned to operate with the army to clear Bolshevik troops from the area at the junction of the Dvina and Vaga rivers, from where they could threaten the Allied advanced base at Bereznik. The naval force consisted of the monitor M25, the British manned steamers *Advokat* and *Razlyff* and two armed motor launches. Their task was to keep any Bolshevik gunboats at bay and to bombard the enemy positions in the village of Chamova prior to its occupation by British and American troops.

The ships weighed anchor at first light. In thick fog, which hid them from the enemy but made navigation difficult, they made their way upriver against a strong current and in a narrow and tortuous channel. When the ships were about 2 miles from Chamova the fog thinned and a large Bolshevik gunboat was sighted moored to the riverbank at a range of only 400 yards. The M25 missed with the first shot from the powerful 7.5in gun, while the enemy's quick-firing guns rapidly opened up in reply. The next two rounds hit the enemy in the stern and amidships and she began to sink. After picking up some survivors the British ships continued on towards their objective.

A single gun firing from near the church was soon silenced. There was no sign of the supporting Allied infantry, but Bolshevik gunboats approached from their base further upriver and began to engage the British ships at long range. Return fire from the monitor forced them to withdraw. Increased activity by Bolshevik artillery, firing from concealed positions in the woods, put Altham's ships in a dangerous position, although firing shrapnel towards where the enemy's guns seemed to be hidden had the effect of making the enemy cease fire – at least temporarily.

The ships had only a finite amount of ammunition in their magazines and a signal that the arrival of the infantry was delayed by several hours brought home the truth of the old saying that ships (and nowadays tanks) can force the enemy to retire but cannot secure territory. The decision faced by Captain Altham was whether to retire or put a landing party ashore and take the village. Lieutenant Commander Green himself took charge of a force of sailors and had almost cleared the village when they came under intense machine-gun fire from the woods. There was no alternative but to retire and this was successfully organised by Green, who showed great gallantry in doing so. The men were re-embarked with only three casualties.

Before the flotilla finally retired back towards Bereznik, prior to sunset, a second attempt by the Bolshevik gunboats to interfere with the operation was repulsed. That evening the infantry marched into Chamova without a shot being fired. In this first engagement the actions by the flotilla had been successful and the enemy had withdrawn. It transpired that the Bolshevik forces, which had engaged the naval landing party in the village, were the main body of the retreating Bolshevik forces.

Later the naval flotilla on the Dvina River damaged several of the Bolshevik gunboats and forced the remainder back to Kotlas. In one such action, in mid-September, a Bolshevik gunboat had suddenly approached the Allied positions and shelled them at close range. The American and British troops in the area opened a brisk fire with rifles and machine guns, causing the gunboat to haul off into mid-stream and then moor on a nearby island. At this stage the monitor M23 appeared and soon hit the enemy craft with several shells and set it on fire.

On 19 September mines were sighted in the Dvina between 15-20 miles south from Bereznik. Minesweeping was difficult, mainly because of the lack of properly designated mine-sweepers, and although the area had been occupied by Allied troops there was still some sniping at the crews from the riverbanks. A channel was finally swept and at the beginning of October the troops pressed on to occupy Seltzo, 35 miles from Bereznik, where it was intended to main-tain a front line over the winter. Immediately after the capture of the town the naval flotilla was ordered to withdraw to Archangel in anticipation of the Dvina freezing over; remaining upriver would have resulted in the ships being caught for the winter in the ice and falling depths of water. To try and offset the loss of the naval flotilla's guns two batteries of recently arrived Canadian 18-pounder field guns were sent to the area.

Both soldiers and sailors were feeling the effects of the beginning of the Arctic winter. Only a few weeks previously they had been basking in the warmth of summer sunshine and beat-ing off the attacks of countless mosquitoes. At Archangel and along the river southwards the temperature had been warm enough for the Admiralty to order the wearing of white uniform by both officers and ratings in the Royal Navy. The sailors had been issued with straw hats with khaki covers to wear instead of their traditional caps. The orders included instructions for the wearing of mosquito nets or butter muslin to guard against the hordes of insects which were prevalent in certain areas. Ratings working ashore had been given the option of blue shorts with boots and blue puttees instead of white uniform. However, September had brought the rain and the weather became ever colder; the men were in desperate need of warm clothing, much of which was in short supply. The advent of winter, with its habitual potential ferocity and the threat of up to thirty degrees of frost, seemed to have caught the supply officers by surprise.

As it turned out, the freeze of the river did not start as soon as had been anticipated. Rear Admiral Vikorist, the Bolshevik Commander of the Russian Naval Forces on the Dvina, seized his opportunity and his flotilla once more became active against the forces holding the outposts around Seltzo. These troops were forced out of the town, as the Russian naval guns outranged the Allied field artillery. The monitor M25 was sent upriver to provide support with her 7.5in gun. However, the level of water in the river had fallen so much that the ship was unable to go beyond Bereznik and returned to Archangel with considerable difficulty. Ten days later another attempt was made to support the army but the M23, like her sister ship, was unable to reach the front line. The monitor returned to Archangel immediately, getting back just as the river began to freeze.

The danger of ships becoming caught in the ice as the river froze – it could form to a foot thick in a night – meant that a specific date had to be set for the ships to get back to

Archangel. Conditions in 1918 directed that this should be 7 October. In order to leave some comparatively long-range artillery with the army some guns were landed from the gunboats and mounted ashore. The French brought up a 4.7in gun mounted on a raft and subsequently a Russian 5.5in gun arrived upriver also mounted on a raft. Both these weapons became frozen in and had to remain in a fixed position for the duration of winter. The Russian gun was manned by a crew from the M25 and was particularly useful until it was knocked out by concentrated fire from Bolshevik batteries. The Allies laboured under the disadvantage that the river froze later and thawed earlier on the enemy side of the front line – simply as a result of geography – precluding the Allied ships from supporting the army at a time when the enemy's ships were still free to move.

The four 'China' gunboats *Glowworm*, *Cockchafer*, *Cricket* and *Cicala*[14] were specially fitted out in British dockyards to winter in Archangel, ready to resume operations in the early summer of 1919 as soon as the ice conditions in the Dvina permitted. The four ships had been rearmed with two 6in guns, two 3in and ten Maxim and Lewis machine guns and arrived in Archangel at the end of October and beginning of November. Their draught of only 4ft made them better ships than the monitors for operations on the river. The twelve ships of this class, all completed between November 1915 and February 1916, were known as 'China' gunboats only to conceal their proposed destination. It had been intended to sail them to Salonika, dismantle them and transport them overland to the Danube for re-assembly. There they would give support to the Serbs and be able to combat the Austro-Hungarian Danube Flotilla. However, by the time the ships had been completed the Serbian Army had been defeated and there was no longer access to the Danube. It was only after the war that they actually went to China for service on the rivers, where the British had valuable trading concessions. The two 'M' class monitors also remained in Archangel for the winter; the remaining warships were withdrawn either to Murmansk or back to Britain. Before the White Sea was closed by ice the Admiralty sent sufficient food and stores to Archangel to provide for both civilians and the military until the port was open again.

At the end of September the Americans decided to send a senior officer to North Russia to take command of their naval forces in the area. The newly promoted Rear Admiral Newton McCully was selected for the post and on 24 October he arrived in Murmansk on board the French cruiser *Amiral Gueydon*. He promptly hoisted his flag in the USS *Olympia*. His instructions included the sentence: 'Your actions should make it clear that you are the sincere friend of the Russian people and the American forces have no ulterior military or political objectives inimical to Russian sovereignty.' On 8 November the *Olympia* left Russia for Britain and the United States carrying on board the Ambassador, David Francis, who was sick, and eighty-four wounded American soldiers. McCully's command had left with the old cruiser but the admiral himself remained.

Major General Poole left Archangel on 26 October to return to London for some leave and discussions concerning future operations. He did not return. Major General Edmund Ironside[15] – nicknamed 'Tiny' for his twenty stone weight and 6ft 4in height – arrived to assume command of forces in the Archangel area. He was fluent in seven languages, including Russian, and particularly impressed the Russians with whom he had to work because he could curse them in their own language. He had vast powers of leadership and, unlike his predecessor, was extremely tactful – qualities that would stand him in good stead in the months to come in dealing with his multi-national force, where morale was at a low point when he arrived. However, he was only to be responsible for operations on the Archangel front, leaving Major General Maynard independently responsible for those south of Murmansk.

The ship which carried Ironside to Russia also had embarked the 16th Field Brigade, Canadian Field Artillery (CFA), consisting of two batteries of 18-pounder guns. The brigade was formed entirely of volunteers from units who had been serving in France and in England. Immediately on landing the brigade provided a detachment to crew an armoured train on the single-track Vologda Railway, armed with one 18-pounder, two small naval guns and machine guns. The train helped stop Bolshevik trains and forces attempting to counter-attack north-wards. The rest of the brigade was sent by barge up the Dvina to Bereznik.

The 11th day of November 1918 is normally remembered as the day the First World War ended. Many soldiers and sailors serving in North Russia were unaware of the great events in France and elsewhere until several days later. For Allied troops at Tulgas, on the west bank of the Dvina and to the south of Bereznik, the day was notable in that it signalled the onset of a strong Bolshevik attack, which was directed both north and south of the small town. The garrison consisted of one company of American infantry, a company of the Royal Scots and some Canadian artillerymen manning two of their 18-pounder field guns. The attack was supported by two Russian gunboats, which had taken advantage of a slight thaw to allow them to reach Tulgas and bombard the Allied positions with 4.7 and 6in guns. The fight lasted all day, with the Canadian gunners often reduced to firing over open sights. The following day the Russian attack was finally repulsed and the Red forces withdrew[16].

The success of the Allied armies in France in the early autumn of 1918 had caused a gradual withdrawal of German troops from Finland as the High Command sought reinforcements to make good the losses of their spring offensive and to try and halt the steady Allied advance. By mid-October all the German troops had left the country and the possible threat to Murmansk and Petchenga no longer existed. It was considered that the White Finns would not seek action on their own, but nevertheless their stance was unclear. Any British withdrawal from the area, or an immediate change in force levels, was not deemed feasible.

The 11 November Armistice should have brought operations in Russia to a halt. The reason for intervention in Russia was originally to protect the vast quantities of stores that had accumulated at Archangel and Murmansk from being removed and perhaps allowed to fall into German hands. It was also the intention to encourage any military resistance by the Russians so that the withdrawal of German troops would not be possible. With the Armistice this plainly was no longer applicable. Nevertheless, as early as 14 November the Cabinet in London approved a Foreign Office proposal that Allied troops should remain in occupation of Murmansk and Archangel; that the British Government should recognise the Government of Admiral Kolchak in Omsk as the *de facto* Government of Russia; and that support should be given to the Czechoslovak forces in Western Siberia. The Government also accepted an obligation to protect and support those elements in Russia which had given aid to British forces in defiance of the Bolshevik Government in Moscow.

There was another important change in command before the end of the year. On 15 November Rear Admiral John Green arrived in Murmansk in HMS *Shannon* and took over the duties as Senior Naval Officer, White Sea from Rear Admiral Thomas Kemp, the latter having spent three years in North Russia in that post.

Two disturbing incidents before the end of 1918 showed the fragile reliability of the White Russian troops. On 29 October General Ironside was due to inspect a company of troops from the 1st Archangel Regiment. When ordered to fall in the men flatly refused. They said that they had held a democratic meeting and decided that it was time to strike a blow for better treatment and working hours. The Russian officers of the company cravenly decided that they were safer in a place away from their men and quietly left the barracks, making no attempt to restore order. Ironside, not wishing to make matters any worse, decided not to use British troops to take on the mutineers. Instead, he ordered two Russian colonels of proven loyalty and bravery to be brought from the front to Archangel; such was the urgency of the situation they were flown back. The two officers went to the barracks and quickly restored discipline with a few curt orders; the first mutiny by an anti-Bolshevik regiment was over.

The same regiment was due to entrain for the front in December, after attending a *Te Deum* in the cathedral. Two companies refused duty. This time American troops were immediately ordered to the scene. After two mortar bombs had exploded in the barracks and the walls peppered with rifle and machine-gun fire the Russian soldiers came out with their hands up. Thirteen ringleaders were identified and promptly shot by a firing squad drawn from the mutinous regiment; a second mutiny was over. Many years later, in his autobiography, Ironside wrote that the mutinies 'had caused me a greater shock than I liked to admit even in my innermost thoughts. I now felt a distinct urge to extricate my troops as quickly as I could'. Whatever Ironside may have felt, there was at that time no question of withdrawal.

FOUR

MURMANSK AND ARCHANGEL, 1919

The opening weeks of 1919 presented the Allied troops in North Russia with the difficulty of trying to cope with the extreme conditions, which were unlike anything they had ever had to experience previously. The cold weather clothing, which had eventually reached the British troops, was very good apart from the shoes, which tended to cause the wearer to slip on icy surfaces. The whole outfit had been designed by Ernest Shackleton, the famous Antarctic explorer. However, frostbite was an ever-present danger; it took only a few moments to strike, such as when a soldier carelessly removed his padded mittens. Men caught outside without shelter could lose fingers and toes; those that fell asleep in the open would not wake.

Probably the men who suffered the most were the RAF mechanics and fitters. The engines of their aircraft froze, despite being constantly warmed with special covers; they had to be flushed through with five gallons of hot water before they could be started up. Bracing wires and struts on the wings could snap as the metal crystallised in the intense cold. Bomb release gear would freeze in flight and aircrew were reduced to carrying small 20-pound bombs in the cockpit and dropping them by hand! In the face of all these additional problems the mechanics found it extremely difficult to work with their hands protected against frostbite.

The soldiers found that the cold also affected their ammunition. The Canadian 18-pounder field gun crews had to set gun ranges which were nearly double those normally needed; the French 75mm guns had similar problems. Grenades often failed to explode as the firing pins had frozen. Machine-gunners found the moving parts of their weapons frozen solid. In addition, the troops had to deal with increasingly hostile attacks by Bolshevik infantry.

On 19 January 1919 the Bolsheviks launched a strong assault with about 8,000 men on the Allied outpost at Shenkursk, on the River Vaga. The town was held by a joint American-Russian garrison, which was eventually driven out after fierce fighting. One battery of Canadian artillery was also involved in the battle, constantly firing in close support of the infantry. The surviving soldiers and nearly 500 civilian refugees fell back nearly 70 miles to Kitsa, near Bereznik. The retreating column made their way through deep snow along forest paths in temperatures of 35 degrees Farenheit below freezing. The Russian troops had proved to be stubborn in defence, but one company refused to advance and counter-attack the Bolsheviks. When the Americans reached the village where they had left all their personal belongings while in the front line, they found that their kitbags had been looted. The men lost almost everything they owned. The village, as with others on the line of march, was burnt by the Cossack rearguard once all the troops had passed through.

The fall of Shenkursk was a serious blow to the prestige of both the Allies and the Provisional Government. It had a devastating effect on morale in Archangel among civilians and the military.

As long as that important bastion, 200 miles away, was held then Archangel itself remained aloof from the war and any possible Bolshevik advance. People became fearful that being seen to support the Allies might be a serious and fatal mistake. It is therefore not surprising that the leader of the Northern Provisional Government, Nicholas Tchaikovsky, took the opportunity to leave – by ice-breaker – for Paris, ostensibly to have discussions with Allied leaders at the Peace Conference. He never returned.

The fall of Shenkursk was followed a week later by a Bolshevik attack further west and once again the Allied outposts were driven back. General Ironside considered that the situation was becoming critical and requested that the War Office in London should send more troops. Reinforcements were not sent but General Maynard in Murmansk was ordered to send a battalion and half a machine-gun company to Archangel. A few of these men were able to travel in the comparative luxury of an ice-breaker; the remainder travelled by train to Soroka and then marched 200 miles to Onega, their equipment and supplies being carried on a relay of sleighs.

At Onega the men were expected to go south to Kodish to help stabilise the front line. They refused. The officer commanding, Lieutenant Colonel Lavie, who had only been with the regiment for a few days, ordered them to fall in without their weapons. Once the men were on parade two sergeants stepped forward and volunteered the information that the men had had made up their minds not to fight. Lavie immediately ordered a corporal to take a squad and return with their rifles. The regiment eventually marched to Kodish, the sergeants having been placed under close arrest. Both men had recently transferred into the regiment; they had served all the war in the Pay Corps in England. Ironside ordered the court-martial of the two NCOs, who were found guilty of mutiny and were sentenced to be executed by firing squad. This was commuted to life imprisonment with hard labour; King George V had instructed that no further disciplinary executions were to take place, as the war was over.

News of this mutiny by British troops reached the French Colonial Regiment. In turn some of them mutinied on 1 March, the date they were due to leave Archangel to relieve the Americans in the front line. Most of one company refused to leave their barracks, insolently remaining on their beds. They were put under the guard of a detachment of marines from the French cruiser *Gueydon*[1], which was lying in the harbour, and were later evacuated to France once the ice in the White Sea had broken.

While Ironside was trying to halt further Bolshevik advances, General Maynard received approval from London to stage a limited offensive against enemy positions on the railway down to Segeja, about 70 miles south of Soroka. He considered this to be very necessary to counter any reports – which would almost certainly reach the Russians – that his forces had been weakened by sending reinforcements to Archangel. The operation was a complete success and Segeja was captured by the end of February.

The situation in North Russia at the beginning of 1919 caused considerable anxiety not only to General Ironside and the military but also to the politicians. Winston Churchill, by then the Secretary of State for War, pressed for decisive military action but – as was so often the case – his was a lone voice. The Prime Minister, Lloyd George, in particular wished to play down British involvement, while the British public cared little for what happened in Russia, indeed many sympathised with the Revolution. The matter remained continually under review and in March the War Cabinet in London decided to advise Allied Governments that all forces should be withdrawn from North Russia. The rear admiral, White Sea (Rear Admiral Green) was informed of this decision on 11 March, as was General Ironside, and they were told to make secret preparations to plan for the withdrawal of forces as soon as ice conditions in the White Sea permitted.

Admiral Green appreciated that this change in Government policy should not make any difference to preparations already being made to reinforce naval strength on the River Dvina. He thought it very likely that once the White Russian troops learnt that the Allies were leaving they might well desert to the Bolsheviks, making an Allied withdrawal even more difficult. Under these circumstances a strong and well-disciplined naval force would be essential to hold the Bolshevik riverine flotilla in check while the troops were withdrawn down-river to Archangel; it would also be available to help deal with any turncoat Russians. Clearly, a complete withdrawal would not be possible until the middle of June and the troops at Murmansk could not pull out until after the evacuation of Archangel was complete.

The naval force, which had been retained at Archangel for the winter, would remain only a distant threat to Bolshevik forces on the Dvina until the break up of the ice on the river allowed both sides the freedom to move. There would then be a delay of five or six weeks until the ice broke in the White Sea. In the meantime, the Admiralty had to ensure that strong reinforcements were available at Murmansk, ready to move as soon as conditions allowed. The size and number of ships that were to be prepared by the Admiralty depended on a Government decision as to the extent of operations in 1919. War Cabinet approval was given on 5 February 1919, although there were to be restrictions and the ships were available for 'active defence, in co-operation with the army, and only as far as the positions then occupied by the military forces on the rivers'. At this time Ironside's forces were in position on the River Dvina at Kurgomen, south of Bereznik and about 200 miles from Archangel.

The new naval expeditionary force totalled twenty-two[2] HM Ships in addition to the six already in Archangel, together with a large number of auxiliaries and barges for stores and repair bases. The river force would be under the command of Captain Edward Altham, who had commanded the River Flotilla so successfully in 1918. HMS *Haldon*, a paddle minesweeper of the Ascot class, was fitted out as the SNO's headquarters ship, but in the event she had to be diverted to other duties in the White Sea, as her draught of over 7ft would have restricted operations on the river. As a replacement vessel Captain Altham chose what must arguably be one of the strangest looking ships which has ever been graced with the prefix HMS: it was the local paddle steamer *Borodino*.

Another peculiar vessel destined to join the River Flotilla was HMS *Hyderabad* – a one-time Q-ship built specifically as such in 1916. For her new task the ship was converted to become a 'mother ship' to assist the fighting ships upriver and to be able to carry out many ancillary duties. To keep the draught of the ship as small as possible, all the guns, magazines and Q-ship superstructure were removed, while a sick-bay, operating theatre, bakery, refrigeration spaces and a large number of showers and baths were added. At one time the ship would provide the only operating theatre for emergency cases for the army, where the nearest field hospital was 50 miles downriver.

Once Government approval for the force had been given, the organisation and preparation was pushed forward with all possible speed. Ships required work done to make them ready for the conditions they might meet in North Russia, and many shallow-draft vessels had to be brought home from the Mediterranean and Mesopotamia before being sent out to operate on the River Dvina.

HMS *Fox*, an elderly light cruiser[3] only lately returned to Chatham after service in the East Indies, was chosen as the parent ship for the whole force. The ship finally left Rosyth on 4 May 1919, calling at Murmansk to await suitable weather conditions before sailing for Archangel. The *Fox* left Murmansk on 10 May in company with the naval repair ship HMS *Cyclops* and the Royal Fleet Auxiliary store ship *Bacchus*. The ice-breaker *Sviatogor*, raised from the bed of the Dvina River at Archangel the previous autumn and commissioned with a Royal Navy crew, went with them to assist their passage through the ice. The ships made a steady 12½ knots until the afternoon of the 11th, when pack ice was encountered. The ice floes quickly grew larger and thicker and the *Bacchus* was soon surrounded by thick ice and brought to a halt. The *Sviatogor* was unable to help and all the ships had to await the arrival of two more ice-breakers, which had been sent from Archangel. The *Kosma Minim* and *Kniaz Pojarski*, with Russian crews, were sighted that evening but it was six hours before they were in company and the little flotilla began to make slow and intermittent progress once again.

It was a terrifying time for the crews of the British ships, who were totally unused to this type of weather and these conditions. The temperature dropped to 10 degrees Farenheit below zero. The ships were creaking and groaning as the ice pressed in on the hulls. Sleep was almost impossible because of the bumps that reverberated throughout the ship as unusually large chunks of ice hit the hull. Progress was less than walking pace and they sometimes managed as much as 3 miles in four hours. The interior of the ship became soaked with condensation.

These conditions prevailed for three days as the ships made their way slowly through the frozen sea towards their destination. Eventually, the ice began to get thinner until they were able to make good 10 knots, reaching Archangel after six days in the ice field.

When the War Cabinet decided that British troops should be withdrawn from North Russia, Winston Churchill was given authority to 'make any preliminary arrangements necessary to bring about the safe evacuation of the troops'. He ordered the War Office to prepare two brigades, which would be sent to Archangel. Their purpose was to relieve those British troops who had spent the previous summer and winter in North Russia; to make good the numbers of troops caused by the American withdrawal, planned for June; and to ensure that the evacuation went smoothly and unhindered. Churchill also wanted it made clear to the men who formed the brigades that they were going only to 'extricate their comrades and not for a long occupation'.

The American Admiral McCully feared that the situation at the front to the south of Archangel was becoming precarious and requested an increase in the size of the US Navy presence in Murmansk and Archangel. He felt that the most immediate critical time would occur between mid-April and mid-May, when the ice on the upper reaches of the Dvina would have thawed, allowing the free movement of Bolshevik gunboats. To counter this and to protect the flank of American troops he asked that twelve submarine chasers be sent to arrive by 1 May. After some debate with Admiral Sims in London there was a compromise and McCully was sent three of these small (500 tons) Eagle class ships, imaginatively named *Eagle 1*, *Eagle 2* and *Eagle 3*. The Americans appear to have overlooked the fact that the British already had a far more powerful flotilla of monitors and gunboats at Archangel but they would be unable to move south until the ice broke in the lower part of the river; the same limiting factor would also have prevented any movement of the Eagle boats. In the event, the American ships arrived but remained at Murmansk.

At Tulgas, on the left bank of the Dvina below Kurgomen, the Allies suffered another setback at the end of April. The 3rd North Russian Rifle Regiment had taken over a section of the front line from the Americans; however, about 300 men of the regiment mutinied, murdered their officers and deserted to the enemy. They immediately turned round and attacked the rest of their erstwhile comrades and soon the Bolsheviks were firmly established in the small town. Canadian artillery, firing from the other bank of the river, helped the surviving Whites to escape.

Bolshevik gunboats had been able to move freely even before the later break-up of the ice in the lower reaches of the river at Archangel allowed the British ships to move. Fortunately, the Canadians had transported three heavy guns – 60-pounders (5in calibre)[4] – by specially constructed sleighs from Archangel, using a total of 118 ponies to pull the enormous weight through 120 miles of deep snow in only ten days. The guns had arrived at the front just as the thaw began.

These large guns out-ranged anything that the Bolsheviks had mounted on their river flotilla. During the first week in May the Canadians were able to show that the enemy gunboats no longer had the ability to hit the Allied troops with impunity. The nine ships of the Bolshevik flotilla, mounting 5.1in or 6in guns, retired hastily back upriver to Puchega as soon as they came under fire. The only time the Canadians were troubled by the enemy was when the Bolsheviks mounted some 6in guns on barges and brought them into action. These too were repelled.

The monitor M23 (Lieutenant Commander St A.O. St John) slipped from her winter berth on 3 May and skilfully forced her way upriver through the thick ice in the lower reaches of the Dvina, the first Allied naval ship to reach the front line in 1919. On 6 May the ship made her presence known to the enemy when Tulgas was bombarded. The following day the monitor was joined by the four smaller 'China' gunboats *Cricket* (Lieutenant Commander A. Worsley), *Cockchafer* (Lieutenant Commander C. Hester), *Cicala* (Lieutenant Commander E. Grayston) and *Glowworm* (Commander A. Ackland); the last two began operations by going up the Vaga River and bombarding the enemy positions. The arrival of the naval ships at the front after the ice had broken proved good for the morale of the troops.

A number of minor engagements took place during May between the gunboats of the two sides. On 11 May the *Glowworm* scored the only notable success of these skirmishes when a Bolshevik ship was badly damaged by shellfire. In the middle of the month aerial reconnaissance reported a total of forty-two various Bolshevik vessels at Seltso, some 15 miles upriver from the Allied forward positions. The British gunboats were in action almost daily during the ensuing summer and in one month fired over 1,000 rounds of 6in ammunition apiece. Besides the Bolshevik gun barges, targets included cavalry units and entrenched positions. The Bolsheviks retaliated by making regular – but ineffectual – air attacks.

The crews of the gunboats and monitors working on the river near the front line had to put up with excessive summer heat, inadequate food and conditions for which their ships had not been designed. In June the crew of HMS *Cicala*, dissatisfied with their lot, refused to sail up the Dvina to engage the Bolshevik batteries. Captain Altham, acting on behalf of Admiral Green, ordered the other ships to train their guns on the *Cicala*. The threat of being fired on by their own ships – and perhaps coercion from those on board the gunboat who were willing to obey orders – restored the situation. The ringleaders of this mutiny were court-martialled and returned to England.

Churchill's 'Russian Relief Force' of 8,000 men was formed of volunteers who for one reason or another were prepared to rejoin the army, having been demobilised at the end of the war. Jobs were hard to find and they discovered that, contrary to what they had been told, Britain was not 'a country fit for heroes'. Re-enlisting seemed a good alternative to life on the dole. Efforts were also made to attract men from the Dominions who were still in Britain awaiting transport to their homelands. Between 2-300 Australians were recruited, but only a few from New Zealand, Canada or South Africa. Most of the Australians were veterans of Gallipoli and the Western Front and were enrolled into the 45th Battalion of the Royal Fusiliers and the 201st Battalion, the Machine Gun Corps. Before they could be enlisted they first had to be discharged from the Australian Imperial Force, since the Dominion Government refused to become embroiled in Russia. However, the Australian Government did agree to sponsor their return to their home country once their service in Russia was over.

A number of these Australians had clearly volunteered on impulse and, given time to reconsider, withdrew their enlistment. Among the many reasons cited for changing their minds were the harsh conditions likely to be met in North Russia, the loss of rank on joining the British Army, the fact that they would be serving under British officers and, perhaps strongest of all, the lure of returning home. Nevertheless, there were enough applications for General Sir William Birdwood, who had been the commander of ANZAC troops on the Western Front, to write to the Governor-General of Australia in Canberra:

> It really seems astounding that apparently such large numbers of men should be keen on this, while presumably the same men are ready to make a tremendous fuss if not returned to their homes without delay.

The two brigades were named after their Commanding Officers; Brigadier G. W. St George Grogan and Brigadier L. W. de V. Sadlier-Jackson. Grogan's brigade arrived in Archangel on 26 May. Part of Sadlier-Jackson's brigade arrived on 5 June, the remainder four days later. The first unit in action was the 2nd Battalion the Hampshire Regiment who were taken upriver to relieve the Americans at Tulgas, the village having been recaptured on 18 May.

Meanwhile the Royal Fusiliers, with the Australians, moved up the Dvina to a camp at Osonova. The months of June and July were taken up with training exercises, in conjunction with White Russian troops, and small-scale patrols south of Troitsa. These were planned to keep the Red Army at bay and to give the White Russians confidence in their own ability to take on the Bolsheviks[5].

The situation regarding the Americans grew more obscure. In early May Admiral McCully requested that more of the Eagle class boats should be sent to North Russia if the American troops were to take part in operations on the Dvina front in the coming months. Once again the established presence of the comparatively heavily armed British River Flotilla seems to have been overlooked by McCully; the American boats were armed with only two 4in and one 3in guns. This was, perhaps, symptomatic of the lack of a common policy in North Russia between the Allies, the complete absence of consultation and a general feeling of resentment by the Americans at British overall command.

In Washington the Chief of Naval Operations, Admiral William Benson, sought clarification of policy from President Wilson before considering McCully's request. He was told that 'there are no plans for active operations, and what is intended is merely to ensure the safe withdrawal of our land force'. The President had, in fact, already agreed to withdraw the American troops as soon as the thaw allowed. However, unbeknown to the President, at that time the 339th Infantry Regiment was heavily engaged in fierce fighting. It was several weeks before the troops in the front line learned of their intended withdrawal.

Gradually, all the Americans were relieved from front line duties and sent back to Archangel. On 14 June they boarded their transports and sailed for the USA. They had fought well, suffered over 200 casualties but met with little acclaim on their return home. As a result of pressure from the Government in Ottawa, the Canadians too sailed for home; the 16th Field Brigade CFA fired its last rounds on 28 May and headed north to Archangel. The Canadian's final parade in Russia took place on 11 June, when they were inspected by General Ironside. The gunners had won universal praise for their professional qualities and spirit, and in bidding them farewell the general said 'Over and over again the CFA had saved the Dvina force from destruction'.

The Royal Air Force in North Russia had also been reinforced. The first priority in the early months of the year was seaplanes, since during May no landplanes would be able to operate because of the marshy nature of the ground. On 31 March six seaplanes arrived in Murmansk on board the SS *War Grange*. The ship had to wait for nearly a month before the ice was thin enough for her to make the passage to Archangel, escorted by the watchful *Sviatogor*. The aircraft were uncrated, made airworthy and went into action almost immediately.

Among the pilots at Archangel was Major Alexander Kazakov, an ace of the old Tsarist Air Force. He had with him thirty-seven other Russian pilots and ground crew as well as a small unit of RAF aircrew, half of whom were Canadians – some with as little as twenty-four hours flying experience. In addition to the seaplanes there were eight DH4 bombers sent direct from Britain. Kazakov also discovered some Sopwith 1½ Strutters and Nieuports still in crates in a stores dump near the railway station at Bakaritza; they had arrived before the Revolution and had been missed by the Bolsheviks before they left Archangel.

The RAF established an airfield at Bereznik, some 140 miles south of Archangel at the junction of the Dvina and Varga Rivers, from where they could operate the landplanes. The aircraft included a motley collection of DH4s, DH9s, Camels, Snipes and Sopwith 1½ Strutters. The seaplanes were eventually based on an island in the Dvina near Troitsa. Initially, the RAF attacks consisted of bombing and strafing. While there was little air opposition, enemy ground fire was effective. The greatest fear aircrews had in these operations was not in engaging the enemy, but being shot down in enemy territory and captured. They were advised to carry a pistol and shoot themselves rather than risk capture, for the Bolshevik troops were known to show barbarity towards their attackers.

An example of this occurred in mid-August, when seven DH4 and DH9 bombers were sent to attack Red forces in the village of Gordook. Flying into fog, the aircrews lost direction and only two planes returned to base. One of the missing aircraft made a forced landing in enemy territory. The pilot made the mistake of asking a nearby soldier where he was and then, on realising he was behind enemy lines, he sprinted back to the aircraft. In his haste to take off he choked the engine and it would not start. He climbed out of the cockpit and attempted to swing the propeller, but by this time enemy soldiers had arrived in force and he was viciously bayoneted to death. Fortunately for the second member of the crew, he had a mechanic's overalls covering his uniform and so was not recognised as being an officer. He survived and was sent to a prison camp.

The British policy of withdrawal from North Russia did not last for long. The success of Admiral Kolchak's armies in Siberia in April and May 1919 made the possibility of a junction with them at Kotlas once again seem a viable proposition. At this time Kolchak and his White Army was at Perm, less than 500 miles from Kotlas. General Ironside was accordingly given approval by the War Cabinet for an offensive towards Kotlas, supported by the naval River Flotilla. The policy of intervention in North Russia was thereby substantially altered; it was now to become much more active in support for the anti-Bolshevik forces. It also implied that the evacuation planned for the beginning of summer would have to be postponed at least until just before the ice formed in the White Sea about November.

An advance by the army towards Kotlas would have given the naval river force a difficult task in providing support. The distance from Bereznik to Kotlas was about 200 miles but would have to be undertaken through unknown channels, which could be mined by the enemy. It would need a very large minesweeping force – for which no provision had been made. The depth of water in the Dvina, before September when the rains might be expected to swell the river, was also problematical; not more than 3ft 6in could be expected in the upper reaches.

Captain Altham, as SNO of the river force, had only four 'Tunnel' minesweepers of the Dance class with which to clear any Bolshevik mines in the Dvina[6]. These ships had their propellers protected to enable sweeping to take place in shallow waters without the risk of damage to the screws striking the bottom. Three Russian-manned paddle tugs which had been fitted for minesweeping proved to be unsuitable for the task; they had insufficient power. The minesweepers – HM Ships *Sword Dance*, *Stepdance*, *Morris Dance* and *Fandango* – reached the front in the middle of June and began their task as soon as the army had cleared the enemy from both banks of the river. The sweepers were constantly harassed by fire from the Bolshevik gunboats, which retired as soon as the supporting British gunboats returned fire. By the 27th a channel had been opened up as far as Troitsa (on the right bank, a little further upriver from Tulgas), which would become an advanced base for gunboats, CMBs[7] and seaplanes. Another problem that the four sweepers had to contend with was the turbid state of the river, which made it almost impossible to spot mines, even from a seaplane.

Two of the minesweepers were sunk during these operations. The *Sword Dance* (Lieutenant A. Halliley) struck a mine on 24 June and the *Fandango* (Chief Boatswain T. Vosper) met a similar fate on 3 July. One rating was killed in the former and one officer and seven ratings in the latter. A total of over forty mines were swept and destroyed.

The Bolsheviks later used the tactic of floating their mines down the river with the current and a net defence across the width of the Dvina was constructed to foil these efforts. Before the net could be laid, a mine was sighted drifting down towards a hospital barge. Lieutenant R. Fitzherbert-Brockholes and four ratings were killed when the mine exploded as they attempted to tow it clear before rendering it safe. Captain Altham proposed Fitzherbert-Brockholes for a posthumous Victoria Cross, which the Admiralty 'could not see their way to recommend His Majesty to award'.

HMS *Cicala* became another casualty when the leadsman inadvertently struck a mine as he made his cast. The resulting explosion so close to the ship damaged the bows to such an extent that it required several weeks' repair in Archangel.

Attempts were made to salvage the *Sword Dance*. With the help of lifting 'camels' the ship was raised off the bottom and secured between two lighters. The minesweeper was then pumped out, a task which was aided by the fact that some compartments were still intact. However, the damage to the wreck was found to be too extensive and the hulk was later sunk again and ultimately blown up as the final evacuation commenced.

The navy also assisted ashore. Thirty-five seamen, under the command of Lieutenant M. Spalding, were landed to protect the riverine flotilla's anchorage and the seaplane base, near Troitsa. Lieutenant R. Martin commanded another party of twenty seamen which manned two 60-pounder guns; one of these had actually been salvaged from the bottom of the river.

The War Office in London made poison gas available for use during General Ironside's offensive – a perfectly legitimate weapon of war at that time, ever since its first use by the Germans on the Western Front in April 1915. The gas sent to Russia was a new variety and therefore still secret, and there were concerns that its formula could be acquired by the Russians. There were also problems of a more practical nature. It was found to be impossible to empty the canisters by hand, particularly when the wind was light. It also required a northerly wind to ensure that the gas flowed towards the Bolshevik lines, and this was surprisingly infrequent at that time of year. Ironside requested that special new gas projectors should be sent out, but these were found to be useless as they arrived broken. However, an officer of the Royal Engineers designed a bomb for delivering gas which could be made locally in the workshops of the naval repair ship, HMS *Cyclops*.

By the time Ironside's troops began a cautious advance, the situation in Central Russia had changed drastically – and for the worse. Admiral Kolchak's forces, under the command of the Czech General Rudolf Gajda[8], had suffered a severe defeat and were soon in full retreat. Any chance of linking up with them at Kotlas had vanished. In addition, there had been more mutinies among the Russian troops under Ironside's command; these were in regiments that had been raised, trained and armed by the British and should have been considered reliable.

On 30 July 1919 a meeting in London considered the effects of Gajda's defeat and the Russian mutinies on British policy. It came to the conclusion that the original plan of a total withdrawal from North Russia should be implemented. General Sir Henry Rawlinson was sent to Archangel to make the final arrangements and to co-ordinate both Maynard's and Ironside's forces in what might prove to be a hazardous operation. Rawlinson[9] sailed from Newcastle on 4 August on board the SS *Czaritsa*, reaching Archangel on the 11th. HMS *Haldon* was placed at the General's disposal during his time in North Russia and the Government in London gave him full discretion as to the time and method of implementation. Also on board the *Czaritsa* were six tanks, which were to help cover the final withdrawal from Archangel.

The morale of the White Russian troops was greatly strengthened by the arrival of General Eugene Miller as Commander-in-Chief of the Russian forces in North Russia. He had fought successfully against the Austrians and Germans in Poland and Galicia and had been well regarded by his troops. His first task was to create a strong anti-Bolshevik army and by the end of April he had 16,000 men under arms. Despite the earlier mutiny of a battalion at Tulgas, the regiments appeared to be well disciplined and ready for battle. Ironside decided to order a small offensive operation using these troops. In fact the Russian attack was a great success, achieving all their objectives and causing the Bolsheviks over 500 casualties. It was therefore all the more disappointing that on 7 July a company of Dyer's battalion in the Slavo-British Legion, named after its first Commanding Officer – a Canadian who had died of overwork and the Arctic cold – mutinied and killed five British and four Russian officers. One, Captain Barr, made a brave bid to raise the alarm by swimming out to the monitor HMS *Humber*. He had ten bullet wounds and, not surprisingly, he soon died but not before General Ironside had personally decorated him for his gallantry. A hundred men of the battalion deserted to the Bolsheviks.

On 19 July another Russian unit mutinied at Onega. Captain J.B. Wilson, one of the regiment's British officers, was handed over by the mutineers to the Bolsheviks and eventually imprisoned in Moscow. He was later exchanged for Commissar Raskolnikov, who had been captured by the British in the Baltic at Christmas 1918 and was held in Brixton Prison in London. Another British officer, Captain G. Roupell, also ended up in prison in Moscow and he was not released until May 1922.

Events on the front line south of Bereznik also affected the troops of General Maynard's force south of Murmansk. The changes in policy regarding the evacuation from North Russia were unsettling for the troops and the possible extent of Maynard's operations became increasingly uncertain. In February he had already initiated a minor advance down the railway to Segeja, where a strong position between Lakes Segozero and Vigozero had been established.

Further operations were deferred until the status of the Finns in the area had been clarified. In 1918 a force of Red Finns had been enlisted in Murmansk by the British to help fight off any attacks by the White Finns and their German allies. On the other hand, by 1919 the British were so involved in active hostilities with the Bolsheviks in Russia that the mood and allegiance of the 1,400-strong Finnish Legion was becoming doubtful. There was also a local Karelian force, of about 2,000 men, to be taken into account. The Karelians, who wanted their own independent homeland[10], could be expected to join with the Red Finns in the event of trouble. Maynard's intelligence suggested that a revolt would take place on Sunday 6 April.

As a result of these expectations Maynard requested that one or more warships, each with a capability of putting a landing party of 400 men ashore, should be sent to Murmansk. Two

American cruisers, the *Chester*[1] and the *Galveston*, arrived on 5 April. The 6 April came and went without any undue trouble. However, pressure was put on the Finnish Government to enable the Finns at Murmansk to be included in any amnesty given within their country so that they could return to their homes. The Finns were eventually repatriated, but not until August.

With his base at Murmansk relatively secure, General Maynard felt able to move his HQ south to Kem, on the shores of the White Sea, which meant that he was nearer the centre of operations. At the end of April the War Cabinet informed Maynard that he might advance to the northern shore of Lake Onega, which dominated the approach to Petrograd from the north, if the situation was favourable. There was a proviso. White Finns were carrying out operations to the south of the lake and it would be politically undesirable for his troops to join up with this Finnish army. The Government was trying to obtain an undertaking from the Finnish Government that they had no territorial ambitions in the area. No such undertaking was received, but by then the matter had become academic.

At the beginning of May the troops at Segeja launched a pre-emptive assault on the Bolsheviks gathering at Urosozevo, who were preparing to go on the offensive. For the loss of one man killed and five wounded the Allied troops routed the enemy force, capturing some field guns and a large quantity of ammunition along with twenty-two railway freight cars loaded with valuable track repair equipment. The French troops manning an armoured train played a large part in the operation. Forty Bolshevik prisoners were sent back to Murmansk to be accommodated in the old battleship *Chesma*, which had been converted to house POWs.

On 4 May Maynard reported that his troops had captured the small town of Meselskaya, about 40 miles south of his previous advanced positions at Segeja. The Allied force of Royal Marines, Russians, Canadians, French and American troops had captured the town after fierce resistance. On the 18th the Allied force had taken Povienetz on the eastern shore of Lake Onega, and on the 21st Medvyeja Gora, situated on the railway opposite to Povienetz, was occupied.

Once established on the northern shores of Lake Onega General Maynard gathered together a varied collection of ships to form a navy on the lake itself, to wrest control from the Bolshevik flotilla already there. Maynard's flotilla consisted of the three American Eagle class submarine chasers, two British and one Russian 35ft open motor boats, and a motor boat each from the American ships *Galveston* and *Yorktown*. All had to be loaded on railway flat cars and taken south to the newly captured lake-port of Medvyeja Gora. Apart from the American ships and motor boats they were given crews of army and marine personnel. The flagship was one of the submarine chasers, which was armed with a 37mm gun and renamed *Jolly Roger*. She was an unlucky ship and had no chance to live up to her name; her engines frequently broke down and eventually she burst into flames and her ammunition exploded, killing five men.

The RAF gave good support to the ground troops, as far as it was able. The RE8 bombers had become a spent force by the time the troops reached Lake Onega, with just one aircraft still capable of flying. The seaplane carrier *Nairana* (Commander R.G. Moore) arrived in Murmansk with a flight of Short seaplanes and another of Fairey IIIc seaplanes. The aircraft were sent by rail to the lake and arrived on 4 June. They showed their worth in their first encounter with the enemy only two days later. Four armed Bolshevik steamers approached Medvyeja Gora; they were larger and more heavily armed vessels than any in the British flotilla. However, the Bolshevik ships were surprised when the seaplanes took off and attacked with bombs and machine guns.

On 23 June General Maynard took a party of VIPs by train up to the front to see conditions for themselves. The party included the American Rear Admiral McCully, a Russian general and a War Office film photographer. Accompanying them was a petty officer (officers' cook) from the *Nairana*, and he recorded the event in his diary. He describes the seaplane camp as being on the edge of the lake, with the aircraft themselves standing on a sandy beach. From the original two flights, one plane had crashed into the lake and sunk, as it had engine failure after reaching 100ft on take-off. Another had been damaged while doing some low-level bombing; a 250lb bomb had been released unintentionally instead of a 50-pounder and the aircraft had been caught in the blast. Other aircraft had been hit several times by rifle or machine-gun fire, but were repairable. At the time of the visit there were only four seaplanes ready for action.

Naval reinforcements arrived from England in July in the shape of twelve CMBs. There were six 40ft boats, each armed with a 3-pounder gun, and six 35-footers armed only with machine guns. The boats had arrived in Murmansk and had then to be shipped down the railway to Medvyeja Gora, where they arrived on 26 July. Commander R.W. Curteis was in command of the naval crews and maintenance parties, a total of fourteen officers and 120 ratings. On arrival he took over command of the whole of the flotilla.

The reinforced flotilla had its first success on 3 August in a combined operation with White Russian troops against the port of Tolvoya. Four Fairey seaplanes attacked three Bolshevik ships which were helping to defend the port. Although undamaged by the aircraft bombs, the ships hurried from the area; one ran aground and the remaining two surrendered to the 40ft CMBs, which had harried them with their guns. The Russian troops then captured the town. One 300-ton steamer and a small warship armed with two 3in guns were the prize for the naval flotilla for this gallant skirmish. As a result the whole of the northern part of Lake Onega was under Allied control.

While Maynard's forces were successfully advancing and gaining a foothold on the lake, Ironside's offensive down the Dvina came to a halt. In fact, in another change of British policy, Ironside was directed by the War Office that Archangel should now be evacuated at the earliest possible time, that the operation should be total and that preparations should be made to destroy everything of value. He was also told that Murmansk would only be held until all the small craft from Archangel were safely on their way back to Britain, at which time the remaining troops in North Russia would be withdrawn. To ensure the safe evacuation of all personnel, additional forces were prepared in England for despatch to Archangel and Murmansk, if required.

The Provisional Government in Archangel was told of the planned withdrawal and as a consequence they decided that it would be impossible for them to continue to oppose the Bolsheviks on their own. However General Miller, the Russian Commander-in-Chief, had other ideas and told Ironside that he considered it his duty to fight on[12]. This, in turn, led to a change in the decision to destroy all stores before departure – many would have to be left for the use of Miller's troops.

There was an ongoing demand for seaplane replacements to ensure that there were enough aircraft to support either any continued advance up the Dvina to consolidate the forward positions or a complete withdrawal. On 24 July HMS *Argus*, a new aircraft carrier with hangars and a complete flight deck for flying operations, left Britain for Archangel with seventeen seaplanes and RAF personnel. Twelve of these aircraft were disembarked to HMS *Pegasus*, the seaplane carrier and depot ship at Archangel, for service with the Dvina River Force. Another carrier, the *Nairana*, sailed from Kem and collected the other five machines for use on the Murmansk front.

Although the decision had been made to withdraw there was no possibility of acting upon it until the level of water in the Dvina rose with the rains at the end of August, or even early September. The British flotilla in the upper reaches of the river could still give support to the troops and it was planned to launch a heavy attack which would, it was hoped, deter the Bolshevik forces for enough time for an orderly disengagement of British forces to be made. The attack was planned for 10 August.

In co-operation with army guns, four monitors, the *Humber* (Lieutenant Commander A. Johnstone), M27 (Lieutenant Commander G. Parker), M31 (Lieutenant Commander F. Black) and M33 (Lieutenant Commander K. Mitchell) opened a heavy bombardment of forty minutes duration on the enemy positions. Seaplanes gave assistance by bombing the enemy and by spotting the fall of shot. A kite balloon, tethered to a barge, was brought into position for reconnaissance and also for spotting. On the right bank, the attack was immediately successful and the *Humber* and *Cicala* (Lieutenant Commander E. Grayston) carried out a further bombardment to enable the next objective to be captured.

On the left bank, the attack on Seltso stalled initially, chiefly because of the reluctance of the Russian troops to advance in the face of heavy Bolshevik resistance. The town was captured in the evening, but only after a further bombardment by the monitors *Humber*, M27 and M33. As a result of this successful attack both banks of the river were captured as far south as Borok on the right and Puchega on the left. Heavy casualties had been inflicted on the Bolshevik defenders and over 3,000 prisoners had been taken.

During the fighting the heroic deeds of an Australian, Sergeant Percy Sullivan, serving with the 45th Fusiliers, won him the award of the Victoria Cross. While his platoon was crossing the 100 yard-wide River Shika by a small plank bridge four of the men fell into the swampy water. Under heavy enemy fire, Sullivan jumped in and rescued all four soldiers.

A second Victoria Cross was won nineteen days later when the Australians were again in action, this time on the railway at Emsta. The Australians routed a Bolshevik force in a fierce bayonet charge. However, a group of Russians held the railway station and a nearby block-house. Sergeant Samuel Pearse cut his way through the barbed wire defences under heavy rifle and machine-gun fire, then single-handedly charged the blockhouse, killing all the occupants with grenades. Minutes later, Pearse was cut down by machine-gun fire from another position. The citation for his award concludes with the words: 'It was due to Sergeant Pearse's courage that the position was captured with few casualties.'

It was found that the Bolsheviks had mined the river to the south of Seltso, but as no further advance by the army was intended it was decided not to sweep this barrier. Some Russian mines that had been floated down the river had been caught and defused. These were now taken by lorry upriver past the Bolshevik mines and then reactivated and re-laid. Neither this minefield nor the one laid in the Varga River was swept by the Bolsheviks until after the British had finally departed from Archangel and so achieved their purpose in keeping the enemy gun-boats away from the river traffic during the withdrawal.

As predicted, the river began to rise at the end of August and the *Glowworm* and *Cockchafer* were ordered downriver on 24 August. The next evening, while the two gunboats were at Bereznik, a barge loaded with ammunition caught fire from a cooking stove being used by the Russian caretakers. There was nothing to indicate the nature of the cargo and the *Glowworm* slipped her moorings and went alongside to put the fire out. Without warning, the barge blew up. Three officers, including one from the RAF, and fifteen men were killed immediately; another three officers and fifteen men were wounded. The Commanding Officer of the *Glowworm*, Commander S. Green, was one of those injured and he subsequently died of his wounds, as did two of his men. A second barge, also loaded with ammunition, was riddled with shrapnel but did not explode, although one rating was killed and another four injured. Damage to the *Glowworm* was extensive and the ship had to be hastily patched up in Archangel before making the passage back to England.

A second, though fortunately less serious, casualty was HMS *Cricket*. Enemy gunfire damaged the ship's bow below the waterline. The inrush of water caused the forward bulkhead to collapse and the ship ran aground, where she remained for four weeks, undisturbed by the Bolsheviks, while being patched up before she was towed to Archangel for more permanent repairs.

The CMB28 (Lieutenant Walter Beckett) was one of several CMBs stationed on the Dvina near the front line to give any close support needed by the infantry. On 14 September Beckett received orders to take a badly wounded officer back to Archangel. The boat's fuel tanks were filled and an additional 200 gallons of fuel in cans were embarked. The wounded officer was strapped to a stretcher, which in turn was secured in the torpedo trough. Beckett set off after sunset with little moonlight to show the way. Several of the marker buoys on the river were out of position and early the following morning the CMB ran hard aground. It was found that the boat had developed a leak and was filling quickly and Beckett decided that the only way of preventing the boat sinking was to run at full speed into the riverbank. This ripped the bottom out of the boat but saved the passenger from further injury and possible drowning. At first light Beckett made contact with a naval motor launch, which undertook to complete the journey to Archangel with the unfortunate wounded officer. After removing anything of value from the CMB it was set alight and destroyed.

Eventually, all but three ships of the flotilla were able to make their way downriver. It had meant much hard work in lightening the ships by removing fuel, stores and even gun barrels before they were able to get through the shallows. The three left behind were the two monitors M25 and M27 and the yacht *Kathleen*. Dredging was carried out over the bars to try and clear a passage and a number of depth charges were exploded in the riverbed for the same purpose. Some progress was made in getting the monitors to safety, but after the last convoy had passed their position the ships were abandoned and completely destroyed. The *Kathleen* got through to Archangel.

Once the gunboats and monitors of the River Flotilla had departed down stream to Archangel the troops began to pull back from their advanced positions. The only opposition from the Bolshevik forces was when the troop barges were passing the mouth of the Varga River. Here the White Russians had failed to hold the line, which allowed the Reds to place machine guns on the riverbanks to fire on the British forces as they went by. An armed launch and several CMBs were sent at once to meet this threat and a marine detachment was landed to clear the enemy from the area. What Ironside feared most was a mass desertion by General Miller's troops, but nothing of the sort happened. Once clear of the junction with the Varga the only delays were when some of the barges went aground in shallow winding reaches of the river. The convoy was covered all the way by CMBs until it reached Siskoe, about 70 miles from Archangel, where the gunboat *Mantis* was stationed as escort; further downriver the *Moth* was waiting to guard the troops. When they were only some 20 miles from their destination the two monitors M31 and M33 were stationed until the evacuation was complete.

Meanwhile, the advanced positions were held entirely by Russian troops. The Bolshevik Army showed little inclination to attack or try to advance. Whether this was because they realised that it was likely that the front would crumble as soon as the British had gone or for some other reason will never be known, but what is known is that the evacuation went more smoothly than had been anticipated.

On land the 45th Fusiliers and a machine-gun company formed the rearguard. On 27 September General Rawlinson and Major General Ironside boarded the transport *Czaritza* and a convoy of forty-five ships sailed from Archangel in half a gale. The rearguard was taken out to a transport by a tug. The ships took with them over 4,500 Russian civilians, who desperately wanted to escape from the Bolsheviks. Watching over a deserted city was HMS *Fox*, at action stations and with guns trained on the shore. Just one CMB had to be left behind and scuttled – there was no room on any of the ships to embark the boat.

General Maynard's forces were kept in action south of Murmansk whilst the withdrawal from Archangel was being completed. At the time when Ironside's troops were beginning their retirement from the advanced positions, Maynard was being reinforced with the 6th Battalion Royal Marine Light Infantry, under the command of Lieutenant Colonel Kitcat. They arrived in Russia in the SS *Czar*, which sailed back carrying a battalion of Italian troops which had been giving trouble and were no longer considered as fit for any action.

The marines had been earmarked for ceremonial duties in Schleswig-Holstein in August 1919 in connection with a plebiscite regarding the future status of the State, but instead found themselves in action in North Russia. The battalion consisted largely of returned POWs and new recruits. On 10 September they were ordered to attack enemy positions near Lake Onega. It was a failure. The marines had become disorientated while attacking a village, demoralised under fire and some refused to obey orders. The enemy had been expected to retreat as soon as they came under attack from both land and air. They did not; they defended fiercely. It was probably the first, and only, mutiny among men of this proud, highly disciplined and professional corps. The ninety-three marines involved were court-martialled and thirteen ringleaders were sentenced to death, later commuted to seven years of penal servitude. Others received shorter prison sentences. One officer was cashiered[13]. Colonel Kitcat was placed on half pay and then on the retired list. The battalion left Murmansk on 6 October and on arrival in England the convicted men were taken away to serve their sentences in the naval prison in Bodmin, and the battalion was disbanded. Since then the numeral '6' has not been used to designate any Royal Marine unit. The sorry episode became the subject of questions in the House of Commons and, on review, all the sentences were reduced.

On 14 September General Maynard began an offensive against the Bolshevik positions at Kapeselga, about 10 miles south of Medvyeja Gora. The object was to deter the Bolshevik forces from any aggressive operations during the withdrawal. The attack, which was carried out by British, Russian and Serbian forces, supported by the naval flotilla on the lake and the seaplanes, was entirely successful. The troops then occupied the town of Lijna.

By 29 September General Skobeltsin's Russian troops had taken over the whole front line and the Allied troops then began their retirement to Murmansk. Kem was evacuated on 29 September and the last British troops left the shores of the White Sea on 4 October, when the *Nairana* and the SS *Santa Elena* sailed from the port of Kandalaksha. The remaining troops concentrated on Murmansk.

It had originally been the intention to carry out the complete destruction of the port of Murmansk and to destroy all remaining stores in the area. However, as had been the case at Archangel, this order had to be changed; the Russian commanders had indicated that they would fight on. In the circumstances it was necessary to ensure that the Russians were left with sufficient food, stores and ammunition to enable them to continue their struggle against the Bolsheviks. The Admiralty did not approve a Russian request for four CMBs, complete with torpedoes, for operations on Lake Onega. All the boats were taken to Murmansk to be loaded on ships for passage to England.

Initially, the Russian troops left in the front line at Lijna suffered a setback and the town was recaptured by the Reds. However, the Bolsheviks did not follow up their success and the line remained static for many weeks.

As at Archangel, the final evacuation was carried out smoothly and without loss. The with-drawal was completed on 12 October 1919 when HMS *Glory*, flying the flag of Rear Admiral John Green, sailed from Murmansk. A number of vessels were deemed to be too unseaworthy to make the passage home. Two paddle-wheeled hospital carriers, the *Edinburgh Castle* and the *Lord Morton*, were stripped of any valuable gear and then taken out to sea and scuttled. Two small tugs, four lighters and five motor launches were handed over to the Russians in Murmansk. The CMB77 was due to be shipped out on the American transport *Wisconsin Bridge*, but the floating crane required to lift the CMB was not available until after the American ship had finished loading. By the time the crane was ready the cargo ship was seen to be proceeding out of harbour, and the American master refused to turn back. The CMB was taken clear of the harbour and sunk by gunfire.

One hundred and fifty Royal Marines had landed in Murmansk in April 1918. A year later 18,000 British and Allied troops were involved in and around Murmansk or Archangel. There were never enough troops to be decisive on these two fronts; the Governments of the nations involved lacked any enthusiasm for the small commitment actually made and had no wish to add to their obligations. The inevitable outcome had cost over 300 British servicemen their lives.

The story ends in February 1920. During the winter the Red Army, as it had become, crept steadily closer to both Archangel and Murmansk. On the 17th of the month General Miller explained the situation to what was left of the Provisional Government in Archangel. The end was inescapable and nigh; he had sent an emissary to the enemy to seek terms, which had been refused: 'Unconditional Surrender' was demanded.

A powerful ice-breaker was in harbour and General Miller embarked his staff, a select group of army and navy officers, members of the Government and certain wealthy merchants and their families. Perhaps not surprisingly, the captain of the ice-breaker was the ubiquitous Captain Georgi Chaplin, who had masterminded the coup that took over Archangel prior to the Allied landings in August the previous year. The ice-breaker reached Tromso, in Norway, on 26 February and disembarked its passengers. General Miller went to live in Paris. In September 1937 he was kidnapped, supposedly by agents of the Soviet Union, and was never seen again.

On 21 February 1920 the 154th Infantry Regiment of the Red Army marched into Archangel. Murmansk fell two days later. The retribution began.

Above: The Tsar and his family taken during the war. Standing: Marie, the Tsarina and Anastasia. Seated: Olga, the Tsar, the Tsarevich and Tatiana.

Left: Commander Francis Cromie. Despite being on detached duty during the war, Cromie is photographed in full dress uniform, probably for a meeting with the Tsar. He is wearing the DSO and China Service Medal plus three Russian decorations on his left breast, another Russian medal around his neck and the Royal Humane Society Bronze Medal on the right breast.

Rear Admiral Richard Phillimore, the British naval representative at Imperial Headquarters from 1915 to the end of 1916. The admiral is seen here during a visit to a Russian Naval Air Station on Oesel Island. (Nik Cornish)

Building the railway from Murmansk to Petrograd involved the use of Chinese labourers and huge numbers of German and Austrian POWs. The number of those who died is not known but the figure may have been as high as 20,000. (Central Museum for the Armed Forces, Moscow)

The problems of winter ice: an 'E' class submarine in Revel during the winter of 1916/17 with the gun completely iced up.

The depot ship for the British submariners, the *Dvina*, hoists the Red Flag and once again resumes the proud name *Pamiat Azova*, which was removed by order of the Tsar after the mutiny of 1905.

The revolution arrives in Revel. Russian sailors gather on the jetty to hear speeches from leaders of the Sailors' Revolutionary Committee.

An entire ship's company stands in awe as the Red Flag is hoisted. At this stage the proceedings appear to be carried out in an unusually disciplined manner.

The Russian cruiser *Askold*. The distinctive five thin funnels earned the ship the nickname 'Packet of Woodbines' from the British sailors. (Maritime Photo Library (MPL))

The battleship HMS *Glory*, which served successively as the flagship of both Rear Admirals Kemp and Green in Murmansk from September 1916 to October 1919. (MPL)

The seaplane-carrier HMS *Nairana* at Murmansk in July 1918; a Sopwith Camel is visible on the forward flying-off deck and a seaplane can be seen aft under the crane. Note the very unusual camouflage. (Fleet Air Arm Museum)

The light cruiser HMS *Attentive*, which led the expedition to capture Archangel in August 1918.

The old American cruiser *Galveston*, which arrived in Murmansk in April 1919 in response to a request by General Maynard, who wanted extra armed forces in the town to deal with possible trouble by the Finns. (MPL)

Major General Edmund Ironside and a group of staff officers after a parade to celebrate the King's official birthday in 1919. Included in the group are Rear Admiral John Green and Captain Altham, seen here wearing a commodore's uniform. On the right is a French Liaison Officer and Colonel George Stewart, commanding the American 339 Infantry Regiment, is third from the right. (Imperial War Museum (IWM) Q16349)

HMS *Sword Dance* lying wrecked in the River Dvina after striking a mine on 24 June 1919.

The monitor HMS *Humber* in the River Dvina in 1919. The low freeboard is particularly noticeable. The ship was fitted with a twin 6in turret forward and a single 6in gun aft; these are clearly visible in the photograph. The ship was one of three originally built for the Brazilian Navy but were taken over by the Admiralty in August 1914. (MPL)

The monitor HMS M27. The ship was originally armed with a 9.2in gun but this had been replaced during the war and for service in North Russia the ship was fitted with a triple 4in mounting. (MPL)

General Eugene Miller, who became Commander-in-Chief of the White Russian forces in North Russia in April 1919.

An Allied security patrol ready to move off in Vladivostok, consisting of Czech infantry, Japanese marines and British sailors. There appears to be a lone American present. (*Illustrated London News* Photo Library (ILNPL))

The vast harbour of Vladivostok, almost devoid of shipping in early 1919. The British cruiser *Kent* is lying alongside nearest to the camera, with the American *Brooklyn* the other side of the jetty. The Japanese ships are at buoys in the centre. (ILNPL)

A group of Allied officers at a function given by General Otani, the Japanese commander of his nation's troops in Siberia, who is seen here seated in the centre. Also present are British, Chinese, Czech, French, Italian, Polish and Romanian officers.

FIVE

SIBERIA

Intervention in Siberia became mainly an army commitment rather than a naval one; it also involved British forces to a lesser extent than elsewhere. It arose from the same basic necessity as intervention on the other fronts – namely, the great anxiety felt by the Allied Supreme War Council and the British War Cabinet over the consequences of the collapse of the Eastern Front in the autumn of 1917. As was the case at Murmansk and Archangel, the Allied aim was greatly influenced by the presence at Vladivostok of immense quantities of valuable war material, almost all of which were of American origin.

The German presence in the Far East had been eliminated on 7 November 1914, when Germany's enclave at Tsingtao, on the Chinese mainland, was captured by a joint Japanese-British force. Vladivostok became a port that could freely be used to handle the supplies which were arriving to keep Russia in the war. These were urgently needed; they had been ordered by the Russians and despatched in good faith, but they piled up in Vladivostok and eventually in dumps all around the city. The largely single-track Trans-Siberian Railway could not cope with the massive increase in traffic which was required to carry this vast storehouse towards the front in European Russia. The construction of the railway had begun in 1891 and the ambitious enterprise had not been completed until 1905, when the last section around Lake Baikal had opened. The main obstacle once war broke out was that the railway had been built with financial constraints and it was estimated that the light track-bed could not carry more than three trains a day. By the summer of 1916, like many other railways in Russia, it had come almost to a halt. Along its length could be seen whole trains or individual freight cars, broken down and abandoned either beside the track or in sidings

Surprisingly, in view of these problems, in 1916 the railway had carried eleven submarines. The boats had been built in Vancouver, using an American modified Holland design and American parts. They had then been crated for delivery to Vladivostok, from where they were transported across Russia to be re-assembled in Russian shipyards. They were known by the Russians as the AG type (Amerikanski Golland for American Holland) and were the same as the 'H' class submarines which served in the British, Italian and United States Navies. The first five were assembled for service with the Baltic Fleet and had been completed by the end of 1916. The other six were to be rebuilt at Nikolaev for the Black Sea Fleet, although only two entered service with the Imperial Navy before the Revolution.

Early in the war President Wilson had recognised the problems on Russia's railways, in particular the Trans-Siberian, and had sent an advisory team to help. The men, led by the railway engineer John Stevens, had stayed on after the Revolution to help the Provisional Government. Wilson had also promised to send more than 1,000 new locomotives and 30,000 railway wagons of various types to replace the existing worn-out and damaged equipment. More men were required and railway workers were specially recruited in America to work in Russia – a Russian

Railway Service Corps, civilians in uniform. They arrived unannounced in Vladivostok on 14 December 1917, just as ice had begun forming on the harbour and Bolshevism had begun to arrive in the city. There was no accommodation for these railwaymen-soldiers, there was no security for them and officials did not know what to do with them. The ship promptly steamed out of harbour and took the men to Japan. John Stevens told the President that his whole team would be unable to continue to work without the presence of armed American soldiers to protect them. In reality, he was asking the American President to intervene in Russia. President Wilson remained unconvinced. The British Government proposed that Japanese troops should be transported across Siberia to bolster up the Eastern Front, either in Galicia against the Austrians or in the Caucasus against the Turks. Apart from the dubious practicality of such a scheme, neither the Japanese nor Russian Governments were consulted before the proposal was made and in any case it had no appeal to the rulers of Japan, who were determined to pursue their own aims to dominate Manchuria and Korea. Nor did the Americans show any enthusiasm for a second proposal, put forward in December 1917, that they should send troops to Vladivostok to safeguard 600,000 tons of stores and ammunition lying there. President Wilson had no wish to become embroiled in Russian politics.

By the end of 1917 conditions in Vladivostok had become chaotic and the Bolsheviks appeared likely to gain control and remove the stores for their own purposes. Accordingly, on 30 December the British Ambassador in Tokyo informed the Foreign Office in London of the situation in the port and asked that a British cruiser be sent. It was a tried and tested axiom of the Foreign Office that, when trouble brewed abroad and there was any doubt as to the action to be taken, the answer was 'send a gunboat'. Consequently, HMS Suffolk[1] was promptly ordered by the Admiralty to proceed to Vladivostok from Hong Kong; the ship arrived on 15 January 1918. The Japanese reacted immediately by sending two of their old battleships, the Asahi[2] and Iwami[3], but it was not until February 1918 that the Americans sent a ship of their own, the cruiser Brooklyn[4].

It was still not clear what the Allies were to do once they had forces in Vladivostok. Towards the end of January 1918, the British Government proposed that Japan should undertake the duty of safeguarding the Trans-Siberian Railway. The large, well-trained Japanese Army had done nothing since the capture of the German base at Tsingtao and many of the German Pacific colonies in 1914. The French were agreeable to the idea but the Americans rejected the plan. The Japanese, for their part, had no desire to become involved in this situation. At the same time Bruce Lockhart, the British Foreign Office representative in Moscow, was endeavouring to obtain the agreement of Lenin and Trotsky to the Allied presence in Vladivostok.

While the Allies dithered, the mere presence of the warships in the harbour brought an air of stability to the city. A young English governess, who had been living in Moscow before the war and had worked as a Red Cross nurse with the Tsarist Army, travelled on the railway to escape from the menace and chaos of Bolshevik controlled areas. She described her feelings on arriving in Vladivostok on 2 April 1918, twenty-seven days after leaving Moscow:

> In that harbour four large cruisers were anchored and one of them was flying the Union Jack. Oh the relief! The comfort! The security! Who will ever know all that this glorious flag symbolled to us travel-weary refugees? It was though we had heard a dear familiar voice bidding us 'welcome home'[5].

Early in February 1918 the British, who had been on the look-out for a local leader who would rally the anti-Bolshevik factions, decided to give a subsidy of £10,000 a month to a self-styled general named Gregori Semenov, a Cossack, and supply him with arms and military advisers. This proved to be an unhappy choice, for Semenov's men were little better than bandits and support for him was the prime cause of the Soviet authorities' mistrust of Allied intentions. Support for Semenov was renounced by the British in April and the subsidy was stopped; nevertheless, he did retain some limited help from the French. However, he remained on the scene, becoming a complicating factor in an already difficult situation, and eventually acted as a willing puppet for the Japanese[6].

In the middle of March, Captain Payne of the *Suffolk* reported that the Bolsheviks in Vladivostok were trying to move the stores and munitions westwards and proposed that the dumps should be placed under Allied protection. As these arsenals were located in fifteen large depots disposed over a radius of 15 miles, this would present a considerable undertaking.

Then, in early April, the murder of some Japanese citizens during an armed robbery brought on a crisis in Vladivostok. Admiral Kato, the Japanese Commander-in-Chief, ordered his ships to land 500 marines to protect Japanese interests in the city. Captain Payne sent fifty Royal Marines to guard the British consulate. The Americans took no action at all; Rear Admiral A.M. Knight perceived no danger to American lives or property. The Admiralty supported the action by the *Suffolk's* captain, but the landings caused some diplomatic embarrassment in both London and Tokyo as the Bolshevik Government opened a strong propaganda attack on its nominal allies. The British marines withdrew after a few days and the Japanese on 25 April. The Bolsheviks subsequently took control of the city.

At the end of April 1918 about 350 Belgian soldiers arrived in Vladivostok. They were the men of the Belgian Corps of Armoured Cars – Corps Belge des Auto-Conons Mitrailleuses (ACM). The unit had been formed from a single primitively armoured car, which had operated with some success in Belgium against the advancing German Army in 1914. A more sophisticated car was developed and the ACM was recruited from Belgians in France. After training in the Boulogne area the corps was sent to the front in Belgium in April 1915. By then conditions had changed from those prevailing when the corps was conceived. The muddy fields of Flanders, coupled with a static front line, were no place for armoured cars. In June 1915 an agreement was reached with the Russians for the unit to be deployed to the Galician front. The Corps, with ten vehicles, left Brest for Archangel in September 1915.

Like their opposite numbers in the Royal Naval Armoured Car Division, the unit found they had no useful role once the Russians ceased fighting after the Revolution. In the second half of February 1918, after lengthy negotiations in Kiev, the Bolsheviks agreed that the unit could travel to Vladivostok to be repatriated, providing they left behind their cars. The Belgians agreed but managed to sabotage the cars and any guns they could not take with them. From Vladivostok the Belgians travelled to America and then back to Paris, where the corps was disbanded.

The Czechoslovak Legion in Siberia was a big unknown quantity in all the uncertainty at the time. The original strength of the Legion was a brigade of exiles who had left their country – occupied as part of the Austro-Hungarian Empire – and were living in Russia when war broke out. Their numbers had later been swollen by thousands more, who had either deserted from the Austrian Army or had offered their services after becoming POWs. By the end of June 1918 they had gained control of the greater part of the Trans-Siberian Railway as they headed for Vladivostok, where they had been told ships would be present to take them to France to fight as part of the French Army.

In fact, no shipping had been sent to Vladivostok to move them to Europe and, fearing that their comrades who had not yet reached the city would be cut off in the middle of Siberia, they seized control. The Bolshevik takeover of Vladivostok had lasted just fifty-eight days. Some of the Czechs had not even started their journey eastwards and remained thousands of miles away to the west of the Urals and fighting Bolshevik attempts to disarm them. The Czechs in Vladivostok then turned westwards to rescue their comrades – a number of German and Austro-Hungarian former POWs had been armed by the Bolsheviks and had seized control of Irkutsk, for a short time blocking any movement along the railway.

The success of the Czechs stirred the Allies into further reluctant action. In early July 1918 Sir Eric Geddes, the First Lord of the Admiralty, proposed to the Cabinet that an Allied force of 100,000 men be sent to Vladivostok and for troops to be landed immediately to guard the town and store depots while the Czechs returned westwards. There was little likelihood of a force of that size being made available; the demands of the Western Front were insatiable. Nevertheless, the Foreign Office gave approval for the Czechs to receive arms from the base stores and for men to be landed to guard the depots. The *Suffolk* landed 200 men, the Japanese 100, and on the 11th the Americans authorised Admiral Knight to order the *Brooklyn* to give support. This was the first active involvement of the Americans in the area.

In an apparent change of policy President Wilson approved the despatch of 7,000 American troops to the area to join with a similar number of Japanese. In early August a British battalion from Hong Kong – the 25th Middlesex – and a French colonial battalion from Indo-China reached Vladivostok. The British troops on board their transport, the SS *Ping Suey*, were escorted into harbour by a Japanese destroyer and were then ceremonially met with a Czech band. In the middle of the month, the 27th United States Infantry arrived from the Philippines; the 31st Infantry followed a few days later.

The Middlesex battalion consisted of men in medical category 'C3', meaning they were unfit for active service in a theatre of war. This led to their being given the nickname of the 'Hernia Battalion'. They had been expecting to return home for demobilisation; instead they were to be plunged into a civil war. Also arriving in Vladivostok at this time was the British Military Mission, headed by Major General Alfred Knox, who had previously been the Military Attaché in Petrograd. He spoke fluent Russian, a factor which had stood him in good stead in Petrograd and would continue to do so in his new role.

The arrival of the American troops gave the Japanese the opportunity for which they had been waiting. By October 70,000 Japanese troops had not only landed in Vladivostok but had taken control of the Chinese railway through Manchuria to Chitra, where it joined the Trans-Siberian. The real Japanese aims were thus unmasked, but that made it no easier to frame and implement a common Allied policy. President Wilson became more determined not to involve America in Russian affairs; he stressed that the American troops that he had authorised were 'solely to help protect the Czechs and that there was no intention to interfere with the internal affairs of Russia or to infringe upon Russia's territorial sovereignty'.

The Canadian Government planned to send a brigade composed of both infantry and cavalry. An advanced party of unhappy troops arrived in Vladivostok in the autumn and, until the rest of the brigade arrived, they were used for administrative and guard duties. The remainder of the brigade was still assembling in Vancouver at the time of the Armistice in November. The fact that they were going to what was potentially a war zone just when peace had arrived in Europe led to a rapid deterioration in morale and discipline among the soldiers, many of whom had only recently completed their initial training. More importantly, the Canadian Government felt that they had not been fully consulted about this deployment of their troops and used the opportunity to cancel the move unilaterally; indeed, they also ordered the advance party back to Canada.

The Czech's need for artillery resulted in the *Suffolk* fitting out an armoured train and manning it with sailors and marines. One 6in gun and four 12-pounder guns taken from the cruiser were mounted on the train, which consisted of twenty-four trucks and carriages, complete with living accommodation, provision cars and ammunition wagons. The train was commanded by an energetic and enterprising officer from the *Suffolk*, Commander J. Wolfe-Murray. The Czechs greeted its arrival as a 'joyful event'.

The unfortunate men from Middlesex were sent to the Ussuri River front; they were intended to support the Czechs, but soon found themselves in the front line. Well-trained and efficient Japanese infantry also went into action, the whole force being supported by the *Suffolk*'s armoured train, where the 6in gun in particular assisted in driving the Bolshevik forces further into the wastes of Siberia. Travelling west along the railway the train continued in action, particularly between Omsk and Ufa, which lie either side of the Ural Mountains. Wolfe-Murray and his men won high praise from the Czech General Ditrich and also General Janin who led the French Military Mission which was assisting him. It seems unlikely that naval officers and men have ever before been in action so far from salt water, over 6,100 miles from Vladivostok.

Meanwhile, the Czechs had gained a substantial success over the Bolsheviks near Lake Baikal. By early September they were in control of the whole railway from the eastern seaboard to Samara on the River Volga and Kazan to the west of the Ural Mountains. The upsurge of optimism for the anti-Bolshevik cause led to the selection of Admiral Kolchak as the leader who was most likely to unite all the various factions[7]. On 13 October 1918 Kolchak reached Omsk and a month later he accepted leadership of the White Government established in that city. At first Kolchak was responsible for bringing a sort of unity to the various White Russian factions, while his armies gained considerable success. At one stage, in the spring of 1919, they had reached a point only 300 miles east of Petrograd and 60 miles south of Kotlas, where they were expected to join up with the British advancing from Archangel. Unfortunately, personalities came into play; he was neither liked nor trusted by the Czechs, who consequently gave him no support. He was regarded with jealous suspicion by many of the White Russian officers.

By the end of November 1918 the recoil cylinders of the naval guns on the armoured train froze up and further fighting became impossible. The train and its gun crews withdrew to Omsk. At that time the men were suffering badly from extreme cold and poor food and the Admiralty ordered their withdrawal to Vladivostok – except for Commander Wolfe-Murray. He was given the rank of acting captain and ordered to join Admiral Kolchak's staff to assist in the formation of a patrol on the River Kama as soon as the ice conditions made this possible.

A second British infantry battalion arrived in Vladivostok on 28 November 1918. The 1st/9th (Cyclist) Battalion of the Hampshire Regiment landed – without their bicycles – in an ice-cold city fresh from a tour of duty in India where they had faced temperatures of 116 degrees Farenheit in the shade. They were originally sent to Omsk, where they did little soldiering until May 1919, when they joined Major General Knox's training team in Ekaterinburg. The Hampshires, together with the Middlesex Battalion, were withdrawn in November 1919.

While Wolfe-Murray and his men had been fighting on the railway in the centre of Russia the cruiser HMS *Kent* (Captain John Edwards) had sailed from Plymouth in June 1918 to relieve the *Suffolk* at Vladivostok. The need to undergo extensive repairs to the ship's engines involved an extended stay of two months in Hong Kong Dockyard. The ship reached the Russian port on 3 January 1919. It is a tradition that ships arriving in a foreign port parade a guard and band, which will salute the vessels of an ally and also the nation in whose port they are arriving. This was done by the *Kent*. What no one had counted on was the extreme cold. As could be expected, the arms drill of the Royal Marines was faultless as they saluted the American cruiser. The band began to play the 'Star Spangled Banner' but within a few notes only the drums carried on; the wind instruments all froze into an embarrassed silence.

Wolfe-Murray arrived back in Vladivostok with the proposal, already agreed by Kolchak, that the guns landed by the *Suffolk* for use on the railway should be transferred to vessels on the River Kama and manned by a detachment from the *Kent*. The ships would form part of the Russian flotilla being formed at Perm. The Admiralty gave its approval to the plan and volunteers were sought from the *Kent*'s ship's company, primarily the Royal Marines. Captain Thomas Jameson RMLI was told that he would command the force. Out of sixty-four NCOs and marines on board the *Kent*, sixty-three volunteered for service as the landing party and guns crews; the one exception was serving a sentence in cells and could not take part. The number selected was based on manning the 6in gun and the four 12-pounders. In total the party, thirty-five strong, consisted of: one captain RMLI, one lieutenant (mate) RN, one gunner (warrant officer) RN, seven NCOs RMLI, twenty-two privates RMLI, one petty officer armourer, one sick berth attendant RN, and one surgeon lieutenant RNVR. An additional officer was later added to the party: Lieutenant Ewing, who was to serve as an interpreter.

Lieutenant Ewing had been born of an English father and an Italian mother and was working in Russia when war broke out. He was found to be medically unfit for the British forces on account of his eyesight. He applied to join the Russian Navy and was eventually commissioned as a sub-lieutenant. After the Revolution he found himself in Vladivostok, where he was appointed to edit the English language newspaper on behalf of the British High Commissioner. He was released from that task to become an interpreter in Jameson's force, with a temporary commission in the Royal Naval Volunteer Reserve[8].

No one knew how long they would be away, or what conditions they would have to face while miles away from regular naval support. Before leaving, Jameson wisely added two months' iron rations to the stores that were to accompany the party. They also purchased a large quantity of what he described as 'luxury items' from the ship's canteen. Jameson could not be sure that they would have returned to Vladivostok before the onset of the cold weather at the end of 1919 and the Canadians were persuaded to issue a supply of their excellent winter clothing. Each man was given a complete outfit of special Arctic boots, breeches, lumber jacket, a thick sheepskin-lined waterproof coat and a musquash fur cap with ear flaps.

Jameson and his men left Vladivostok by train on 6 April 1919 to travel the 4,500 miles to Omsk, where they arrived ten days later. At Chita, where the train left the Chinese Eastern Railway to join the Trans-Siberian, they found that the Cossack General Semenov was in control. Passports of all passengers were inspected, bribes collected and anyone suspected of being a Bolshevik was shot. British forces were exempt from such treatment; however, a Russian officer, Commander Fedotoff-White, was about to be taken off the train as a suspected spy when Jameson claimed that this officer was one of the British party, undoubtedly saving him from an ugly fate. In fact, Fedotoff-White was on his way to Omsk, where he was to join the Russian Rear Admiral Nikolai Smirnov, who was in command of the Kama River Flotilla – which was also the destination of Jameson and his party.

The locomotives required copious quantities of wood, which meant the train had to stop once or twice a day while its crew restocked with fuel. These stops provided a welcome break from the tedium of the journey. The stations became the social centre of each town or village as the local inhabitants set up a market to sell their produce. In addition, singing and dancing to the music of accordions and balalaikas provided welcome entertainment for all the travellers.

After ten days in Omsk Jameson's men left for another 1,000 miles travel to Perm, a journey which involved crossing the Ural Mountains. At Perm the British marines and sailors joined the vessels that were to be their home for the next few months. They had been allocated a Kama River paddle wheel tug for the 12-pounders and a large barge with its own tug for the

6in gun. The tug was 170ft long and had a beam of 40ft; this included the paddles, which were each 8ft wide. In better times both the tug and the barge were part of a vast amount of shipping that plied the Kama River and then into the Volga with cargoes for Astrakhan, a port on the Caspian Sea. For their own convenience they named the tug *Kent* and the barge became the *Suffolk*! Both vessels flew the White Ensign and each had its own Russian crew, leaving the British to man the guns with Jameson himself in overall command.

The Russians had organised the Kama River Flotilla into three divisions, each consisting of six ships carrying 3in or 4.7in guns, except for the British ships with their own armament. Two divisions were prepared at Perm and the third at Ufa, on a tributary of the Kama and 300 miles to the south. Jameson and his small force became unique in the story of British intervention in Russia. They were the only British unit to fight as part of a Russian force and under Russian operational command.

Converting a tug boat into a ship of war requires a lot of work as additional accommodation has to be provided, store rooms and magazines have to be constructed and armour plating must be fixed around vulnerable positions. In this particular case, fitting the guns necessitated a lot of improvisation, skill and hard labour, especially with the 6in gun to be mounted in the *Suffolk*. The whole procedure was accomplished in seven days of ceaseless work, much of it undertaken by Russian women, as men of military age had been conscripted into Kolchak's army.

Before leaving the flotilla's base Jameson wanted to test-fire his guns on different bearings and elevations to ensure that all the fittings were adequate for the task. He was immediately given permission for this and told to fire towards the hills on the other side of the river, being assured that the local peasants inhabiting the area were of no consequence! Only one bolt was found to be in need of further strengthening.

The land battle had been waged with savage ferocity throughout the winter of 1918–19. In late December Kolchak's army had begun to march westward over the Ural Mountains and had taken Perm. The Red Army had reacted by an offensive over the River Volga, which led to the capture of Ufa. Kolchak's forces recaptured Ufa in March and then advanced to seize the important Volga River ports of Kazan, 280 miles north-west of Ufa, and Samara (now Kuybyshev), which lies 250 miles south-west of Ufa. There the attack stalled and in April the Red Army counter-attacked. Kolchak's supply lines were stretched and his forces were unable to stop the Red Army's advance. In June Ufa fell once again. The Kama River became an important battleground as the Red Army strove to push the Whites back across the Urals.

On 8 May 1919 HM Tug *Kent* and HM Barge *Suffolk* sailed from Perm ahead of the other gunboats. The river, swollen by the thaw, varied in width from ½ to 2 miles. From time to time the two vessels passed under the enormous bridges which spanned the river even when in flood. There were unexpected shoals but the Russian skippers knew the river well and were able to avoid any disasters. The following day the two vessels passed through the town of Sarapul and on the 10th they reached Elabouga, where they went alongside the Russian base ship *Nitalia*, a converted river steamer. Jameson called on Admiral Smirnov to discuss operations. Politics and the military merged, for by this time he was not only the commander of the flotilla but also Kolchak's Minster of Marine.

Within days of arriving at Elabouga the British vessels were under attack. A pair of Bolshevik seaplanes bombed them as they lay at anchor. Two of the three bombs straddled the *Suffolk* but did no damage. The second aircraft was met with a barrage of fire from all the ships present and came down on the river; there was little actual damage but the engine was labouring and clearly in trouble so the pilot surrendered. The first aircraft, seeing his comrade come down by the flotilla, thought that the ships must be Bolshevik, and so it too landed, and was captured. Both pilots, former Tsarist naval officers, were taken away to be shot – one of many sad consequences of a civil war.

The same day Bolshevik gunboats made their debut, making contact with the White ships in the Kama River just above the junction with the Viatka. The *Gregiasshi*, which was acting as guardship in the area, engaged with her single 3in gun but was out-gunned by the enemy; a shell in the boiler room put an end to the action. Meanwhile, the two British vessels and the rest of the flotilla steamed west down the Kama to meet the enemy. The engagement was inconclusive, neither side causing any damage before the Reds withdrew – though Jameson reported that the enemy shooting was more accurate than he had expected. The action was part of the Bolshevik offensive designed to capture Elabouga.

A more effective encounter occurred on the 24th, when the Bolsheviks made a determined effort to gain control of the river as they advanced on Elabouga. Their leading ship, the *Terek*, took hits from the *Kent* and was set on fire; she subsequently beached herself. The remaining Bolshevik ships turned to go downstream and several more were hit and destroyed, including the flagship *Roosal*. The *Kent* and the *Gordi* attempted to follow the retreating enemy ships, but as they steamed round a bend in the river the Russian ship was hit by several shells, which damaged the bridge and put the forward gun out of action. Both ships had to retire, with the *Kent* protecting the two of them with a smoke screen.

The following days provided a similar routine of defending the river from any advance by the Bolshevik ships while the enemy troops were engaged as they moved eastwards. Both the *Kent* and the *Suffolk* had to go to the base at Sarapul for repairs, the former needing the engine overhauled and the latter requiring attention to the 6in gun. The *Kent* was ready within forty-eight hours and it was found on trials that the ship could now reach 11 knots against the stream and 15 or more with it. On 2 June the *Kent* was ordered to rejoin the flotilla about 25 miles downstream. As she passed under the Sarapul bridge it was noticed that some artillery were digging in, with the guns apparently laid towards the town. It seemed strange that this could be a Bolshevik unit so close to where the White Army HQ and the Naval Command had established themselves.

However, it was indeed the case. Admiral Smirnov ordered the *Kent* and the *Grosni*, his two fastest ships, back to Sarapul to stop the Bolsheviks – or the retreating Whites – blowing up the bridge, which would prevent the rest of the flotilla from passing under it to safety. When they arrived they found that the main span was still intact, though the others had already been blown. The two ships maintained an uneasy watch on the bridge for two hours until the rest of the flotilla arrived. All the ships then went at full speed until the town had been passed. Bolshevik artillery, some of which was by then positioned actually on the waterfront, fired at almost point-blank range at the ships as they sped by. A Bolshevik field gun was seen to be firing through the door of a house by the riverside; a shell from a 12-pounder on the *Kent* blew both house and gun to pieces. The *Startni* was hit and sunk, but the next ship in line stopped and picked up survivors. The *Kent* received a hit, which damaged the port paddle wheel box; the broken timbers were soon cleared away and the delay and reduction in speed were of little consequence. Another shell burst near the forward gun and slightly injured one of the crew, the ship's only casualty.

The fall of Sarapul was unexpected and was indicative of the parlous state of Kolchak's armies at this time. The morale of the soldiers was poor, there was little willingness to fight and desertions were becoming ever more common. On the other hand, the Bolsheviks were concerned about the presence of the British ships on the river, as an intercepted radio report stated: 'Our naval manoeuvres on the River Kama are being seriously hampered by the British destroyers.' Jameson's party were delighted by the flattery.

Admiral Smirnov's headquarters arranged for rations to be supplied regularly to all the ships of the flotilla, including the British. The food supplied – mostly black bread, bear meat and vegetables – was monotonous and lacking in taste, despite the best efforts of the cooks. Often the bread was sour and green in the centre. The meat had frequently become inedible because of faulty packing in the casks. Naturally, the sailors and marines bartered luxury items, such as soap and chocolate, for food to supplement their diet. One marine swapped a small piece of soap for a bag of white flour, both peasant and marine being delighted with the exchange. There was no yeast available with which to make bread but he improvised by using the fermented green centre of a black loaf as a substitute. The result was declared to be a resounding success!

A new base for the flotilla's ships was established at Galova. In 1918 the town had held out against the Bolsheviks and was only captured after a long siege. Surrender was followed by mass executions, a fate which seemed likely to be repeated in 1919 as the Red Army closed in again on the town. Galiana, another town on the river, changed hands several times but was finally captured by the Bolsheviks on 7 June. The two British ships and the rest of the flotilla were constantly engaged in giving support to the army, but it was disappointing work. The army frequently failed to follow up any advantage that the fire of the ships gave them.

While these actions were taking place the British High Commissioner in Siberia met with Admiral Kolchak and told him that the British Government could no longer recognise the Omsk Government and as a consequence all British forces in Siberia were being withdrawn. Unfortunately for Jameson and his men, only a few days previously Kolchak had awarded a number of medals to them after the courageous and gallant work on the river. Sir Charles Eliot, when informed of this, told Jameson that the decorations were to be handed back – a petty decision, as British servicemen in other parts of Russia were still being given Russian awards.

Despite Sir Charles' statement that British forces were being withdrawn, no orders were received from the Admiralty and the two British vessels continued in action, the whole time being forced to withdraw towards Perm. The only sign of disaffection in the flotilla took place during this period when one of the Russian mechanics in the *Kent* was found to be a Bolshevik sympathiser. The Russian engineer officer was transferred to another ship and the mechanic met the inevitable fate for Bolshevik agents.

At the end of June, Jameson met with Admiral Smirnov and Captain Wolfe-Murray, who were about to move back to Omsk. Jameson was given the responsibility of deciding when the *Kent* and *Suffolk* should be withdrawn from action and the British marines and sailors evacuated. Admiral Smirnov left him in no doubt as to the seriousness of the situation, which was deteriorating rapidly. Although it was stated that the withdrawal of the British vessels would affect the morale of the troops at the front, it was also agreed that the *Suffolk* should be brought back towards Perm and a start made on removing her equipment. At this time the Red Army was only about 70 miles from Perm. When the *Suffolk* rejoined she had expended all her ammunition, having fired 256 rounds of 6in ammunition in two days.

The work of off-loading all the equipment, stores and any remaining ammunition from the ships and then loading them onto a train was done by the marines and sailors, with the help of a labour force composed almost entirely of women. Including the guns and their reserve ammunition, the total weight to be moved amounted to some 225 tons; the 6in alone weighed almost 7 tons. The two vessels were then scuttled to prevent their use by the Bolsheviks.

The city of Perm was in chaos as refugees struggled to keep ahead of the vengeance of the advancing Red Army. Jameson estimated that over 8,000 horse-drawn carts, piled high with families and their possessions, were passing through each day; every train was packed to capacity. Jameson took an armed party to the railway depot to commandeer an engine to attach to the special train allocated to the British. They left early in the morning of 29 June with the prospect of travelling 1,000 miles before reaching Omsk. Three hours after their departure the Red Army captured Perm.

The following morning the engine pulling the train broke down and there seemed to be no possibility of repairing it. The Red Army were not far behind them and safety was at least 300 miles away across the Ural Mountains. Jameson considered obtaining horses to travel eastwards along the railway, or to head north-west to join the British forces believed to be advancing towards Kotlas. In either case most of their equipment and supplies would have to be abandoned. Fortunately, Admiral Smirnov had learned of their non-arrival and had sent another locomotive back along the line to find them.

At Omsk Jameson received approval from the Admiralty to hand some of the equipment over to Admiral Smirnov and his staff, thereby saving space on the crowded trains. As the men left Omsk they were warned that bands of Bolshevik sympathisers were constantly sabotaging the line and attacking trains. Jameson himself was informed that a large amount of gold bullion was being transferred to the bank in Vladivostok and had been put aboard his train. Typhus and cholera were endemic where any of the thousands of refugees had travelled or camped. Jameson took desperate measures, including the threat of armed force against railway officials, to ensure that his men did not become infected. This time the stations were empty, the local inhabitants had little or no produce to sell and the threat of typhus prevented any social gathering. The journey was slower than before but they reached Vladivostok without major incident on 18 August 1919, some fifty-two days after leaving Perm. They were met by the band of the Middlesex Regiment, who led them to HMS *Carlisle*[9], the guardship in the port. Their own ship, the cruiser HMS *Kent*, had already returned to Britain.

Kolchak attempted another offensive in September, but this too failed and on 14 November 1919, Omsk, the seat of his Government, fell to the Red Army. In November he withdrew to Irkutsk on Lake Baikal. By the end of 1919 it was plain that Kolchak's cause was lost. In January 1920, with his forces retreating in confusion, he proclaimed General Denikin, the Russian commander in South Russia, his successor and leader of all the White armies. He sought refuge with the Czechs, but, with the tacit agreement of the French General Janin, he was handed over to the Bolsheviks. He was shot on 7 February 1920. Janin's actions were condemned in his native France.

The fact that Kolchak was handed over to the Bolsheviks by the Czechs may seem surprising. However, there was little love lost between Kolchak and his allies. As early as the end of 1918 he had regarded the Legion as a spent force and did not take into consideration the conditions that caused the Czechs to be exhausted and war-weary. Earlier, Sir Charles Eliot reported to the Foreign Office that Kolchak had spoken harshly of the Czechs and how he wanted them out of Russia as soon as possible. This lack of understanding was a critical mistake, and one that would ultimately cost him his freedom and his life. The Japanese did not like him either and did nothing to aid him. In fact, once the British withdrew their support there was little he could do to avoid his fate. The Czechs could have saved him, but did not wish to delay their railway evacuation and sought tacit Bolshevik support for their journey.

The Czechs' long retreat across Siberia ended at Vladivostok, from where some 16,000 were repatriated between January 1919 and February 1920. This left about 50,000 near Irkutsk along with about 11,000 Poles, Yugoslavs and other East Europeans who were intermingled with the Czechs. In October 1920 eight British troopships arrived at Vladivostok to complete the evacuation of these soldiers[10]. In the meantime, the last of the American troops had left in April 1920.

Allied intervention in Far Eastern Siberia did not finally end until October 1922, when Japanese forces withdrew from Vladivostok. The Japanese should have left once the Czech evacuation had been completed, but in March 1920 the Japanese garrison, a number of Japanese civilians and the local inhabitants of the town of Nikolaevsk, at the mouth of the Amur River, were slaughtered by local bandits. The Japanese Government issued a statement that the disturbed situation in Siberia threatened the lives of Japanese citizens and the general peace in Korea and Manchuria. As a consequence, it was impossible for the Japanese forces to withdraw.

At the same time as the Japanese departed, a disparate collection of ships evacuated the remnants of the Siberian armies and thousands of White Russian refugees. Most went to Shanghai, from where they gradually moved on to Singapore, America, Canada, Australia and even to Europe. Admiral Nikolai Smirnov was one such refugee. He had been Kolchak's Minister of Marine, and the admiral commanding the Kama River Flotilla, and as such had once proudly flown his flag at the masthead of HM Tug *Kent*. He had also been made an honorary Commander of the Order of St Michael and St George. Somewhat bizarrely, he ended up making and selling ladies' hats in Cannes. Admiral Smirnov was, perhaps, one of the more fortunate of those thousands fleeing from the horrors of Bolshevik rule.

On 23 October 1922 the Bolshevik Army entered Vladivostok, witnessed by the British cruiser *Carlisle*[11], which was carrying out a second tour of duty as guardship in the city. She was herself withdrawn a week later. Captain Gerald Dickens, who was commanding the cruiser, could therefore perhaps have claimed to be the last member of the British armed forces to have been involved in the Russian intervention imbroglio.

SIX

THE CASPIAN SEA
AND THE CAUCASUS

Following the cessation of hostilities by the Russians in 1918 the British Government decided to send forces into the area of the Caucasus. There were no stockpiles of war material to guard, as there was at Murmansk and Archangel; however, there were vital oil supplies. It was crucial to ensure that they did not reach Turkish or German hands. In the spring of 1918 the Treaty of Brest-Litovsk between Russia and Germany ceded three Trans-Caucasian states to Turkey – including Azerbaijan, with the vast oilfields around Baku.

In December 1917, a secret Anglo-French agreement had established the limits of the spheres of influence of the two countries in southern Russia. Britain assumed responsibility for the Cossack-dominated areas, the Caucasus and the Transcaspian region, which covered the approaches to the British-dominated oil fields in Persia and Mesopotamia (now Iraq). As a consequence of the Turkish acquisition of the Caucasian states, the British Government expected that the Turks would also try to make use of the important oil fields around Baku. Accordingly a number of troops, at about brigade strength, were ordered from Baghdad to Enzeli (later Bandar-e Pahlavi and now Bandar-e Anzali), the primary Persian (now Iranian) port on the south Caspian coast. Major General Lionel Dunsterville, who commanded the troops, was ordered to proceed from there to Baku, using whatever shipping he could find, where he was to support the local Bolsheviks in resisting the Turks. As had been the case at Murmansk, British intervention was initially to give military backing to a local Soviet.

Among the troops allocated for this mission was the Armoured Car Brigade – five squadrons each of eight cars – which had arrived in Mesopotamia in the summer of 1918. Many of the crews had returned home from Russia only at the end of 1917, where they had served with distinction since 1915 as the Royal Naval Armoured Car Division, giving support to the Russian armies. At that stage the unit had been transferred from the Admiralty to the War Office and then sent overseas again.

In support of this fanciful plan the Royal Navy was asked to consider the feasibility of taking a Fly class gunboat[1] in sections and transporting it on lorries from the River Tigris to the Caspian Sea, where it would be re-assembled. These craft had arrived in Mesopotamia in their component parts, having originally been built in Britain and then put together in Abadan. However, the proposal had to be dropped as no lorries were available which were large enough to carry one of these gunboats, even in a dismantled state, nor were the roads in any way suitable. The distance from Baghdad to Enzeli was nearly 700 miles and some of the passes to be crossed reached 7,000ft. Intelligence regarding the Caspian was minimal at the Admiralty – there had never before been a reason to consider this inland sea for operations by the Royal

Navy. There were no charts and little information about climate. However, it was well known that sturgeon were caught – for there was a thriving caviar industry – hence it was deduced that there were fishing boats!

'It is both the duty and tradition of the Royal Navy to engage the enemy wherever there is water to float a ship.'

The remark is attributed to the First Sea Lord, Admiral Sir Henry Jackson, in 1915 when plans were being discussed to send two armed motor boats to attack German maritime dominance on Lake Tanganyika, in East Africa. It was equally apposite on this occasion three years later. Indeed, a precedent for activities by the Royal Navy on inland waters had been set in 1812, when operations were conducted on the Great Lakes in Canada during the war against the United States.

The basin of the Caspian Sea covers nearly 750 miles from the delta of the River Volga at Astrakhan in the north to the Persian coast in the south and about 200 miles east to west at its widest. Baku lies on the western shore, about a third of the way up. On the opposite coast is the town and rail terminal of Krasnovodsk, from where the railway leads into Central Asia, in what is now Turkmenistan. Roughly halfway between Baku and Astrakhan lies a cluster of small islands, of which Chechen Island is the largest. Around the Volga Delta, and for some distance south, the river silt has reduced the depth of water to one and a half fathoms (9ft) or less, except in the dredged channel leading to Astrakhan. The deepest part of the Caspian is the southern third. In winter the sea freezes over as far south as Chechen Island.

The Admiralty had information on two Russian gunboats, the *Kars* and the *Ardagan*. They were believed to be in Bolshevik hands at Baku. The craft were 200ft long, displaced 623 tons, had a speed of 14 knots, and were armed with two 4.7in and four 11-pounder guns. There were also two smaller gunboats, the *Chasevoy* and *Astarabad*. They formed an impressive-sounding force, but their efficiency was doubtful.

In July additional orders were received from the Admiralty that these gunboats and as many merchant ships as possible were to be seized and taken from Baku to Enzeli; 4.7in guns were to be mounted on suitable merchant ships and a seaplane base was to be set up. No overall command of the Caspian Sea was envisaged; there was to be a rapid move only to Baku to obtain control of the shipping and to deny its use by others so as to prevent the Turks from taking the oil and also from spreading across the Caspian. Lieutenant Commander Harrison, RNR, who was the Senior Naval Officer (SNO) on the Tigris, was instructed to put these arrangements in hand.

A party of two officers and twenty-two ratings of various specialist trades were landed from the two Insect class gunboats *Moth* and *Mantis*[2]. This was believed to be enough to run one steamer initially. The men were all armed and wore khaki shirts, shorts and helmets. The army were to provide food, transport, lodgings and – surprisingly – pay. One 4in and two 12-pounder guns were landed from the gunboats and were to be taken to Enzeli with the naval party. They left Baghdad early on 27 July. Commodore David Norris, who was to act as SNO Caspian Sea, left the next day with his broad pennant flying on a Ford car, his coxswain following in a Ford van containing much spare equipment for the force. The naval party joined up with General Dunsterville on 2 August; nobody at his HQ was expecting the navy to arrive, much less knew what they were to do when they got there!

On 26 July 1918 the Bolsheviks in Baku were ousted in a coup and replaced by the Central Caspian Dictatorship. They too sought help from General Dunsterville in defending the city.

Three steamers in Enzeli were chartered – the *President Kruger*, the *Kursk* and the *Abo* – and detachments of British troops began to move to Baku on 5 August. Dunsterville himself sailed for Baku on board the *President Kruger* on the 16th.

An example of the petty problems which faced the force as it began to move to Baku was a dispute over which ensign the ships should fly. Both Dunsterville and Commodore Norris totally rejected the idea that a red flag should be flown, although the ships were Russian manned. Eventually a compromise was reached when it was agreed that the ships would fly the red, white and blue of the old Russian Imperial flag, but that it should be flown upside down. Apparently no one realised that this was then the Serbian flag! In this manner British troops travelled to war: on board a merchant ship, named after an erstwhile enemy Boer President, flying an inappropriate ensign, to defend a revolutionary Russian city on the shores of an inland sea, where the Royal Navy had never previously sailed.

Meanwhile, reinforcements for the naval party were being found. With the consent of the Government of India most of the British crews of the Royal Indian Marine (RIM) ships *Northbrook* and *Harding*[3] were sent from Bombay with seven 4.7in, three 4in and two 12-pounder guns. Some men from the old cruiser HMS *Fox*[4] and another RIM troopship, the *Dalhousie*, subsequently augmented the party.

In Baku the situation was chaotic. The new rulers of the city had also taken over thirteen Bolshevik ships in the port and stopped the commissars from leaving with a contingent of 1,200 men and a considerable quantity of military stores. Eventually, they were allowed to leave by ship for Krasnovodsk, where the commissars were arrested and then executed. The defenders of the port were mainly Armenian with some Tartars and Russians; none were really prepared to fight and in any case hated each other to a greater or lesser extent. The Azerbaijanis did little to help protect their town. The discipline of many units was almost non-existent, the Armenians being the worst.

The British troops which arrived to defend this political and ethnic maelstrom initially included a battery of artillery and men of the 1st/4th Hampshire Regiment and 7th North Stafford Regiment. They were joined later by the 9th Royal Warwickshire Regiment. None of these units was up to full strength and in any case the whole force remained greatly inferior in numbers to the advancing Turks, who were estimated to be 12,500 strong.

Attempts by Norris and his small group of naval personnel to requisition and arm any merchant ships other than those that they had brought from Enzeli were frustrated at every opportunity by various committees and Captain Voskerensky, the commander of the Centro-Caspian Flotilla. Neither Dunsterville nor Norris were prepared to give ground on their principal demand that the British would arm and provide the guns' crews, the ships could be commanded by officers from the flotilla, but the British would be in overall control.

The main Turkish attack began on 26 August. The few British troops, unsupported by their notional allies, were unable to do much other than postpone the inevitable. On 7 September it was agreed that the *Ardagan* would sail to bombard some of the Turkish positions and a British naval officer would be on board to observe proceedings. The officer arrived at 5.20 a.m. and found the crew still asleep. At 6.30 a.m he was told that they could not leave as half of the crew was still ashore! Nevertheless, he persuaded the captain to sail. The Ship's Committee would not allow the ship to be taken closer than 5,000 yards from the shore, even though this would reduce the accuracy of the gunfire. Surprisingly, a train was hit and stopped and a number of bridges attacked. The guns were reported as being well maintained, but otherwise the ship was filthy.

Finally, on 14 September, Dunsterville ordered the withdrawal of all British troops, although he was informed that his ships would be fired on by artillery under the control of the Dictatorship, including the four gunboats, if they should attempt to leave.

The wounded were embarked on the *Kursk* and the *Abo*. All the reserve ammunition was put on board a small steamer, the *Armenian*. Late at night Dunsterville led his men in absolute silence on board the *President Kruger*. At the last minute it was decided to take the guns rather than dump them in the sea. To the chagrin of the gunners it was not possible to take their mules and they had to be left to fend for themselves. The rearguard was formed by the North Staffords, who broke contact with the Turks and joined the remainder of the force on board the *President Kruger*.

As the ship cleared the jetty a Russian sailor rushed on deck shouting and sobbing that his wife had been left behind. The remainder of the crew insisted that the ship went back, which it did, and the lady in question was picked up. The *President Kruger* left once again, but then the same thing happened when the chief engineer realised his sister was not on board. As the ship passed near the guardship one of the Russians – of suspect loyalty – switched on the lights on the bridge. The guardship ordered them to stop. The captain put the telegraphs to stop; the commodore immediately put them to full ahead. The guardship fired a few rounds, which all missed. Ending the excitement, the *President Kruger* narrowly missed collision with an oil barge, which was drifting off the harbour mouth.

On board the *Armenian*, which followed astern of the *President Kruger*, the crew heard the gunfire ahead and sent the chairman of the Ship's Committee to order the captain to return to harbour. Colonel Rawlinson, one of Dunsterville's staff officers, was on the bridge covering the captain with his pistol. A guard of four British soldiers promptly 'downed' the chairman as he reached the bridge. The guardship challenged and opened fire. The slow-moving *Armenian* made an easy target for the guardship's guns and seven shells fell on the superstructure before she moved out of range. If the shells had been high explosive the ship would undoubtedly have been sunk but they were only charged with gunpowder so did little damage and caused no casualties. Enzeli was reached safely the following evening.

Dunsterville's expedition to hold Baku to prevent the oil fields coming under Turkish control was over. The British had been ignominiously ousted from the port. Too few troops had been sent to hold the town and the local troops had proved to be useless. The North Staffords alone had landed at Baku with twenty officers and 480 other ranks. They lost thirteen officers and 143 men were killed and wounded. The Turks subsequently admitted to 2,000 casualties.

With the departure of the British, law and order in Baku broke down completely. The Turks promised the Tartars the opportunity to exact their revenge for their massacre by the Armenians in March 1918 and so waited for three days outside the town. About 16,000 Armenians are believed to have died in this tit-for-tat orgy of death.

Besides the ships carrying the British troops from Baku, some forty other vessels had escaped and anchored off Enzeli; on board were about 2,000 refugees who had to be found accommodation and food in the port. The naval party, by then reinforced from the original twenty-two ratings, made a start on choosing suitable craft and converting them into warships with the meagre resources available. By the end of October five ships had been taken over and armed. Ammunition for the guns was in short supply and additional rounds had to be brought from Baghdad, mostly by camel. Each camel could carry eight 4in shells. The facilities at Enzeli were barely able to cope with all that was required of them; the harbour was silted up and needed dredging, there were few proper workshops and there was a shortage of alongside berths for the ships.

The *President Kruger* had been armed with four army field guns, lashed to bales of cotton and secured on the forward cargo hatch. The commodore decided to visit Krasnovodsk, on the eastern shore of the Caspian, where it was believed that the workshops of the railway terminal would make a more suitable base for the navy. He sailed on board the *President Kruger*. Taking passage to Krasnovodsk with Commodore Norris was Major General Andrews, who had relieved Dunsterville. The local Social Revolutionary Government enthusiastically welcomed the *President Kruger* and the two senior officers who had arrived to review the town's facilities. A brass band was on the quayside as the *President Kruger* berthed alongside. The self-styled President Khun was present to meet the British officers in person. He was the head of the local Revolutionary Government, a former ticket collector by trade and a man of strong character who was very pro-British. As expected it was found that the workshops were much more extensive and better suited to the navy's needs than those at Enzeli. The visit ended with Andrews and Norris being entertained to dinner which concluded with the brass band playing 'God Save the King' to demonstrate the allegiance of Khun's Government! As a result the navy began to move to Krasnovodsk, the benefits there far outweighing the disadvantages of the extra mileage on the lines of communication.

Developments elsewhere, however, caused a change of plan. At the end of October 1918 Turkey surrendered. The main reason for a British presence in the area disappeared as the ink dried on the signatures on the surrender document. There was no longer any need to try and thwart Turkish plans for expansion into the region, or to stop any Baku oil reaching Turkey and thence to Germany. Indeed, on 11 November Germany too surrendered and what would come to be known as the Great War was over. It would have been a good time for the British contingent to have withdrawn altogether from the Caucasus and Caspian Sea area, but the benefit of hindsight was not available to the politicians and military commanders of the time. First, the withdrawal of Turkish troops from the area had to be supervised. Governments were seeing Bolshevism as a menace and began to support anti-Bolshevik forces in the vicious civil war that was raging. At the same time the Baku oil looked attractive to the British Government. As had been the case for over 100 years, the Government of India remained concerned about any possible activity by the Russians in the frontier regions of India. No orders to withdraw from the Caspian were given and indeed further troops, of 27 Indian Division, were made available for any necessary operations in the Caucasian States, once a presence in the Black Sea had opened up the port of Batum.

On 6 November a squadron of six British ships under the command of Captain Washington, Norris' deputy, arrived off the port of Petrovsk (now Makhachkala), to the south of Chechen Island. General Bicherakov, a one-time colonel in the Tsarist Army, held the town with a strong force against the Turks. His troops were mainly Russian, and although Bicherakov was nominally under the White Russian commander in South Russia, his loyalty to the cause was less than his loyalty to his own interests. In addition the efficiency of his troops was symptomatic of the time, with only a fragile discipline remaining. The situation was surreal. The Turkish commander claimed not to have heard of the Armistice, but in any case his troops would go on fighting as they would be serving the Baku Republic. Bicherakov sought British help in his battle against the Turks and was not best pleased when this was refused. It was impossible for the British to get involved, he was told, because of the Armistice. Eventually, Bicherakov abandoned Petrovsk and returned towards Baku.

Meanwhile the *Asia* (Lieutenant Mare RIM), an armed merchant ship with four 4in guns, was sent to Gurieff, a town in the far north-east of the Caspian beyond Astrakhan. This was the furthest afield that any of the British ships could go and was the base of the Ural-Cossacks. The Cossacks were delighted but very surprised to see a British ship. The *Asia* made a second trip to the port later in the year; and as before they found only friendly Cossacks and there was no sign of the Bolsheviks.

The policy of the British Government at this time is reflected in a statement made to the Eastern Committee of the War Cabinet on 2 December 1918 by its chairman, Lord Curzon, who was the Lord Privy Seal and one-time Viceroy of India[5]. He considered that it was essential to the interests of the British Empire, and of India in particular, that Britain should exercise some measure of control over Transcaucasia – the area to the east of the Caspian. He believed that anarchy or Bolshevism would react unfavourably upon British interests in Persia and India. However, Edwin Montague, Secretary of State for India, felt that it was not acceptable that Britain should take full responsibility for the area, although Britain had to keep open the lines of communication with India. He even suggested that France or America might be interested in helping. They were not. While the politicians argued, the British forces stayed.

As the Royal Navy's Caspian Flotilla was to stay indefinitely, there was clearly little point in retaining a base at Krasnovodsk with all its disadvantages. A large convoy of seventeen transports, escorted by all the armed ships, sailed from Enzali for Baku. They were led by the *President Kruger*, which by then was flying the White Ensign. They arrived on 17 November and the troops landed without opposition, the Turks having withdrawn to a position outside the town. Also based in Baku was the Centro-Caspian Flotilla – a number of armed ships including the four gunboats originally belonging to the Tsarist Navy.

In early December four British armed merchant ships, led by the *Emile Nobel*[6] (Commander K. Guy), left Baku for the north. Their mission was to try and find out the strength and activities of the Bolshevik ships at Astrakhan. Nothing was seen of the Russians but the operation shows the extent to which the British had already taken control of the Caspian. Three more ships completed the task of arming and arrived at Baku at this time, bringing the full strength of the flotilla to eight ships.

Intelligence reports indicated that the Bolsheviks were planning to establish a base on the mainland near Chechen Island. The *Zoroaster*[7] (Lieutenant Charsley) and the *Alla Verdi*[8] (Lieutenant J. Snow) were sent to the area to investigate. On the morning of 8 December they were lying at anchor off Chechen Island when they were attacked by three Bolshevik armed ships, escorting three transports. The British ships immediately weighed anchor and sailed to give battle. The enemy retreated and in the running battle which ensued the *Zoroaster* was hit three times; the enemy ships were also hit and one was seen to be on fire. All six escaped back to Astrakhan. The most worrying fact of this minor skirmish was the heavy expenditure of ammunition, since reserves were very limited and difficult to replace. Nevertheless, it was a great morale boost for the flotilla.

This attempt by the Bolsheviks to form a forward base near to Baku at Staro-Terechnaya was brought to an end on 29 December when Lieutenant Commander Harrison, with three ships under command, closed on the empty village, bombarded and then burnt it. The British also set up patrols in the area. They met no enemy ships but they intercepted radio signals from ships which could only be from the Centro-Caspian flotilla at Baku to the Bolsheviks in Astrakhan. As a result, Commodore Norris knew for certain that there was a potential enemy in his own base port and made plans to take action at a suitable moment.

In the meantime, the northern part of the Caspian froze in January 1919, which ensured that the Bolshevik ships were immobilised until the spring thaw. It was hoped to use the winter as a break from operations and a time to consolidate the remaining work of arming the ships and making the port of Baku into a firm base. However, there were a sizeable number of Bolshevik sympathisers in the town. This was due in part to the Bolshevik propaganda which flooded into Baku from outside. A more important influence was the shortage of food and other goods, added to the rampant inflation. The Government printed more and more paper roubles. In

1914 a rouble had been worth the equivalent of 11½p; it was worth 1½p in January 1919 and just ½p in September. Work was available but for the most part this was controlled by British requirements; the workers were discontented and strikes were numerous.

Norris received welcome reinforcements in the shape of twelve 55ft CMBs. These had been shipped from England and then taken by rail from Batum, on the Black Sea, to Baku. In command of these boats was Commander Eric Robinson, who had won a Victoria Cross in 1915 at Gallipoli[9]. The *Sergie* and the *Edinburgh Castle* (the renamed *Alla Verdi*) were converted to carry two CMBs each. The boats had to be hoisted out by means of a derrick, which had been specially made and fitted to each ship.

The first of a long-awaited number of aircraft finally arrived at Baku. The RAF contingent was commanded by Lieutenant Colonel Frederick 'Ginger' Bowhill[10]. The first aircraft, DH4 and DH9 bombers, were sent up to Petrovsk, where Major Malcolm RMLI had set up an advanced base. Gradually, the number of aircraft increased to about forty – both land and seaplanes. Another merchant ship, the *Yusanoff*, was taken over and converted to carry two seaplanes.

In early 1919 Commodore Norris and General Andrews planned to deal with the personnel of the Centro-Caspian Flotilla. The ships had been lying at Baku since the British returned in November 1918. They had steadily decreased in efficiency, reliability and discipline. Some of the crews had deserted. Their political loyalty was very doubtful, if not openly pro-Bolshevik – as had been shown the previous December. The flotilla owed a nominal loyalty to General Denikin, who commanded the White forces in South Russia. However, Denikin was not keen on the idea that he should pay a body of sailors who did nothing and whose work was done for them by the British; he was in any case short of money. General Erdeli was sent to Baku to pay off the ships, but arrived without any money. He sought help from the British, but they were reluctant to become involved. Many plans were considered and rejected until finally Erdeli confessed that he was unable to cope. Rumours of what was afoot reached the Russian ships and the two gunboats and three armed steamers put to sea and then anchored outside the port. Another four armed merchant ships remained at their berths; British guards were put on board, the crews made prisoners and the ships and their armament immobilised. The commander of the flotilla, Captain Voskerensky, a one-time cavalry officer and described by one of Norris' officers as a first class rogue, was summoned to Andrews' HQ. He was put on a train and sent to Batum. Only the ships outside the harbour remained.

Four CMBs armed with torpedoes were sent out to deal with them; they carried a representative of Voskerensky and interpreters. The ships were given an ultimatum; either to surrender and return to harbour, or be sunk. They were given ten minutes to comply. Nothing happened and two torpedoes were fired. To Robinson's embarrassment both ran deep. The effect, however, was the same. The situation was made clear by two very brief entries in the log of the *Ardagan*:

> 3.25 *They fired a torpedo.*
> 3.28 *Decided to surrender.*

All five ships weighed anchor and returned to harbour.

The four naval gunboats were not considered to be worth taking over and adding to the British flotilla. However, three of the armed merchant ships were in a better condition; their armament was serviced and supplemented and the engines overhauled. The *Lieutenant Schmidt* was renamed *Windsor Castle* and given an armament of four 4in guns, the *Orlionoch* became a seaplane carrier, while a third was renamed *Jupiter* and given two old 6in guns.

While the ships had been based at Krasnovodsk the SS *Tula* had been commandeered as an accommodation ship; she was transferred to Baku at the end of 1918. Over the months the ship proved inadequate for her task as increasing numbers of men arrived to man, maintain and administer the growing flotilla. A block of flats was requisitioned and converted to become Royal Naval Barracks, and was commissioned, in accordance with Royal Navy custom, as HMS *Theseus II*[11]. It originally had accommodation for twenty-five officers and 104 ratings, including a sick bay, dental surgery and cells for any delinquents. The barracks was soon found to be too small and the rooms had to accommodate extra men; additional houses were then taken over. It was all a far cry from the small party of the commodore, two officers and twenty-two ratings that had accompanied General Dunsterville and his men the previous year. At their peak strength in July 1919 the flotilla totalled forty-seven officers and 1,063 ratings and Royal Marines. The navy also employed 307 Russians, Armenians and Tartars as ships' crews and shore staff.

It was not until the middle of April 1919 that the northern part of the Caspian Sea became free of ice, giving the Bolsheviks the chance to resume operations. All through the winter the British ships had carried out limited patrolling as far as the ice edge to ensure that there was no unexpected activity by the enemy. From April at least four ships were kept constantly at Chechen Island, using Petrovsk as an advanced base. The seaplane and CMB carriers remained at Baku at short notice to join the other ships if they were required.

As soon as they were able the Bolshevik ships began to patrol, at first only off their own base at Astrakhan but as the month went on they ventured further south. It was known that they had actual fleet destroyers, which were much faster, more heavily armed and more manoeuvrable than the makeshift British ships. There was no doubt that the Russians had a distinct theoretical advantage, but they never succeeded in winning control of any areas of the Caspian. When the two sides met there was usually an exchange of gunfire before the Russian ships retired back to their base.

On 21 April the RAF mounted a series of daring reconnaissance missions over the base at Astrakhan. The aircraft had to cover about 200 miles each way, a considerable distance for the aircraft of the time; the aircrew had little hope of rescue if the aircraft had to ditch as the water was generally too shallow for the British ships. One aircraft failed to return, having been forced down near Astrakhan. The crew of two were recovered by the Bolsheviks and became POWs. The Bolshevik strength in the port was determined as between six and twelve destroyers, six armed merchant ships and a number of smaller craft – it was believed that they also had two or three submarines.

The next important operation took place in mid-May. The RAF reported that most of the Bolshevik ships had left the base at Astrakhan and had moved to Alexandrovsk, a port on the eastern side of the Caspian about 150 miles across from Chechen Island. The first task of Norris' ships was to examine the coast around Alexandrovsk, where there were believed to be many uncharted shoals and where all the navigation marks had been removed. Aircraft were used to survey the harbour and it was then planned that the two CMB carriers would be brought up to hoist out their boats, which would attack the ships in their berths. First, fog interrupted the plans of attack; then, the weather became too rough to hoist out the CMBs. However, a Bolshevik convoy of three armed steamers and two barges was encountered. The British ships immediately attacked and the escorting Russian destroyer made off at speed. The barges were sunk but the ships escaped in the fog.

It was subsequently learnt from Russian deserters that the Bolshevik Fleet had intended to attack the Chechen anchorage at that time. They were thwarted by the fog and returned to Astrakhan and Alexandrovsk. The British and Bolshevik forces must have passed close by each other unaware during the foggy night.

The British mounted another attack after air reconnaissance on 18 May reported that eight destroyers, fourteen armed motor boats and two gunboats were in Alexandrovosk. In fact, the aircraft had missed two small submarines[12], a minelayer and two depot ships. The British approached the port early on 20 May and a seaplane was launched in marginal weather conditions after daylight. A second aircraft crashed on take-off. The aircraft had been armed with bombs to attack ships in harbour as convenient and to report back on the conditions there. The weather prevented both tasks from being achieved.

The next day Commodore Norris took his force towards Alexandrovsk in fine weather. Three destroyers were sighted to the north but they did not contest the advance of the British ships; they disappeared at high speed. In the best traditions of Admiral Lord Nelson, Commodore Norris led his slow and ungainly fleet directly towards the harbour, banking on the Bolsheviks' usual lack of appetite for a battle. Some ships near the harbour mouth opened fire but failed to make any hits.

The only British ships that were within range during the approach were the *Emile Nobel* (with 6in guns) and the *Ventuir*[13] (with modern 4in guns). The two vessels scored several hits on enemy ships and a barge mounting two 6in guns. Large armed merchant ships moored near the harbour entrance were set on fire, forcing the Bolsheviks to abandon them. The other ships retired up harbour, a distance of some 6 miles. The *Emile Nobel* was hit in the engine room, causing some damage and several casualties among the Russian crew.

The Bolshevik shore batteries continued to fire at Norris' flotilla. The Russian ships were out of range, and if the British tried to get closer they would be unable to manoeuvre their cumbersome erstwhile merchant ships in the narrow harbour. At 1.30 p.m., after a brisk seventy-five minutes of action, Norris decided to withdraw.

It was a perfect opportunity for the CMBs to show their worth, but fate intervened. The old radio sets in the CMB carriers, *Sergie* and *Edinburgh Castle*, failed to pick up the signals summoning them to bring the CMBs to the action. Norris sent the damaged *Emile Nobel* back to Petrovsk while he took the rest of his force to seek out the CMB carriers.

The following day the seaplane carrier *Yusanoff*'s one remaining seaplane managed to fly five sorties against Alexandrovsk, but achieved little. The final flight nearly ended in disaster when fog returned before the seaplane arrived back with the force. The two airmen were found next day clinging to the one remaining float of their aircraft, having been in the water for almost twenty-four hours.

The *President Kruger* and the *Ventuir* met with two large Bolshevik destroyers on the 23rd, but after a brief exchange of fire the two Russian ships disappeared at speed to the north. It was the last time that the British Caspian Flotilla saw the enemy. It was later found that this action had led to the sinking of the destroyer *Moskvityanin*[14], a depot ship and some smaller craft. The Bolshevik ships left Alexandrovsk and returned to Astrakhan, while the British were left to spend the hot summer patrolling fruitlessly off Chechen Island.

In mid-June the Bolsheviks decided to attack the British ships off Chechen Island, using their only serviceable flying boat. The story of this sortie illustrates the lunacy of events in the Civil War that engulfed Russia. The aircraft had a crew of two: the pilot and a 'watchdog' who sat behind with a drawn pistol to ensure that the other did his job as ordered. During the flight the watchdog realised that if he had to shoot the pilot his own life would be endangered in the subsequent crash. The two men discussed their problem. Astrakhan was not a place to which they wished to return and they decided to surrender. The British would surely provide better food and living conditions – and probably greater life expectancy.

They landed their aircraft near their targets. The machine was hoisted on board the *Yusanoff* and taken to Baku. Once the captured aircraft had been made ready by Colonel Bowhill's men it was flown to join General Denikin's forces in South Russia, as were the two aircrew. History does not record their ultimate fate or how many of their expectations on surrendering were met!

In March 1919 the Allied Powers at the Peace Conference in Paris decided that Italy should assume responsibility for the Caucasus and surrounding areas. The Italians seemed keen to assume this role, but as time passed nothing happened. The War Office became increasingly anxious to withdraw from the area and the Admiralty offered to hand over all their ships and material in the Caspian to the Italians. In June the Admiralty reviewed the entire position there. They pointed out that the naval force based at Baku was essentially a part of General Denikin's White Army rather than a part of British forces in the Caucasus. The Naval Staff proposed that, regardless of anything the Italians might decide to do, the British force should be withdrawn. However, as General Denikin's forces were about to start an offensive a decision would be left until July, by which time it was hoped that the White Army would have captured Astrakhan.

On 15 July the Admiralty informed the Commander-in-Chief of the Mediterranean Fleet that all naval material was to be handed over to General Denikin, and British personnel were to leave Baku by 15 August. Although the Italians continued to show only lip service to their responsibility for the Caucasus and Caspian Sea[15] and Denikin had failed to capture Astrakhan, these orders were put into effect.

There was one final task for the British Flotilla. They assisted local troops from Baku in ousting a party of armed Bolsheviks from the islands around the Persian port of Ashurada (now Bandar-e Torkman) in the south-east corner of the Caspian. The Bolsheviks were not exactly under the orders of any central, or even local, government but were acting on their own behalf – with a little private enterprise piracy.

General Denikin found enough naval officers and ratings to take over from the British. All ship, aircraft, stores and ammunition were handed over in July and August. The first ship to be turned over was the *Asia* – on 28 July 1919, exactly a year from the time that the first party left Baghdad for Enzeli. On 2 September the White Ensign was hauled down at the barracks, HMS *Theseus II* ceased to exist and the remaining personnel left for Petrovsk and then on to Novorossisk.

There the matter should have rested. However, on 6 January 1920 the First Sea Lord, Admiral of the Fleet Sir David Beatty, told the Cabinet that there were indications that 'the Bolsheviks are turning their eyes to the Middle East and particularly the Mohammedan population there'. He went on to say that the British had 'assumed responsibility for Persia, whose interest in the Caspian Sea is great'. He explained that British control of the Caspian Sea would be essential if military operations for the defence of India, Persia and Mesopotamia became necessary against any southward advance of the Bolsheviks. He proposed that the Royal Navy should take over as many of Denikin's ships on the Caspian as was possible and man them from the Mediterranean Fleet. He concluded that this would mean the re-occupation of Baku as a base. Unsurprisingly, the Cabinet remained unimpressed with Beatty's arguments and nothing was done to implement his proposals.

Nevertheless, the Royal Navy – or at least some of its personnel – had not seen the last of the Caspian Sea. As the Bolshevik armies swept aside General Denikin's White forces in late 1919 and early 1920, a White fleet began to take shape in Enzeli, using the ships so recently handed over by the Royal Navy. The fact that Enzeli was nominally in Persia was overlooked by Admiral Gerasimov and his staff as their preparations went ahead. In April 1920 there was a decision to send a small British naval party to Enzeli to aid the Russians in their task. The force was to travel via Batum and Baku. Five officers and twenty-six ratings were led by Commander Bruce Fraser, later to be Admiral of the Fleet Lord Fraser of North Cape.

They left Constantinople on 19 April and finally reached Baku in the early evening of the 27th. Unfortunately for them, the Azerbaijani Ministers had done a deal with the advancing Red Army, agreeing to hand over power without further resistance in return for saving their skins. A *coup d'état* took place that night and in the morning Fraser and his men were arrested. Despite Fraser's best efforts, his attempts to get his men released failed and the whole group spent the next eight and a half months in the most terrible conditions in Baku's gaol. On 5 November 1920 they were finally put on a train to take them back to Batum, where the battleship HMS *Centurion* was waiting to take them to Constantinople[16]. The British Government was only too thankful that the matter was safely concluded with no casualties and little publicity.

This signified the end of the Royal Navy's extraordinary involvement in the Caspian, with its motley flotilla on an inland sea.

SEVEN

THE BLACK SEA

The surrender of Turkey, which came into force on 31 October 1918, opened up the access to the Black Sea and gave the Allied Powers the opportunity to intervene in South Russia. They had watched helplessly as German and Austrian troops advanced ever further into Russia following the Treaty of Brest-Litovsk in March that year, which to all intents and purposes had ended the war between the Central Powers and Russia. The Ukraine and the Crimea had been occupied, including the great naval bases at Sevastopol and Nickolaiev. A puppet Ukrainian Government was set up in Kiev and German troops maintained law and order until 11 November 1918.

Prior to the Armistice the main concern for the British and French had been the fate of the Russian Black Sea Fleet. The Germans made every effort to take over some of the ships and man them with German personnel. Their expectation was to sail through the Dardanelles with a stronger fleet than that of the British and French in the Aegean, giving them the chance to disrupt supply lines through the Mediterranean. They were thwarted from the beginning by Vice Admiral M.P. Sablin, the Russian Commander-in-Chief. As the Germans advanced on Sevastopol, the Commissars and the Fleet Committee begged Sablin to save them and the fleet. Confusion reigned as the individual ships of the fleet, and their Sailors' Committees, were uncertain as to who was in command. Eventually, Sablin ordered the Ukrainian flag to be hoisted, as this was supposedly an independent state recognised by the Germans. It made no difference and the German advance continued. Sablin took to sea as many of the fleet as would follow his orders and they safely arrived at Novorossisk.

Under the terms of the Peace Treaty the Germans demanded the ships return to Sevastopol, otherwise they would continue into Russia. Trotsky, as Minister for War, wanted to keep the fleet from falling into German hands and resorted to deviousness. In an open signal to Sablin – which could be read by the Germans – he ordered the fleet to return to Sevastopol, while at the same time a coded message was sent ordering Sablin to scuttle his ships. Sablin, fearing for his life if he made the wrong decision, left for Moscow to seek clarification of his orders. Back in Novorossisk, two factions were left with opposing views. One side wanted to go to Sevastopol, while the other favoured scuttling. The flagship *Volya* (ex-*Imperator Aleksander III*) duly sailed with half the fleet, the remainder being scuttled outside the harbour.

Having got control of at least some of the ships, the Germans found that they were unable to do much with them. They eventually managed to commission the *Volya*, which made a short cruise to the Bosphorus and back, but the ship was in no way fit for operations. The submarine *Utka* carried out trials as the US3, and the *Gagara* started trials in November 1918 as the US4. Neither boat became operational.

There was a great shortage of sailors to man the ships and crews had to be brought from Germany, meaning the new ships' companies had to make themselves familiar with the vessels and their different operating systems. The Germans were reluctant to bring in crews from Austria to ease the manning situation as they believed that this would weaken the Austrian Fleet, which might then seriously affect operations in the Adriatic. However, the British and French naval commanders remained worried; actual intelligence of what was happening to the Black Sea Fleet was almost non-existent, but they were aware that at least one battleship at Sevastopol was being made seaworthy.

A large number of Russians who had supported the old Tsarist regime, or at least hated or feared the Bolshevik Government, managed to escape the chaos of Petrograd and Moscow and moved south. General Mikhail Alekseev, who had been the Chief of Staff of the Imperial Army, and General Lavr Kornilov, who had attempted a coup in Petrograd against Kerensky's Provisional Government, began to form a 'Volunteer Army' in December 1917. Initially, it was only a small force, but it was dedicated to driving both the Bolsheviks and the Germans from Russian soil. The process was viewed with grave suspicion by the Don Cossacks, who feared that they would be absorbed against their will into some vast bureaucracy similar to that of the Tsar, and also that the Volunteer Army would bring down the wrath of the Bolsheviks on the area. The two Russian generals were at odds with one another, and together were faced with Peter Krasnov, the *Ataman* – elected leader – of the Don Cossacks. On 9 January 1918 the two generals issued a statement in which they summed up their common policy, which ended with the hope that one day 'the Russian people can express their will through the election of a Constituent Assembly'. This agreement had been negotiated by General Denikin, Alekseev's Chief of Staff; he also managed to pacify most of Krasnov's fears. It went some way to pointing out a degree of unity.

As a result of the Armistice between the Allies and Turkey, an Allied Fleet passed through the Dardanelles and anchored off Constantinople (now Istanbul) on 13 November. It was a massive force of seven battleships: four British, two French and one Italian, with cruisers and destroyers in support. A Greek battleship later joined the force. Flying his flag in the battleship HMS *Superb*, Vice Admiral Sir Arthur Somerset Calthorpe was in command of the British ships.

On 19 November the Admiralty signalled to Admiral Calthorpe: 'It is desirable that large British forces should enter the Black Sea as soon as convenient in order to impress not only the Ukrainians but also General Denikin and his forces.' Calthorpe sent an advance party, led by the cruiser *Canterbury* (Captain Percy Royds), to Sevastopol. They entered the base without hindrance on 24 November. A force of 500 Royal Marines were landed to maintain order in the town and to supervise the evacuation of nearly 10,000 German troops and sailors. The orders given to Royds before he sailed from Constantinople were to take over the battleship *Volya*, it being thought that the ship was under German control – which indeed it had been only twenty-four hours prior to his arrival in the Russian base. By the time the *Canterbury* entered harbour the battleship was once again flying the Tsarist St Andrew's flag. Nevertheless, a British party went on board and summarily hauled down the Russian flag and ordered the Russian Admiral, his officers and crew to leave the ship. It was a tactless act of rigid obedience to orders given by a senior officer who was not present at the scene. It was a humiliation for the loyal Russians, the very people the British had been sent to support. Worse was to follow.

The *Canterbury*'s boarding party found four German U-boats in the base. Two were allocated to the British and two to the French. HMS *Adamant*, a submarine depot ship, and the submarine E21 were ordered to sail from Constantinople to Sevastopol to take over the two British prizes. While there, the submariners tracked down a small party of loyal Russian submarine officers and men who were lovingly caring for the Russian boats as best as they could. Commander Pogeretsky, who had been awarded the British Distinguished Service Order during the war, was the leader of just twenty-eight officers and a few petty officers; the remainder of the men of the submarine flotilla had either been murdered by the Bolsheviks or had deserted. The submarine *Tyulene* had been in the best condition and Pogeretsky's men had lavished most of their care on keeping this boat clean and in good working order. In a nearby shed were a large number of spare battery cells; these too had been carefully maintained and routinely charged.

Admiral Calthorpe's next order was that all the submarines and the stored battery cells were to be rendered useless. The admiral's aim, no doubt, was to ensure that nothing of value was available to the Bolsheviks if they captured the port, but the order did little to show the Russian officers that the British were any better than the Germans who had so recently left. The distress of the Russians was obvious once it became clear what was to happen to their precious boats and batteries. Weeks of devoted work were made worthless in the space of a few hours. Though all the spare battery cells were wrecked the submarines only had their main motor starting switches removed. The only exception that the British made was the submarine *Tyulene*.

The two German submarines allocated to the British were the UB42 and UC37. Lieutenant Leslie Ashmore, who had commanded one of the 'C' class submarines in the Baltic in 1917, was to command one of the prizes and relates how the British crews carefully inspected their new boats for booby traps but found none. They did, however, find that the UC37 was in a much worse state than the corresponding French boat. As the French had not arrived the British officers, on a first come first served principle, appropriated the better one for themselves by the simple expedient of hoisting the White Ensign on the UC23. When the French arrived they were furious at the deceitful behaviour of their Allies and, after several protests to ever higher authority, Ashmore and his crew were ordered to return to the submarine originally allocated to them.

Post-Armistice euphoria was not over for the British crews. In place of the 'UB' and 'UC' on the conning towers they painted 'UN' since the Germans had seldom been known as anything but 'Huns'. All was well until the new symbol was noticed by a senior officer, who wanted to know about the new type of U-boat! Belated explanations were accepted with good humour.

The earlier agreement between General Krasnov, the *Ataman* of the Don Cossacks, and the White Russian forces commanded by General Denikin was proving difficult to implement. General Alekseev had died of a heart attack and General Kornilov had been killed in a skirmish with Bolshevik troops. While Admiral Calthorpe's main force had been sent to Sevastopol the cruiser HMS *Liverpool*, accompanied by a French cruiser and two Australian destroyers, sailed to Novorossisk with Military Missions from the British and French Governments to General Denikin. This was the first formal contact with White Russian forces in the South. After initial Anglo-French meetings with the Russians the French left to carry out their own agenda, leaving Lieutenant Colonel A.P. Blackwood, the head of the British mission, to compile his own report of Russian requirements and an assessment of the situation. Blackwood's report, containing as it did the extraordinary inflated Russian requests for military assistance, ought to have served as a warning to the British Government that the cost of any involvement would be neither short-lived nor cheap. Any such warning went unheeded.

The Allies still wanted Denikin to lead all the anti-Bolshevik forces in the South and sent another low-ranking delegation to report on the state and potential value of the Cossack troops. For this important mission two destroyers were allocated: HMAS *Swan* (Commander Arthur Bond[1]) and the French *Bisson* (Capitaine de Corvette Cochin). Bond led the team and was accompanied by three other officers and six ratings. The French ship was similarly represented and two Cossack colonels and a former staff officer to the Tsar, General de Svetchin, were also assigned to the party.

The two destroyers reached Kerch on the Sea of Azov in early December 1918 and, although the mission was well received by the local population, Bond thought that the White forces there were poorly armed and disciplined. The two ships then crossed the shallow waters to Marioupol and on to Taganrog. At this point the party was joined by two additional interpreters: a senior

Russian naval officer and an army officer. The team went on to Rostov by train and from there to Novocherkassk, the capital of the Don Cossack territory, where the mission met General Krasnov. Commander Bond continued with a tour of the Cossack-held area and saw the various military installations. At Tolovia they saw where the Cossacks were holding back a superior force of Bolsheviks, and noted that they were dependent for artillery and ammunition on what they captured from the enemy.

Back at Ekaterinodar, Bond made his report to Major General Herbert Holman, the head of the Military Mission aiding General Denikin. The hopeless position of the Cossacks if left to fight on their own, a fact which Bond stressed in his report, was probably a key factor is enabling Holman to convince Krasnov to join forces with Denikin.

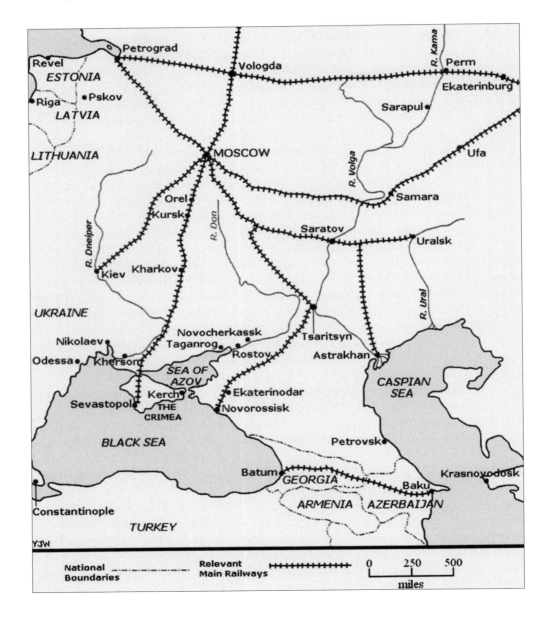

In addition to the *Swan*, three other Australian destroyers were initially deployed to the Black Sea at the end of the war in 1918. HMAS *Yarra* and *Torrens* were the first two Allied destroyers to be sent to Novorossisk and Batum. The *Parramatta* carried despatches and mail between Sevastopol and Constantinople and at the end of November 1918 acted as an escort for a group of Russian warships, which were handed over to the anti-Bolshevik forces in Sevastopol[2]. On 3 January 1919 the Australian destroyers sailed for Plymouth, from where they returned to Australia, arriving in Sydney on 21 May.

The French occupation of South Russia began when about 1,800 troops went ashore at Odessa on 18 December, less than a week after the Germans had left the city. Their intention was to preserve good order in the area; however, the Bolsheviks viewed the invasion as an overt attempt to assist General Denikin's armies. The French presence soon grew to the size of a full division, including many Algerians and Senegalese. The Greeks sent two divisions to the area; there was also a Polish brigade and the Romanians sent two divisions across their border into Russia. It was a formidable force – on paper. About 90,000 men held the coastal strip about 50 miles wide between the Romanian border and the port of Kherson on the River Dnieper. They expected to be doing garrison and security duties while General Denikin's White Russian troops fought the Bolsheviks. Events were to prove otherwise.

Early in January 1919 the Red Armies advanced into the Ukraine, meeting little effective opposition either from the troops of the so-called Independent Republic of the Ukraine or from any of Denikin's forces. In a vain attempt to put an end to the Civil War, President Wilson proposed that all sides in Russia should call a truce and meet with representatives of the Allies at some mutually convenient place. A small island in the Sea of Marmara – Prinkipo – was suggested. The White Russians would have nothing to do with the scheme and flatly refused to negotiate with the Bolsheviks.

The French-led occupation of the Ukraine disintegrated almost as soon as it was begun. The war that raged was actually four-sided, with the Bolsheviks, the White Army of Denikin, Ukrainian Nationalists and Cossack bandits, led by their leader General Grigorev – who was fighting on one side or the other according to the situation he deemed best. Although superior in numbers, this Allied army was low in morale. After the years of slaughter on the Western Front, the French soldiers had little will to risk their lives again in a confused situation which they found hard to understand and seemed to be of little value to France. At Kherson, the port on the River Dnieper, the Greeks fought strongly at first against Grigorev's marauding Cossacks, but as they retreated they committed an appalling massacre of 500 civilians. As his men entered Kherson, Grigorev ordered that every Greek prisoner should be shot in reprisal[3]. On 6 April 1919 Odessa fell to the Bolsheviks. The French evacuated all their own troops as well as Greeks, Poles, some 30,000 Russian refugees and 10,000 of Denikin's White Russian soldiers. Before they finally departed, the French destroyed vast quantities of military stores and equipment – but crucially left six tanks, which were later used by the Red Army.

The capture of the coastal areas of the Ukraine was only one part of the Red Army's offensive; at the same time as they were forcing the French to flee from Odessa they were also attacking the isthmus at Perekop, which defends the northern approaches to the Crimea. Sweeping aside General Denikin's army, the Bolshevik troops fanned out into the Crimea. The guns of the monitor HMS M17 and aircraft from the seaplane carrier HMS *Empress* gave support to the White troops, but to little avail.

With the Red Army likely to occupy the whole of the Crimea at any moment, the Dowager Empress Marie had to be evacuated from her palace near Yalta. The battleship HMS *Marlborough* was made available for this task. Sergeant A. Davenport, Royal Marine

Artillery, leaves us with a unique and moving record of this chapter of the end of the Romanov dynasty. Davenport was the senior NCO of a marine detachment landed to guard the palace grounds while the Empress embarked. In front of the palace a single row of White Russian officers – in smart new British khaki uniforms – were present to say goodbye to their Empress. After the Empress had left, Davenport asked the Russian officer in charge – who spoke perfect English – what they would do, as there were no instructions to take them out to the *Marlborough*. The Russian explained what their fate would be if they were caught by the Reds, especially as they were officers. To avoid this, they were going to shoot themselves. He then said that as they were in single file he would order a right turn and blow his whistle at which point every man would draw his pistol and place this against the neck of the man in front. When he blew the whistle a second time they would all fire; finally he would shoot himself.

As Sergeant Davenport and the marine rearguard went down the cliff to the boat he heard the whistle blown twice, followed by a volley of shots.

Prince Roman Petrovich and his younger brother were also evacuated by the *Marlborough*; Prince Roman was the father of Nicholas Romanovich Romanov, who claims to be the present head of the Romanov family. The Tsar's grandfather, the Grand Duke Peter, together with his wife and fourteen other members of the family, was also taken on board. They brought with them many – too many – of their respective retinues. This may, in part, explain why the Russian officers had to be left behind to their poignant fate.

The destroyer HMS *Speedy* evacuated some more members of the former Imperial family who were living in the Caucasus and now feared for their safety, in view of what seemed to be an unstoppable advance by the Red Army. Among them was the Countess Praskovia Sheremetev, who later married Prince Roman Petrovich.

On 13 February 1919 the French battleship *Mirabeau* ran aground off Sevastopol while manoeuvring to enter harbour during a snowstorm, leaving about four fifths of the ship's length on the bottom. The ship was not refloated until early April, by which time the forward twin 305mm (12in) turret had been removed as well as the side armour, coal, ammunition and many stores. The ship was dry-docked in Sevastopol for repairs, but with the approach of the Red Army strenuous efforts were made to make her seaworthy.

Under the terms of the secret agreement between Britain and France concluded in December 1917[4], the Crimea was part of the French area of influence. French troops had taken over from the Royal Marines in Sevastopol and it would be their responsibility to maintain the security of the great naval base, given the likelihood of it being threatened by the advancing Red Army. On 23 April Vice Admiral Jean François Amet, acting on behalf of the French Government, met with delegates from the Red Army on board the battleship *Jean Bart*. The French demanded a cease-fire while an evacuation of all Allied forces from the base took place. Rear Admiral Michael Culme Seymour[5], who had arrived at Sevastopol in his flagship, the *Emperor of India*, had been invited to join the talks but declined to do so. An agreement was signed on the 26th which allowed the French to evacuate their own and Greek forces, White Russian troops and many civilians along with 1,600 tons of equipment.

There were just 3,500 French and Greek troops ashore to defend Sevastopol and, although the Greeks were ready to fight if necessary, the mood of the French soldiers was less bellicose. They knew of the debacle at Odessa and wanted to go home without the risk of any further casualties. While the fact that Admiral Amet was willing to sit down and talk to the Bolshevik emissaries may have seemed reprehensible to Admiral Seymour, it was in fact an audacious bluff to give him more time to make the *Mirabeau* seaworthy.

Admiral Amet was very much on the defensive during these negotiations as the French Fleet off Sevastopol had mutinied on 20 April – without doubt the most serious mutiny of all throughout this period of intervention by any of the Allied forces. Trouble had broken out on board the destroyer *Protêt* in the Romanian port of Galata on 16 April. A mechanic (2nd class) named André Marty planned to seize the ship and join the Bolsheviks. He was betrayed and arrested before his plan could be executed. He was sent to the cruiser *Waldeck-Rousseau* to await trial[6].

Meanwhile, the battleships *France*, *Jean Bart* and *Justice* at Sevastopol hauled down their ensigns on 20 April and the *France* went as far as hoisting the Red Flag. Later in the day they were joined by the *Mirabeau* and the *Vergniand*. The mutineers said that they would not obey orders and demanded to be sent back to France. The following day two more of the French ships raised the Red Flag. The *France*, considered to be the source of the mutiny, was sent back to Toulon on the 23rd where twenty-three of the crew were court-martialled and received varying sentences. The crews of the other mutinous ships returned to duty after they were told that they were to return to France very shortly and that in the meantime they would not be involved in active operations. The last French ships to leave Sevastopol were the *Mirabeau*, towed back to France by the *Justice*.

During this time the situation in and around Sevastopol was chaotic. As mutinous French sailors roamed the streets of the naval base there was increasing friction between them and the Greek forces. The Bolshevik troops hovered outside the city and the British set about preparations to destroy what was left of the Russian Fleet. Fifteen submarines were taken out to sea and sunk, while the remaining battleships, cruisers and destroyers were sabotaged and made unseaworthy. Commander Pogeretsky and his devoted band of submariners were allowed to take the submarine *Tyulene* to Novorossisk. It seemed fortuitous that the old flagship *Volya* had been taken to Constantinople soon after the British had arrived the previous year.

As an indication of the seriousness of the situation Vice Admiral Calthorpe, who was both the British Commander-in-Chief, Mediterranean and a High Commissioner at Constantinople, arrived in Sevastopol in his flagship, the *Iron Duke*. Captain William Fisher[7], commanding the battleship, wrote in a letter how some French sailors were actually fired on by a patrol of Greek soldiers, though without giving details of any casualties. More humorously, Greek sailors on board the battleship *Lemnos* hoisted a dummy figure of a French seaman being hanged at the yardarm for mutiny. Captain Fisher's letter does not tell the whole story.

A procession in the city in support of the Bolsheviks was dispersed after Greek troops had opened fire, killing and wounding a number of the protesters. Some of the mutinous French sailors had joined the procession and a few of them were among the casualties. The remainder, infuriated with the Greek troops, rushed back to their ships, determined to revenge their fallen comrades. French sailors, who were in a state of mutiny as they had no wish to continue fighting, were now prepared to start another war – against Greece. They intended to open fire at point-blank range on the Greek battleship in the harbour. The results for the Allies as a whole would have been catastrophic. Fortunately, French officers acted swiftly and removed vital parts of the guns to prevent this potential tragedy.

Unaffected by Amet's truce with the Bolsheviks, British ships and the *Lemnos* gave assistance to Denikin's troops by shelling Bolshevik positions. Yet, inevitably, the Bolshevik advance continued to spread throughout the Crimea and the Red Army entered Sevastopol after it had been evacuated on 28 April. The Royal Navy was active in helping 33,000 civilians and over 3,000 troops reach Novorossisk. The British declared that they would not allow the Red Army to advance east of Theodosia, a warning that was ignored. Their relentless progress was finally brought to a halt in May by fire from the warships and the fierce resistance of the White troops defending the Kerch peninsular. On 2 May 1919 the battleship *Emperor of India*, the cruiser *Caradoc*, two destroyers and a monitor were all in action. Four days later these ships had been joined by the battleship *Marlborough*, the destroyer *Tobago* and the Russian cruiser *Kagul*. All were soon bombarding the Bolshevik positions.

At this time Admiral Kolchak's forces in Siberia were only 400 miles from Moscow and General Denikin placed himself under Kolchak's supreme authority. Due to the threat from Kolchak's forces Trotsky switched the main emphasis of the Red Army's operations to the defence of Moscow; this left General Denikin free to launch a counter-attack in the South.

On 19 May Denikin's army attacked in the territory of the Don Cossacks and also in the Donetz Basin. As a result he controlled an area stretching as far as the Volga River to the north of Tsaritsin (later Stalingrad). A squadron of RAF DH9 bombers and Camel fighters supported the White Army in this offensive. The squadron was commanded by Major R. Collishaw[8] and the aircrew were involved in some extraordinary exploits. On one occasion four Camels caught an estimated force of 5,000 cavalry in open country and destroyed many of them, the survivors being ridden down by White Cossacks. Collishaw himself attacked a gunboat on the Volga near Tsaritsin and sank it with two 230lb bombs. More importantly, in September the squadron attacked a fleet of forty gunboats, which had been gathered at Dubovka ready to bombard Tsaritsin with an assortment of weapons, some as large as 9.2in howitzers. In the course of three days, eleven were sunk and the rest forced to withdraw upriver.

An attack by this squadron at the end of July led to an act of outstanding bravery by the crews of two aircraft. Captain Walter Anderson and Lieutenant John Mitchell in a DH9 were photographing the results of a squadron attack on Bolshevik infantry north of Tsaritsin when enemy ground fire hit the starboard fuel tank, which began to leak petrol. Mitchell promptly climbed out on to the wing to plug the hole with his fingers. In another DH9, Captain W. Elliott and Lieutenant H. Laidlaw, who had acted as cover in the event of attack by any Bolshevik aircraft, flew towards their comrades' damaged aircraft. They too became victims of ground fire, which hit the engine. Elliott was forced to land about 5 miles behind the lines and near a large force of Red cavalry. As they began to advance on the stricken machine Laidlaw fired on the enemy with the Lewis-gun while Elliott set fire to the aircraft to prevent it falling into enemy hands. Meanwhile, Anderson landed close by – with Mitchell still out on the starboard wing – and Elliott and Laidlaw scrambled on board, only just ahead of the charging cavalry. Under intense fire Anderson managed to get the heavily laden aircraft airborne for the 110-mile flight back to base, with Mitchell still plugging the hole in the fuel tank despite being burnt by the exhaust pipe.

General Denikin promptly awarded both Anderson and Mitchell the Order of St Vladimir (4th Class), with swords and bow. When making the award to Captain Anderson he stated:

> Although Captain Anderson was fully aware of the danger of being taken prisoner by the Bolsheviks, in view of repeated threats and from captured newspapers announcing their intention to crucify any British airmen, in my opinion this devotion to duty, performed with the utmost gallantry, deserves the highest praise.

The British reaction was more delayed. Major Collinshaw forwarded a recommendation to Brigadier A.C. Mound of the British Military Mission at Rostov that both officers should be awarded a Victoria Cross. Such awards are strictly controlled and require stringent corroborative evidence from more than one source. By the time this had been collected Denikin's armies were again in retreat and some of the necessary paperwork must have been lost in the hasty British evacuation of Rostov. Although the recommendation was forwarded, no action was taken. The remarkable deeds of these two brave airmen were eventually recognised by the award of the Distinguished Flying Cross.

In mid-June Denikin's army broke out from their defensive positions across the Kerch peninsular and by the end of the month the Whites had recaptured Sevastopol and controlled all the Crimea. On 23 August his forces captured Kiev, the Ukrainian capital, and shortly afterwards reached Odessa. By early October they had captured Kursk and Voronesh. On 13 October 1919, Denikin's forces entered Orel, ending up just 250 miles from Moscow. At this time the commander of a detached flight of Collishaw's squadron, Squadron Leader Joe Archer sought permission from General Holman to bomb Moscow. The request was refused; it had been foreseen and Churchill had told Holman: 'I think it inadvisable that British airmen should be used in present circumstances to bomb Moscow.' He added that 'there was no military value in such an operation'[9].

After the recapture of Sevastopol Admiral Seymour visited the port. He expressed his concern to General Denikin about the submarine threat to his ships, as the Bolsheviks were thought to have at least two boats ready for sea in Nikolaev. He ordered the Russians not to use the submarines *Tjulen* and *Utka* in case they were mistaken for enemy warships and sunk.

Like so many armies fighting in Russia, both before and since, Denikin's forces had extended their lines of communication too far. Supplies began to run short, while Bolshevik partisans managed to seize one town after another, causing disruption and fear. Having routed Kolchak in Siberia, the Red Army turned its forces onto Denikin. Like other White generals, Denikin was forced to retreat at a time when it seemed that total victory was within his grasp. With retreat there began a slow but inexorable decline in morale. The Red Army recaptured Orel on 20 October, then Kursk and Kharkov, and by mid-December had retaken Kiev.

During the summer of 1919 the struggle between the pro-interventionist and the anti-war groups in the British Government intensified and led to a series of changes in policy. On 4 July it was decided that a state of war did in fact exist between Great Britain and the Bolshevik Government in Russia and that British forces should engage enemy forces by land and sea. By 25 July this decision was reversed and it was decided to withdraw British troops from North Russia[10], Siberia and the Caucasus. In August a final grant of aid to Denikin was approved amid increased opposition to intervention by the Labour Party and the national 'Hands Off Russia' Committee. In January 1920 the British Government even persuaded the Allied Supreme Council to relax the blockade they had imposed on South Russia.

In the early months of 1920 the rout of Denikin's armies continued. With incredible speed the Red Army swept into southern Russia. As might be expected in the circumstances, corruption and theft were rife. At a base in Taganrog the situation became so bad that the British officers in charge of the stores recruited Bolshevik prisoners, dressed them in British uniforms, paid them, gave them full army rations and used them to guard the supplies! Losses were dramatically reduced.

By early February it was once again necessary to evacuate as many civilians and White Russian soldiers as possible from Odessa. One of the ships used for this task was the transport *Rio Negro*, under the command of Captain Evan Cameron. When his ship arrived off Odessa, Cameron was hampered by the threat of mines, fog and ice, while a bitterly cold wind brought the temperature down to 26 degrees Farenheit.

Inside the harbour was the light cruiser HMS *Ceres*, whose captain, H.O. Reinold, was directing the whole evacuation. Outside the harbour the battleship HMS *Ajax* was anchored ready to give support if required. As the *Rio Negro* finally berthed, the crew could see that the whole jetty was packed with a swarming mass of people, obviously in terror of the advancing Bolsheviks. Littered around was the detritus of those already embarked: piles of baggage, large numbers of abandoned cars, carriages and numerous carts, many with their horses still harnessed, none of which it had been possible to take on board.

Nearby was a French ship, whose crew was charging the evacuees an exorbitant fee before they were allowed to embark – regrettably not an isolated incident as the war continued to go against the White forces. On another ship, a grand piano, watched by its rich and influential lady owner, was being hoisted on board – for a price – while hundreds of refugees waited pitifully on the jetty. At another berth the Russian transport, the *Vladimir*, was embarking the remnants of the army. On one occasion there was such a mad rush to board that those already embarked had to open fire on their comrades to maintain order.

The *Rio Negro*, when loaded comfortably, could carry 750 people. In the horror that was Odessa, knowing that those left behind faced an uncertain fate, over 1,400 were embarked in every stage of destitution, dirt and misery, many infected with disease and all half-starved and poorly clad in the bitter weather. Even then, Captain Cameron reluctantly had to leave with many hundreds of would-be evacuees still on the jetty. The naval guard from the gangway had to run through Bolshevik machine-gun fire to return to the *Ceres*. The *Vladimir* became stuck in the ice as she cleared harbour and had to be towed clear by a destroyer.

The rear guard defending the city was formed of Don Cossack cadets, some mere boys as young as fourteen. At the last minute the *Rio Negro* took on board some of these cadets, who were later transferred to the *Ceres*. The ship took all these unfortunate people to Constantinople, adding one more passenger on the way as a woman gave birth.

Further east, the Red Army recaptured Tsaritsin and Rostov as Denikin retreated south of the River Don. By the end of March Denikin's forces had to evacuate Novorossisk, an event which led to similar scenes to those that had taken place in Odessa. The scale of the provision of British supplies to Denikin had been enormous, most of it channelled through the port of Novorossisk; tons of equipment, however, had never left and yet more tons were sold and never reached those who needed it. Squadron Leader Archer, who had asked for permission to bomb Moscow, reported that he had seen anti-freeze for the lorries and aircraft being widely sold in the bars of Kharkov and Kiev. As the Bolsheviks came closer to the port vast quantities of equipment had to be destroyed to avoid its capture by the enemy.

Major General Holman, who commanded the Military Mission to General Denikin, stated in his final report that between March 1919 and March 1920 the British had supplied more than 1,200 guns and 2 million shells, 6,100 machine guns, 200,000 rifles and 50 million rounds of small arms ammunition. In addition, they had provided over half a million uniforms, 629 trucks and ambulances, 279 motorcycles, 72 tanks and 6 armoured cars, 100 aircraft, 12 500-bed general hospitals and 25 field hospitals. Also countless amounts of communication and engineering equipment had been supplied. Nearly all of this came from wartime dumps around the Mediterranean and, with the exception of the aircraft, little had come direct from Britain.

As the Red Army advanced and Denikin's army disintegrated, Rear Admiral Newton McCully arrived to take command of the United States Navy's Black Sea Squadron. Since leaving Murmansk in July 1919, McCully had spent a short period as the American naval representative at the Versailles peace talks before being specially selected by the State Department to return to Russia. He arrived in Novorossisk on board the destroyer USS *Biddle* in January 1920. Typically, he immediately set out on a personal fact-finding tour by visiting General Denikin at the front and then going to the port of Odessa. He arrived just as the port fell to the advancing Red Army but achieved what was considered to be impossible by arranging a meeting with one of the senior Bolshevik commanders. Afterwards he described the overall situation as 'not encouraging'. He reported that he had been told by Denikin's staff at least 500,000 Allied troops were needed to reverse the continuing rout of the White armies. The figure may have been a slight exaggeration but it was an unachievable ambition for the Whites; after the conclusion of the bloody war against Germany there were no more troops available to be sent to Russia, even if the political will were present – and it wasn't.

In the final days before the Bolshevik occupation, Novorossisk was full of refugees desperately trying to get to the docks to board a ship that would take them away from the enemy. Typhus was endemic. British sailors and soldiers from the Royal Scots Fusiliers struggled to organise the mob into some form of order while destroying what they could of the piles of equipment. Tanks were used to wreck many newly arrived aircraft by driving over their packing crates; wireless sets were smashed in a similar manner. Lorries were loaded with stores and then driven into the sea. Cossacks even shot their horses. A thick cloud of smoke rose into the sky from innumerable fires as stockpiles of stores were hurriedly burnt.

Helping the evacuation were the United States cruiser *Galveston*, three destroyers and a merchant ship. Commanding Officers had strict instructions, emanating from the White House, that American policy was one of non-intervention in Russian internal affairs and that American naval forces were present only to protect the life and property of American citizens. Rear Admiral McCully modified this directive to allow American ships to evacuate anti-Bolshevik refugees[11], but took great care to ensure that American ships were not drawn into hostilities. One Commanding Officer of a destroyer was told that he might use his searchlight but not his guns. The State Department in Washington was less than helpful over the fate of the refugees and anything that was accomplished by the Americans at this time was due solely to the efforts of Admiral McCully.

As the last ships sailed away on 27 March, shells from the victorious Red Army dropped into the harbour and onto the docks. The guns of the British battleship *Emperor of India* and the cruiser *Calypso*, along with the French cruiser *Waldeck-Rousseau* and the Italian *Etna*, kept the advancing enemy cavalry at bay. As in Odessa and elsewhere, those unfortunate enough not to get on board one of the ships, civilian and military alike, faced an uncertain future from a regime who regarded anyone trying to escape as an enemy of the State.

Appropriately, General Denikin left Novorossisk in a Russian destroyer, arriving at Theodosia a few hours later. Shortly after this defeat at Novorossisk Denikin resigned and was replaced by Baron Pyotr Nikolaevich Wrangel. Denikin left the Crimea for Constantinople in April 1920 on board the battleship *Marlborough*; from there he went to live as an exile first in France and then in America. He died in 1947.

During February and March over 83,000 refugees and soldiers had been evacuated from Novorossisk to the Crimea, 70,000 of them departing on the night of 26-27th March as the Red Army entered the town. Left behind were another 20,000 troops; some joined the Reds, while the remainder continued their retreat down the East Coast of the Black Sea.

On 1 April more troops and refugees were taken off by the cruiser *Calypso* and the American destroyers *Tattnall* and *Dupont* from the port of Tuapse – to the south of Novorossisk – before it too fell to the Red Army. This marked the limit of the Bolshevik advance, since most of the Red Army had to be withdrawn to engage in a war with Poland. This gave the Whites the advantage of six months in which to regroup. During this time Wrangel was able not only to strengthen his position in the Crimea, but also to try and do something with the thousands of refugees who swarmed over every town and village.

At the end of March the ubiquitous *Rio Negro* took off some refugees from Yalta, where Commander L. Crabbe of the destroyer *Montrose* was trying to persuade these unfortunate people to go into exile. However bad the conditions were for these homeless families in the Crimea, where their future depended on the success or otherwise of the dispirited army, there was an understandable reluctance to leave their homeland – possibly forever – to go to a strange land where they would be virtually penniless. Those that did decide to leave were taken first to Constantinople and then on to camps on the Aegean island of Mudros. The British Government arranged for many to be taken to the new state of Yugoslavia, where they were given a small daily subsistence allowance for one year to help them settle in to their new homes.

When the *Rio Negro* arrived off Batum in June, rumours were rife that the British would be leaving in the near future and this led to an increase in the number of Russians wishing to leave the town and go into exile rather than face a Bolshevik occupation. Present in the port and in the anchorage outside were the battleship *Ajax*, the French cruiser *Edgar Quinet*, some British and American destroyers and a small Italian gunboat as well as a number of transports. Security in the town was in the hands of the soldiers of the Punjab Regiment of the Indian Army.

At 7.00 a.m. on the 17th, there was a large explosion and the oil tanker *Sviet* was seen to be belching smoke and burning furiously in the fore part of the ship. From time to time there were loud explosions and fierce flames would leap many feet into the air. The ship had only completed loading the night before. A Bolshevik agent had gained access to the jetty and thrown a bomb, which had exploded on the oil tanks. The tanker was an ex-Russian ship but with a British crew, who abandoned their vessel in a hurry.

The destroyer HMS *Swallow* (Commander Bodham-Whetham), which was anchored outside the harbour at the time of the explosion, quickly raised steam and went alongside the jetty just ahead of the stricken tanker. A small boarding party managed to reach the forecastle of the burning vessel and a towline was passed. It was hot and dangerous work, as with a small change of wind direction flames could have engulfed them at any time, but the task was completed quickly and efficiently. The *Swallow* towed the *Sviet* out of harbour; it was brilliant seamanship by Commander Bodham-Whetham as the burning tanker had no steering and could have veered into the line of anchored transports. The *Sviet* was sunk on a sandbank 4 miles outside Batum; the fires were still burning when the *Rio Negro* sailed a week later.

Vice Admiral de Robeck, who had relieved Admiral Calthorpe as Commander-in-Chief of the Mediterranean Fleet, believed that it was not viable for the White Army to remain in the Caucasus, and that General Wrangel should maintain a stronghold in the Crimea. Back in London Mr Walter Long, the First Lord of the Admiralty, recommended to the Cabinet that the White Russians should be given as much help from the sea as was practicable, with a view to holding the Crimea and coming to terms with the Government in Moscow. The Cabinet did not agree with this idea and de Robeck was told that no help was to be given which might prolong the struggle. The Foreign Office suggested to Moscow that negotiations should be started. This last proposal did not even receive a reply.

In early April Admiral de Robeck told the Admiralty that unless effective help was given, or negotiations for a truce were started, a total collapse in the Crimea was likely. The Foreign Office stepped in once more and told the Russian Commissar for Foreign Affairs in Moscow that unless their earlier proposals for negotiating a truce were accepted there would be a resumption of help to General Wrangel. Again, no reply was received and on 25 April de Robeck was authorised to give assistance to the White forces – but no men were to be landed.

The military situation in the Crimea remained quiet, as the Red Army was fully involved in stopping a Polish invasion. By June the Poles were in retreat. On 7 June Wrangel began an offensive to break out of the Crimea, in spite of a warning from London that this would forfeit any British support. The Admiralty informed de Robeck that British naval forces were therefore to be strictly neutral. In fact, Wrangel was initially successful and in August the French recognised his Government.

Wrangel's success led to a Peace Conference in Riga in September between the Poles and the Bolsheviks, giving the Poles all of the disputed territory east of the River Bug. The Red Army was switched south and Wrangel was driven back to the Crimea. The problem of evacuation loomed once more. As a result of Foreign Office pressure the Admiralty told de Robeck that the policy of strict neutrality should on no account be compromised. No action was to be taken to evacuate refugees, other than British, from the Crimea. The French Government was told that as they had recognised Wrangel's Government – which the British had not done – it was up to them to deal with any problems in the Crimea.

Thousands more refugees faced a doubtful future in Bolshevik hands and Wrangel's army faced extinction. Using Russian, American and French warships and merchant ships, over 120,000 people were taken away to some form of safety; large numbers went to Yugoslavia, Bulgaria and Tunisia, and ultimately dispersed over most of the world. Forbidden by their Government to help, it was a distressing time for the men of the Royal Navy, especially as the British Government had on many occasions been the strongest supporter of the White cause of all the Allied Governments. The evacuation began on 13 November 1920 and lasted for three days, after which the Red Army once again entered Sevastopol. Organised White resistance in Russia had been eliminated.

The units of the Russian Black Sea Fleet which had been in White hands, including the submarine *Tyulene*, sailed to the French naval base at Bizerta in Tunisia, where the ships were interned and eventually broken up.

The final event for the Royal Navy, in this unusual period of intervention in South Russia, occurred on 12 November 1920. The destroyer *Tobago* hit a mine while on passage near the Turkish port of Trebizond. Fortunately, the ship did not sink and casualties were light. The ship was made seaworthy, with the help of HMS *Centurion*, and towed to Malta. It was found not to be economically viable to repair the *Tobago*, and she was scrapped in 1922.

Another phase of Allied Intervention in Russia had come to an undistinguished end. During this time in South Russia, Allied solidarity was notable only for its absence. British help to General Denikin had been enormous and, indeed, of all the White Russian generals he had perhaps come closest to success. He failed because of the weakness and lack of public appeal of his cause as opposed to the determination and ruthless discipline of the Red Army. At one time or another the Royal Navy had deployed most of the Mediterranean Fleet to the Black Sea, but it could only play a minor role in the fighting. This was partly because much of the fighting was away from the Black Sea littoral, but mostly because there was a lack of a constant and viable political policy.

EIGHT

THE ROYAL NAVY RETURNS
TO THE BALTIC

On 13 November 1918, just two days after the Armistice with Germany, a conference took place in the Foreign Office in London under the chairmanship of the Foreign Secretary, Arthur Balfour. It was decided to supply the Baltic States – Estonia, Latvia and Lithuania – with arms and other military material if and when they had governments which would be able to use these supplies. On the same day the War Cabinet decided to send a cruiser squadron, a destroyer flotilla and a number of minesweepers to the Baltic. No troops were to be sent.

The force was commanded by Rear Admiral Edwin Alexander-Sinclair, whose orders were brief, less than explicit and left much to initiative. In short, he was 'to show the flag and support British policy as circumstances may dictate'. The Foreign Office provided a political adviser, Mr V. Bosanquet, to help the admiral interpret the Government's intentions. Later, Mr Balfour indicated that 'Bolshevik forces attacking our friends' might be treated as hostile. The Admiralty signalled to Alexander-Sinclair that 'a Bolshevik man-of-war operating off the coast of the Baltic provinces must be assumed to be doing so with hostile intent and should be treated accordingly'! This perhaps went rather further than the Foreign Secretary had intended[1].

The situation in the Baltic at the time was that the Bolsheviks were firmly in control of the old capital of Petrograd (now St Petersburg). The Russian Baltic Fleet was lying at Kronstadt, though with serious manning problems due to an acute shortage of officers and the fact that many of the crews had either deserted or were ashore controlling the city. The three Baltic States had declared their independence from Russia after the Revolution of November 1917, though occupation by German troops quickly followed. These forces enjoyed the support of pro-German elements of the population, generally referred to as the 'Balts' or 'Baltic Barons'. The Germans were reluctant to evacuate Latvia and Lithuania – as they were obliged to do under the terms of the Armistice – because of the influence of these Baltic Barons. The German troops in Estonia mutinied at the time of the Armistice and were withdrawn, making the situation in that country much easier. The Bolsheviks, on the other hand, were determined to bring an end to the independence of the three states and return them to Russian rule. The Government in Finland – itself newly independent, led by Marshal Mannerheim – was also eager to obtain Allied help. However, the situation there was complicated by the presence of the Red Finns, who had been helping the Allies in Murmansk[2]. The Reds in the South of the country were more numerous than in the North and had no reason to side with the British rather than their political allies, the Bolsheviks in Russia. Any co-operation in the North was based solely on a need for British assistance against the Germans.

This was the political and military minefield into which Alexander-Sinclair led his force. On 21 November the light cruiser *Cardiff* had the honour of leading the German High Seas Fleet into the Firth of Forth, where they began their internment under the Armistice. Five days later the cruiser was flying Alexander-Sinclair's flag and led the other four ships of the Sixth Light Cruiser Squadron[3], nine destroyers and seven minesweepers towards the Baltic. Initially their destination was Copenhagen, where the ships would fuel and then proceed to Libau, where the Germans remained in control, and then on to Revel. The cruisers and destroyers were able to top-up with oil fuel from the force's oilers at Copenhagen and proceed, but the minesweepers required coal, of which there were no suitable stocks. The first collier sent from Britain had run aground; a second, sent as a replacement, had struck a mine in the North Sea. A third ship did not arrive until January 1919. The minesweepers were then employed for a week off Copenhagen before returning to Britain; the Baltic had begun to ice over and would have limited the ships from sweeping efficiently to the north of Windau.

Alexander-Sinclair had no option but to press on since the Estonian Prime Minister, Konstantin Pats, had made an urgent appeal for help to the British Government. The Bolsheviks were advancing into the country and the admiral was instructed to make an early appearance with his ships off Revel 'to prevent anarchy and the inevitable massacre'. The Baltic had been sown with thousands of mines during the war, both German and Russian. Many hundreds had the safety device – whereby the mines became inert if they broke loose – removed, or else it had become inoperative. Large numbers had indeed broken loose and were drifting freely. Russian, German and Swedish charts were available and these showed the safety lanes and swept paths; however, they were not necessarily accurate. In the absence of the minesweepers, the ships had to rely on the security afforded by their own paravanes – a device which could be towed from the bows of a ship and which hopefully would cut the mooring wire of any mines encountered.

There was only time for a brief visit to Libau before the admiral resumed the passage to Revel. The temperature was well below freezing, the weather was foggy and the sea was calm though there was a long swell. The force was steaming in line ahead at 20 knots with the cruisers leading when, just before midnight on 5 December, the *Cassandra* (Captain Edward Kennedy) struck a mine. There was a loud explosion and the ship lost way very quickly, so rapidly in fact that the next ship astern only narrowly avoided a collision. Searchlights from the other cruisers illuminated the scene and showed the *Cassandra* lying low in the water without steam or power. Within twenty minutes the ship's upper deck was awash.

The explosion had killed only ten men, but there were over 400 to be rescued. Lieutenant Commander Francis Glossop manoeuvred the destroyer *Westminster* against the stricken cruiser's weather bow and was able to take off fourteen ratings before the movement of the two ships in the swell threatened to damage the destroyer's thin plating and Glossop had to move away. Commander Charles Ramsey, with consummate seamanship, brought the *Vendetta* against the lee bow of the *Cassandra*. Except for one man, who fell between the two ships, all the remaining members of the cruiser's crew were brought dry-shod on to the destroyer, including a number with broken limbs and other injuries. The abandoned ship then sank by the bow, leaving her stern in the air before she broke in two and sank. A Court of Enquiry concluded that the cause of the explosion was a tethered mine which became caught by the starboard paravane but failed to cut the wire, instead dragging the mine into the side of the *Cassandra*.

The *Calypso* had struck a submerged wreck in Libau harbour and had to return to Britain for docking; she carried the survivors of the *Cassandra* with her. Alexander-Sinclair's force was further depleted by the need for two destroyers, the *Westminster* and *Verulam*, to return for docking after a collision in fog. The rest of the ships reached Revel safely two days later.

The two minelayers HMS *Princess Margaret* and *Angora*[4] also arrived at Revel, carrying large quantities of small arms and ammunition, which were to be given to the Estonian and Latvian Governments. Alexander-Sinclair had been instructed by the Foreign Office that once the arms had been landed he was to inform the two fledgling Governments that they would be responsible for the defence of their own countries. No British troops would be sent.

However, events on the ground often prove very different from those viewed at the Foreign Office miles away in London, and leave a military commander in the area with difficult options. Communications with London were slow and tenuous, relying on a ship being kept in Copenhagen to act as a link. Alexander-Sinclair found that the situation in Estonia was far from that envisaged in London. The Government in Revel was only in control of parts of the country, there were shortages of food, fuel and other necessities, and there was a fear of a Bolshevik uprising in the capital and other towns. Most importantly, the activities of the Bolshevik troops were causing grave concern. Shortly before the arrival of the British squadron, the Red Army had made an amphibious landing with the aid of some ships of the Baltic Fleet, had captured the border town of Narva and two others, and was advancing towards Revel. The Estonians informed Alexander-Sinclair that the Russian troops were only about 40 miles east of the capital, and that civilians in captured towns and villages were being treated with the utmost brutality.

Alexander-Sinclair faced a difficult decision as a result of his directive from the Foreign Office. Merely 'showing the flag' seemed rather inadequate. Consequently, he took the *Cardiff* and *Caradoc* and five destroyers along the coast and spent the day shelling targets to the rear of the Bolsheviks. Gunfire destroyed the only bridge across the river on the frontier, which immediately brought the advance of the Red Army to a halt. The overall effect heartened the defenders such that a small force, led by the Estonian General Laidoner, landed at Kunda Bay on Christmas Eve and began offensive actions behind the enemy's front line.

Meanwhile, the admiral also had responsibilities in Latvia; he had to balance these with the possibility of any Bolshevik moves in the Gulf of Finland as a result of his actions along the coast against the Red Army. He confidently believed that much of the Russian Fleet was immobilised and did not pose a serious threat. He split his forces, leaving two cruisers – the *Caradoc* and the rejoined *Calypso* – with half his destroyers at Revel and taking the remainder to Libau.

He would have been able to make this move more readily had he known that the Russian intelligence about his force was woefully inaccurate. Admiral A.P. Zelonoy, the Russian Fleet Commander in Kronstadt, has been told that the British Fleet consisted of two modern battlecruisers, six pre-dreadnought battleships, eight light cruisers and twenty destroyers plus numerous support ships. The small Estonian force landing at Kunda Bay was reported as being supported by two British battleships. Three brief surveillance patrols to Revel by the submarines *Tur*, *Tigr* and *Pantera* did nothing to redress these misconceptions. The three boats explained their failure with excuses of 'severe weather and damage sustained', or 'defective compasses, and freezing of the periscope' or 'trouble with other equipment including rudders, trimming tanks, batteries and radio'. A sorry tale of inefficiency, brought about more by the reluctance of the crews to become involved in any hazardous operation than actual equipment failures.

However, contrary to expectations, Captain B.S. Thesiger of the *Calypso*, the Senior Officer of the ships remaining at Revel, very soon found that he had to deal with an offensive operation by the Bolshevik Fleet. The Russians hoped to destroy the British ships while they were in harbour, although they were unaware that Alexander-Sinclair had taken half of the force away.

In a topsy-turvy plan three destroyers, the *Spartak*, *Avtroil* and *Azard*, were to enter Revel Roads and carry out the bombardment – hardly a strong force for this task in view of the number of British battleships being as numerous as indicated by Russian intelligence. The battleship *Andrei Pervozvanni* and the cruiser *Oleg* were to remain in the vicinity of the island of Hogland, midway between Revel and Kronstadt, where they would be able to provide distant support for the destroyers. The whole operation was under the command of Fedor Raskolnikov, who was a member of the Revolutionary War Soviet of the Baltic Fleet and a former sub-lieutenant in the Tsarist Navy. The operation was planned to take place on the evening of Christmas Day.

From the beginning little went according to plan for the Russians. Only the *Spartak* was able to sail with the battleship. The *Oleg* and the *Azard* were already at sea off Kunda Bay, and in any case the destroyer was unable to join the force as she was too low on fuel. The third destroyer was in Petrograd and was subsequently delayed by engine trouble and heavy ice. Raskolnikov postponed the operation for twenty-four hours, but on the morning of the 26th he changed his mind and headed for Revel in the *Spartak*.

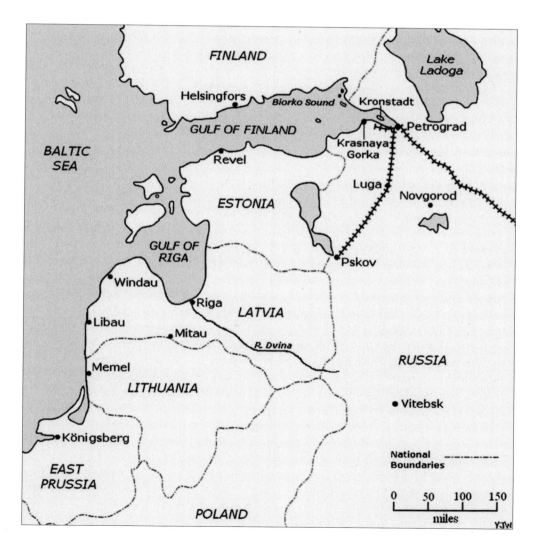

On Boxing Day many of the British officers and ratings were ashore, as the Estonian authorities had invited them to a banquet. Suddenly, with no warning, shells began to fall on the town and the harbour. The single Russian destroyer had arrived and had opened fire with its four 4in guns; it could be seen steaming at high speed off the harbour. The British ships were ordered to raise steam and proceed to sea, a feat which was achieved by the destroyer *Wakeful* in only fifteen minutes. She was quickly followed by the two cruisers. Once clear of the harbour the *Wakeful* opened fire on the Russian ship, which immediately turned away and headed for the distant protection of the two larger Russian ships. The British were then surprised by the fact that the *Spartak* turned through another 180 degrees and hoisted a white flag.

The Russian destroyer had run over a shoal and stripped both propellers and the rudder. She had also developed a bad leak. The destroyer *Vendetta* put a prize crew onboard and towed the *Spartak* back to harbour. When she had anchored a signal was made for the ship to raise steam at once so that she could work her pumps. The Bolshevik crew called a meeting to decide whether to raise steam or not; a quick decision was achieved aided by a second signal to raise steam at once, while the *Calypso* trained her guns on the helpless prize. The ship was found to be filthy and, perhaps not surprisingly, many of the crew appeared quite pleased to have been captured.

Word reached Captain Thesiger that Raskolnikov was on board the *Spartak* but had merged with the crew, hoping to avoid detection. He was later identified by a White Russian officer who had served with him before the Revolution. Meanwhile, papers found on the ship revealed the presence of the two large Russian ships waiting off Hogland and also the fact that there were two more destroyers involved in the operation. Thesiger took his whole force to sea to seek out the Russian ships, notwithstanding the fact that, with only two light cruisers and four destroyers, the heavy guns of the *Andrei Pervozvanni* and the *Oleg* could have blown his ships out of the water before they even got in range of the enemy. However, the seas were empty around Hogland; the Russians had all returned to Kronstadt. All that is except for the *Avtroil*, which met with the British ships, surprised to find them at sea rather than under fire at their berths in Revel. The ship turned and tried to escape from the British destroyers but became surrounded. She showed no sign of wanting to fight, but rather hauled down her colours and hoisted a white flag. The destroyer *Vortigern* put a boarding party on board the Russian ship and escorted her back to Revel.

Raskolnikov was taken to London, where he was initially housed in Brixton Prison. In May 1919, after conditions had improved for British prisoners held in Moscow, he was allowed to live in a hotel. He was highly valued by Trotsky and in June 1919 the Danish Red Cross arranged that he was exchanged for eighteen British personnel: eight officers, three NCOs, three other ranks and four civilians[5]. The two destroyers were given to the Estonians to form part of their navy and became the *Wambola* and *Lennuk*. The Russian crews were also handed over to the Estonians and held as POWs.

While these actions were taking place in the Gulf of Finland, Admiral Alexander-Sinclair and his ships had been trying to bring some sort of peace to Latvia. It was a daunting task. The majority of the population – the Letts – supported the Government of Mr Karlis Ulmanis, which aimed to establish a democratic state independent of Russia. However, the power base of Ulmanis and his Ministers was in the province of Livonia, whose geography prevented the Royal Navy from giving them the same support as in Estonia. In Courland, adjacent to the sea, the population was more in favour of Communism. There were also the Baltic Barons, as in Estonia, who hoped to gain a dominance that would enable them to form a puppet state under the aegis of Germany. Finally, there was the influence of the German Eighth Army, who had already withdrawn from Livonia and expected to return to their native country. Their stores and equipment would provide a massive boost to the Russians if they were left behind. In Livonia the Government's Lettish regiments were poorly trained and badly armed and were having to withdraw ahead of the advancing Red Army.

Alexander-Sinclair sent the *Princess Margaret* (Captain H. Smyth), the *Ceres* and two destroyers to Riga to try and stabilise the situation. While his ship was landing arms and ammunition to help stiffen the resistance of Ulmanis' forces, Smyth, with the help of Mr Bosanquet, summoned the German High Commissioner and the Military Commander and urged them to comply with Article XII of the Armistice terms. This laid down that the Germans were to withdraw from territory that was formerly part of the Russian Empire as soon as the Allies should consider the moment suitable, having regard to the interior conditions of those territories. The Article also laid a duty on the German forces to help maintain law and order in support of the new Government and to oppose the movement of the Red Army into the fledgling state.

The two Germans prevaricated at length with an air of affected innocence. Their only real argument concerned the poor morale of the German troops, which prevented any extensive operations until they could be relieved by volunteers, sent from Berlin. Bosanquet had to be content with urging the Germans to do more to fight the Bolsheviks and adding that if they were unable to carry out the terms of the Armistice then the whole peace process might be delayed. The last threat was a bluff and both Bosanquet and the Germans were aware of the weakness of his case. Negotiations in Paris would be unlikely to stop for such a reason; the Allies not involved in the Baltic – America in particular – were too war-weary to risk everything.

Five days later the Germans had still not acted and the Red Army was only 25 miles from Riga. With a Communist uprising in the capital expected in support of the Russian advance, Smyth embarked 350 British, Allied and neutral refugees on board the *Princess Margaret*. On 29 December two Lettish regiments, which had reached the city from the front line, mutinied. Ulmanis gave the men thirty minutes to surrender, though he had no resources, apart from the British ships, with which to enforce his demand. Smyth considered that this was one occasion when he could exceed his orders and instructed the *Ceres* to open fire on the barracks. The short bombardment had an immediate effect and the men surrendered, though it was doubtful how permanent this would be once the British ships left.

Sailors and marines were sent into the city to patrol the area around the jetty where the ships were berthed and to ensure the continued use of the jetty itself. Alexander-Sinclair himself arrived from Libau in the destroyer *Valkyrie* to see how bad the situation had become. It was very clear that Riga would fall to the Red Army in the near future and Mr Ulmanis' Government was embarked in one of the destroyers. The admiral ordered that the ships make preparations to leave on the morning of 3 January 1919. The *Valkyrie* led the British force down the partially frozen River Dvina[6] as the Red Army began to enter the city. Ulmanis and his Ministers were disembarked at Libau, where they would continue the struggle to form a free and independent state. The admiral had orders to return to Britain with his force, as the winter ice began to inhibit any operations north of the Gulf of Riga.

Even before Admiral Alexander-Sinclair had returned to London the First Sea Lord, Admiral of the Fleet Sir Rosslyn Wemyss, was pressing the War Cabinet for a more positive policy in the Baltic during 1919. He argued that, if the Government was to honour its commitments to the newly formed Baltic States, immediate preparations should be made for a land force of considerable strength to be sent to the area. The Cabinet was firmly opposed to further involvement by British troops but reluctantly agreed to send a new force of cruisers and destroyers to the Baltic under the command of Rear Admiral Sir Walter Cowan. His instructions were similar to those given to his predecessor and included the provision that only in 'exceptional circumstances' was he authorised to land men from his ships. He was also reminded that the blockade of Germany was still in force – Article XXVI of the Armistice – and would remain so until the Peace Treaty was signed and came into effect.

Early in 1919 fresh German troops began arriving in Latvia to replace the dispirited units of the Eighth Army that had been in the country at the end of the war. This was technically admissible since it allowed General Graf Rüdiger von der Goltz to be more active in his operations against the Russian invaders, as he had been asked to do by Mr Bosanquet. However, von der Goltz had great ambitions to set up a series of Baltic States which were controlled by pro-German sympathisers, were dependent on Germany and would ultimately be incorporated as part of Germany.

The Allies, led by Britain, faced a difficult situation in the Baltic, one which would largely fall on the shoulders of Admiral Cowan. It was hoped that the arrival of German reinforcements would obviate the need to send a large British land force to the Baltic States. This was contradicted by the fact that the Allies were determined that all German troops should be withdrawn as soon as possible. However, British hopes did not take into account the ruthless nature of von der Goltz, who had no intention of doing the British Government's work for them unless it fitted in with his own plans. On the other hand, British support for the Baltic States had antagonised the White Russian leaders, who could not accept the separation of these States from Mother Russia. Finally, there was the problem of the blockade. The newly arrived troops of General von der Goltz had been brought to Libau by sea and would have to be supported by sea; German shipping movements were restricted by the requirement to maintain the blockade until the Peace Treaty was signed. The Allied War Council in Versailles were responsible for all political decisions and were fully aware of all the problems in the Baltic, but decided that Britain should assume responsibility for the area and should unravel this multi-problem entanglement[7].

It was into this tangled web of political uncertainty that Admiral Cowan sailed on board his flagship HMS *Caledon* in company with a second cruiser, the *Royalist*, and five 'V & W' class destroyers[8], to meet with Alexander-Sinclair's returning force at Copenhagen on 6 January 1919. Captain the Hon. Matthew Best, in the *Royalist*, was sent on ahead with two destroyers to Libau to report on the situation. He found that since Alexander-Sinclair had left, the Germans had thrown into the sea all the rifles and ammunition landed from the *Angora* for the use of Lettish troops. Ulmanis and his Government feared both the continued advance of the Red Army and also a local uprising in support of the Russians. Prior to the arrival of fresh troops the Germans were powerless to delay the Russian advance, with only some 800 men who could be expected to obey orders. Cowan arrived in Libau on the 17th and learnt that the situation in Estonia was more satisfactory, with local troops clearing elements of the Red Army and their supporters from the country. Any large-scale naval operations north of the Gulf of Riga were, of necessity, out of the question until the spring. The announcement at the end of the month that the Allied force would be strengthened by the arrival of two French warships gave Prime Minister Ulmanis more hope of achieving his aims, as he believed the French ships signified greater Allied involvement.

Another 5,000 rifles and fifty machine guns, with 5 million rounds of ammunition, were handed over on 9 February and were stored in the Government transport *Saratov*, berthed in the Naval Harbour, to prevent a repetition of previous double-dealing by the Germans. At the same time it was learned that Windau, only 40 miles north of Libau, had fallen to the Red Army. Cowan immediately took his flagship north and anchored off the port. The *Caledon's* 6in guns bombarded the batteries guarding the entrance to the harbour and destroyed them, whereupon the Russians evacuated the town and it was reoccupied by Lettish troops.

On 13 February two more light cruisers, the *Phaeton* and *Inconstant*, and five destroyers reached Copenhagen as reliefs for Cowan's ships. The Admiralty had decided that service in the Baltic in winter was such that the ships should be rotated every six weeks or so. Cowan with the *Caledon*, the *Royalist* and the attendant destroyers left Copenhagen for Rosyth on the 21st, and Captain J.E. Cameron in the *Phaeton* assumed the responsibilities as SNO Baltic. On his return Cowan immediately went to the Admiralty, where he was able to discuss the situation in the Baltic with the First Sea Lord and the Naval Staff. Captain Dudley Pound, at that time the Director of Operations[9] in the Admiralty, summed up the situation facing the Senior Officer in the Baltic:

> We cannot expect to achieve much result in bolstering up the Baltic States until our policy becomes a really positive one. At the present time, with the exception of a few arms and a little coal, it is entirely a negative one.

It was a clear case of passing the need for a definitive directive back to the Cabinet and the Allied War Council. However, they failed to give a firm lead and the Senior Naval Officer in the Baltic was left to interpret his orders as best he could. Neither the Cabinet nor the War Council knew what policy they should be advocating.

The Government was unaware of the influence of the German commander in Latvia, where the presence of fresh troops had tightened German control of the area. He allowed the Departments of Justice and Food to be handed over to Ulmanis' Provisional Government but retained control of the railways, ports and communications. In direct contravention of the Armistice terms, he also claimed the right to recruit volunteers, with the officers being provided by the Germans. Captain Marten of the *Inconstant* in Libau was instructed to inform the Germans that he would not allow German supplies to enter the country without prior permission from the Admiralty. This provoked an insolent response that, despite the terms of the Armistice, which required them to oppose the Bolsheviks, the German Army would be unable to continue operations. Misunderstanding the situation completely, the Allied War Council asked if it were the right time to withdraw all German troops from the Baltic States! However, as no Allied troops were available to replace the German forces, the proposal was quietly dropped. More realistically, Marten decide to allow certain supplies to be sent to the German troops.

Cowan's return to the Baltic was the outcome of a Cabinet decision not to increase the naval presence there. It was also recognition that he was best acquainted with the many problems involved, especially that the arrival of spring would free the Russian ships which had been locked by the ice in Kronstadt. Once again the *Caledon*, now commanded by Captain Geoffrey Mackworth, wore Cowan's flag; the rest of his force consisted of the light cruiser *Cleopatra*, five 'V & W' class destroyers and five newly completed 'S' class destroyers[10]. Many of the Commanding Officers found that they had depleted ships' companies – a reduction varying from one fifth to two fifths according to department or ship, a direct consequence of demobilisation. It was also an additional – though unstated – reason for the decision not to keep destroyers in the Baltic for too long a period.

The force visited Christiana (renamed Oslo in 1924), where they landed a consignment of bullion for the Norwegian Government, and Copenhagen on their way to Libau. On arrival their first task was to land a further 20,000 rifles, six 6in howitzers, twelve 18-pounder guns, twenty lorries and a huge amount of ammunition for Ulmanis' Lettish forces. Once again the whole cargo was transferred to the *Saratov* to prevent any interference by the Germans.

Partly as a result of a general shortage of supplies in Germany and partly because of the British maintained blockade, General von der Goltz had ordered his troops to live off the land. This was in direct opposition to Article XIV of the Armistice and caused great hardship and near starvation among the native population. Both Commander Andrew Cunningham of the *Seafire*[11] and Lieutenant Commander John Tovey of the *Wolfhound*[12] commented on the situation. The ships' companies of the destroyers in Libau and elsewhere did what they could to help, using their own provisions and stores.

On one occasion the *Seafire* and the *Scotsman* (Lieutenant Commander J.D. Noble) were alongside the jetty at Libau and had established a line of sentries about 25 yards out from the two ships. Large crowds soon gathered and from time to time someone – usually a child – would dart between the sentries and approach the ships seeking food, rarely going away empty handed. To try and control this, the Germans also placed a line of sentries across the jetty. One day a small girl was making her way back through the German sentries carrying her pitiful portion of food when she was knocked flying by one of the Germans. With a roar of anger sailors from both destroyers swarmed onto the jetty, determined to take revenge on the German. He would probably have been thrown into the harbour had Cunningham and his officers not intervened, not from any feelings towards the sentry but to avoid the provocation which any fighting and possible bloodshed would have given.

The following morning the Germans began construction of a large wooden barricade across the jetty. Cunningham was told by a German officer that it was to stop the ships being troubled by the local population and to ensure privacy for the British destroyers! Two days later the work was completed with a gate in the middle, which was guarded by an armed German sentry. The two destroyers immediately shifted berth further up the jetty, where they were outside the confines of the German barrier and where the local people could reach them again. Within the hour a large staff car arrived on the jetty carrying von der Goltz, who was beside himself with rage, shouting and waving his arms in the air[13].

This incident was followed by another a few days later, which also affected von der Goltz and did nothing to improve Anglo-German relations. The general and his staff rode on horseback down the jetty past the British destroyers. One of the sailors chose that moment to test the *Seafire*'s siren. The piercing shriek emptied every saddle within seconds as the horses bolted. Whether this was an accidental coincidence or a carefully contrived prank was never determined, but either way Prussian pride was severely wounded.

A potentially more serious event took place later in the summer when five officers from the destroyer *Velox*, who had gone ashore to shoot wildfowl, were arrested by a German patrol on the allegation that they had entered a prohibited military area. They were held for three hours before pressure on the Germans brought about their release. Naturally von der Goltz refused British demands to apologise for what had happened and the episode rapidly became a source of contention between Berlin and the Allied Supreme War Council in Paris. Cowan expressed his regret that officers should have been allowed to land with sporting guns at a time when the smallest incident could be exploited by the Germans to embarrass the Allies. He added that 'it was a matter of surprise that British officers should seek to kill game in the breeding season'. Whatever Cowan's feelings, the Admiralty ignored his final qualification and conveyed their displeasure to the *Velox*'s Commanding Officer.

Once Cowan received news that the summer thaw was freeing Kronstadt and the Bolshevik Fleet from the ice he returned to Revel, leaving a small part of his force in Libau to counter the devious moves of von der Goltz. The British ships were reinforced by the small French force of four torpedo boats and four sloops, all under the command of Capitaine de Vaisseau Brisson[14].

Brisson was deeply worried about the loyalty of his sailors, after the mutiny among the French ships in the Black Sea[15]. Too many of the French seamen were believed to be sympathetic to the Bolshevik regime, and so an agreement was reached with Cowan that the French ships would not be asked to fight against the Russians. Instead, they would remain in Latvian waters to help counter the machinations of the Germans – a task more agreeable to the French sailors.

Von der Goltz found an obscure German-Balt lawyer, who declared that the German Army was a *bona fide* army of occupation; he also found an equally unknown Germanophile local pastor, Andrieus Niedra, to become a puppet Prime Minister. Von der Goltz then felt able to plan a military campaign for the capture and occupation of Riga. By that time the Supreme War Council in Paris had at last appreciated the seriousness of Goltz's ambitious scheming and had set up a Baltic Commission to deal with this. Their first move was to send a message to Berlin demanding that the Government replace the general in command. The Commission also required the Germans to state that their forces in Latvia were not an army of occupation but merely an 'auxiliary force'. The politicians in Berlin took their time before answering and eventually forbade von der Goltz from moving on Riga, but otherwise failed to accede to any of the Baltic Commission's demands.

On 29 May the cruiser *Royalist* arrived in Libau and Commodore Alexander Duff was then able to take charge of the situation in the area. Duff soon found that the Germans had moved troops into the area of the Naval Harbour and that field guns had been positioned which would make it untenable to the Allies. It was a difficult situation, but one in which Duff had the full support of the Admiralty and British Government in whatever action he chose. On the other hand, the Supreme War Council cravenly gave in and allowed von der Goltz to remain in Latvia, though this was coupled with a demand that the troops and guns be removed from the Naval Harbour. The Americans went as far as suggesting that Cowan should co-operate with von der Goltz in fighting the Bolsheviks! Unsurprisingly, the British Government instantly rejected the idea.

A 'Weekly Appreciation of matters of Naval Interest' dated 7 June 1919[16] and prepared for the members of the Admiralty Board, showed that the Italian light cruiser *Libia* had left the Thames on the 1st of the month. The ship was not intended as an Allied reinforcement for Cowan's hard-pressed ships; she was merely paying a series of courtesy calls to a number of Baltic ports before returning to La Spezia in September. It was a strange area for the Italians to be visiting at that time. There were hostile warring shores to the east and the whole of the Baltic was still strewn with wartime mines. Italian records[17] show that the *Libia* called at Helsingfors while in the Baltic.

More mysterious are similar reports dated between 11 and 20 June listing an unnamed Danish light cruiser berthed in Libau. In view of Denmark's neutrality no ship of the Danish Navy could take part in any operations in conjunction with Allied warships, either against the Germans or the Bolsheviks. Nor can the presence of the ship be attributed to assisting the Danish Red Cross which worked so hard in Russia on behalf of British POWs. Danish records indicate that their three light cruisers can all be accounted for elsewhere at the time[18]. One report that a Danish warship was in Libau could, perhaps, be ignored as some sort of error in the Admiralty. Continuous reports over a period of ten days are a different matter. It is an interesting puzzle, but one which remains unsolved.

Von der Goltz's open defiance of the Allies in pursuit of his ambitions for Germany in Latvia continued throughout the summer of 1919. That he was thwarted at all was due in the main to the firmness of men like Cowan and Duff, backed by the presence of the Royal Navy and other naval ships in Libau. One other factor became important at this time. The Baltic Commission belatedly decided to send strong Diplomatic and Military Missions to the area. The latter was commanded by Lieutenant General Sir Hubert Gough, who had distinguished himself on the Western Front. With a strong staff at his disposal he was able to base himself in Helsingfors, with subordinate HQs in each of the states for which he was responsible. His orders included the statement that in Latvia and Lithuania he was to promote Allied influence, neutralising that of Germany and to control the movement of German troops with an eye to their ultimate total withdrawal.

The arrival of General Gough gave Admiral Cowan the opportunity to spend more time in the North giving support to the Estonians and remaining ready to thwart any moves by the Bolshevik Fleet in Kronstadt. Commodore Duff's ships in Libau were available to buttress the Latvians if required, while Gough and his Military Mission continued to cope with the machinations of the Germans.

Men of the Middlesex Regiment disembark from their transport, the SS *Ping Suey*, after arriving in Vladivostok from Hong Kong. (ILNPL)

A 6in gun landed from HMS *Suffolk* being readied for use as part of an armoured train on the Trans-Siberian Railway in the summer of 1918. (IWM Q70448)

Admiral Aleksandr Kolchak, who became the titular ruler of the White Russian forces following the death of the Tsar.

The cruiser HMS *Carlisle* was acting as guardship at Vladivostok when the Red Army entered the city on 23 October 1922. The ship sailed for Hong Kong a week later and so became the last unit of British forces to be involved in the War of Intervention. (MPL)

Above: The French battleship *Jean Bart.* The ship was the flagship of the French naval force in the Black Sea in 1919. (MPL)

Left: General Denikin, the White Russian commander in the South, with a group of his senior staff officers. Behind Denikin is General Lukomsky, the Minister of War, while just visible in the doorway is Denikin's Chief of Staff, General Romanovsky, who was assassinated by a disaffected officer in April 1920. One of the French Liaison Officers can be seen extreme left.

Defeated, dispirited and dishevelled soldiers of General Denikin's White Army are evacuated from Novorossisk on board the battleship *Emperor of India*. The men are standing beside one of the 6in guns of the ship's secondary armament.

HMS *Ceres* berthed in Odessa harbour during the evacuation from the city of civilians and White Russian troops in February 1920. An oiler is berthed on the cruiser's starboard beam.

The jetty in Odessa harbour from where the transport *Rio Negro* was embarking refugees. Thousands of people were arriving with all their worldly possessions in cars and horse-drawn carts, most of which had to be abandoned before embarking.

The destroyer *Montrose* berthed in Yalta harbour, in company with the transport *Rio Negro*, where the two ships were embarking refugees to take them back to Constantinople in March 1920.

The destroyer HMS *Shakespeare*, one of five 'S' class destroyers in Admiral Cowan's Baltic Force in early 1919. (MPL)

The submarine L54, sister-ship of the ill-fated L55, sunk by Bolshevik forces in the Gulf of Finland on 4 June 1919. (MPL)

An aerial view of Kronstadt harbour taken before the raid by an RAF aircraft. The guardship, the destroyer *Gavriil* (1), can be seen near the main entrance to the main basin. The submarine depot ship, *Pamiat Azova* (2), was sunk. A hospital ship (3) nearly became a target of CMB88 after Lieutenant Dayrell-Reed was badly wounded. The battleships *Petropavlosk* (4) and *Andrei Pervozvanni* (5) were both damaged by torpedoes.

The Russian battleship *Marat*, which as the *Petropavlosk* had been badly damaged by torpedoes during the attack on Krondstadt in August 1919. The trunked-back fore funnel was fitted during the 1920s to keep the bridge clear of funnel smoke.

The submarines H48 and H51 in Revel harbour in late 1919.

HMS *Vittoria*. The destroyer was sunk on 1 September 1919 by two torpedoes fired from the Russian submarine *Pantera*.

NINE

FAST BOATS, CLOAK AND DAGGER AND A VICTORIA CROSS

O n a day in late May[1] 1919, three young British naval officers in civilian clothes boarded a Swedish steamer in Hull bound for Stockholm. A short time later another officer and two ratings, also in plain clothes, left Tilbury in a second steamer, this time bound for Helsingfors. On board were two 40ft CMBs, carried as deck cargo, which were painted white and hidden under tarpaulins to give them a less military air. All the men were temporarily no longer serving in the Royal Navy, but had been attached to the Foreign Office as part of the Secret Intelligence Service (SIS), or MI6 as it is more commonly known.

The SIS had to rebuild its network of agents in Russia. Captain Cromie had been murdered in the embassy in Petrograd in September 1918, the unpredictable Sidney Reilly had fled the country only minutes ahead of the *Cheka* who were trying to capture him, and Bruce Lockhart had been expelled. All their contacts had been arrested or were too afraid to be of any further use. Captain Sir Mansfield Smith-Cumming, the Head of the SIS – or 'C' as he was known[2] – recruited Paul Dukes[3], a remarkable man. Dukes' task was to return to Russia and report on Bolshevik policy, the possibility of any regime change, the extent of German influence and any military and naval intelligence that he could gather – a formidable undertaking. He landed in Archangel in the summer of 1918 and quietly made his way to Petrograd. At that time Dukes was known within the SIS only by his designated code number, ST25, the ST indicating that he was part of an operation run from Stockholm. At first, he sent his reports out from Petrograd by messengers, who crossed the Finnish frontier before travelling on to Helsingfors by train. Gradually, this became increasingly risky and unreliable as more of his couriers were being intercepted and shot by the *Cheka*, while the Finns took a growing interest in people arriving at the border from Russia – hence the proposal by 'C' to use the CMBs and their crews.

The officers and ratings travelling to Finland were: Lieutenant Augustus Agar, Sub-Lieutenant J. Sindall, Midshipman (later Sub-Lieutenant) J. Hampsheir, Midshipman (later Sub-Lieutenant) R. Marshall, and two petty officer motor mechanics, Beeley and Piper. They had all been detached from the CMB base at Osea Island, which lies in the River Blackwater in Essex. At the end of the war in November 1918 all the CMB crews at Osea Island had been training for an attack on the German Fleet in their North Sea Bases. In December 1918 a flotilla of CMBs was sent out to join the British forces in the Caspian Sea; next, a flotilla was sent to work on the River Dvina in North Russia and another on the lakes south of Murmansk. This latest departure, in great secrecy and only two weeks after Agar had been given the task, involved just the two boats, which were to bring out messengers from ST25 and eventually the man himself.

On arrival in Finland, Agar contacted two British agents already working in the country, known to him only by their cover numbers as ST30 and ST31. After much discussion it was arranged that he and his crews would operate from the village of Terrioki, close to the frontier and only about 25 miles from Petrograd. The village had the advantage of being the home of the one-time Petrograd Imperial Yacht Club, which it was hoped would provide some cover for Agar's boats.

The boats themselves were unloaded at Hango, at the western point of Finland, after their journey from Tilbury with the remainder of Agar's party. The problem was getting the boats from Hango to Terrioki, about 150 miles, without inviting unwanted curiosity from the Finns if they went along the coast or added unnecessary mileage by going too far out to sea. Agar sought help from Rear Admiral Walter Cowan, who was commanding the British naval forces in the Baltic, first explaining the situation and the reason for his presence in the Baltic. He then informed the admiral of his plans to carry out the mission. Cowan then gave his assurance that he would help in any way he could. Agar requested that a destroyer be made available to tow his CMBs from a position off Hango to Biorko Sound, only a few miles to the westward of his intended base at Terrioki.

A second request was more difficult. Agar admitted that he had been told in London that he was to avoid all hostile operations as both he and his boats were meant to be civilian. However, he asked for two torpedoes, one for each boat, in case he got into difficulties with any Bolshevik ships. To allay any fears that Cowan might have, he added that they had permission to carry a set of uniforms in each boat for emergency purposes only – 'C' reluctantly had made this one concession to try and avoid them being shot as spies if captured. After some thought, Cowan agreed with the request and arranged for two torpedoes from the submarine depot ship HMS *Lucia* to be sent to Biorko Sound, where they were kept on board an oiler.

Admiral Cowan made the necessary arrangements and at the pre-determined time and place the destroyer *Voyager* (Commander C.G. Stuart) rendezvoused with the two CMBs and towed them to a position off Biorko Sound. The Royal Navy already used the Sound and Agar believed that the presence of a destroyer off the entrance would not arouse suspicions.

Terrioki is only 30 miles east of Biorko Sound, but before completing the journey Agar wanted to give the engines of both boats a trial run at full speed. It was a fortunate decision as one of the boats developed a serious engine defect, which was mended with the help of the crew of the oiler. The top deck planking of the boat had to be taken off and the engine lifted out using a derrick on the bigger ship, a task that would not have been possible in Terrioki, and one which took many hours of hard work. After a second trial run both boats set off after dark for the final part of their journey to their new base.

The small village of Terrioki had fallen into decay since the Revolution. A few of the old country homes of rich Russians were still in use, mostly inhabited by refugees. A small detachment of Finnish troops, part of the frontier guard, was billeted there. Most importantly, one of Agar's helpers had reported that the Finnish Commandant, Colonel Sarin, was well disposed to the British. The small harbour, adjacent to the pre-war Yacht Club, had sufficient room to moor the two CMBs safely and was protected by a 10ft-high sea wall, which would hide the boats from prying eyes.

Agar had to land his courier to make contact with Dukes in Petrograd; the seaward approaches to the city were at the eastern end of the Gulf of Finland where the width narrowed to about 20 miles. Lying strategically in the narrows and guarding the city was the island of Kotlin, which over the years had become a fortress and the home of the main Russian naval base in the Baltic – Kronstadt. On the north side of the island a chain of ten small forts led to the mainland shore, being connected by a sunken breakwater lying 3ft below the surface of the Gulf. To the south, the island was defended by extensive minefields.

A straight run across the Gulf of Finland to land his courier in Estonia would be the easiest and quickest way for Agar and the CMBs. However, this was not ideal for the courier because of the long route he would then have to take to reach Petrograd. There was also the factor that he would have to cross through an ill-defined area where Bolshevik troops were active against the Estonian and White Russian armies. Agar discounted such an option except as a last resort.

Agar finally decided that the best course of action was for the CMBs to approach a landing place outside Petrograd by creeping at slow speed between two of the northern forts. He hoped that the CMBs draught of only 2ft 9in (84cm) would be shallow enough to pass over the breakwater. Once clear of the forts he would be able to use the full speed of his boats, over 40 knots if pushed to the limit. He estimated that he would be able to land his courier and return within three hours – if all went well. It was an audacious and dangerous plan. The whole outcome of the mission lay firmly in the lap of the Russian engineers who had built the chain of forts and the breakwater between them. A mere 3in was the margin between success and ignominious failure.

Agar's SIS helpers had arranged for supplies of fuel, the boats had been repainted and now showed a more military shade of warship-grey, and, most importantly, the first courier – known only as Peter – was ready to go to Petrograd. The one factor that was missing was the approval of Colonel Sarin for Agar to make a reconnaissance on behalf of the British admiral, for that was all that he could be told – and he had to be told something. Instead, Sarin hesitated and implied that he would have to seek permission from a higher authority in Helsingfors, something that Agar was hoping he would not do; the more people that knew that anything unusual was happening, the greater the chance of the Bolsheviks becoming aware of his plans.

On 10 June 1919 fate intervened. In the fortress of Krasnaya Gorka, on the Estonian coast and guarding the approaches to Kronstadt from the south, the Bolshevik garrison mutinied. They hoisted a white flag and sought help from anyone who would come to their rescue. The importance of this revolt was not lost on Colonel Sarin, for he was quite certain that the Bolsheviks would plan an attack by both land and sea to retake the fortress. Consequently, he requested Agar to make a reconnaissance that night to assess the situation. Agar immediately agreed, as this would enable him to take Peter to Petrograd and make a reconnaissance on the way back, informing Sarin if any of the Russian ships had left Kronstadt.

That evening Agar, with Beeley and a Finnish smuggler who was to act as a pilot, set off for the little harbour to man the CMB. On the way they met up with Peter, who had been hiding in the woods; as a Russian he would have been instantly arrested by Colonel Sarin. All four men were wearing serge trousers with a leather jacket and cap, the general unremarkable clothes worn by most people in Petrograd. Peter had his despatches hidden in the soles of his boots; he also carried a note from Agar to Dukes stating when and where they would pick up both Dukes and Peter for the return.

The sun set and they were ready to leave. The CMB moved slowly and almost silently out of the harbour. Once out in the open sea Agar set a course to take him between two of the forts near the Finnish shore and increased to 20 knots, the engine making only a purring hum at this relatively slow speed. With the forts looming ever nearer, Agar reduced the speed to 8 knots, at which the boat was almost silent. As they approached the gap all four of the men hoped that the depth of water over the sunken breakwater had been accurately calculated, that there really were those vital 3in of clearance they expected. All the time they feared that they would be brought to a sudden halt right under the guns of the enemy. Every heart-stopping moment they anticipated the first stabbing flash of a searchlight to illuminate them, the burst of gunfire that would slice through their frail craft. Gradually, the bearing of the forts drew abeam and then moved astern; they were through. Ahead they could make out the lights of Petrograd. The temptation to increase speed was strong but Agar waited until the forts were about 3 miles astern before accelerating to nearly full throttle and they raced along at 36 knots.

About fifteen minutes later, with the boat approaching the mouth of the River Neva, Agar slowed to a crawl and steered for the northern bank. They unlashed the small dinghy which was carried on the boat's foredeck for Peter to row ashore, where he was able to hide the boat in the line of tall rushes which lined the riverbank. After he had signalled that he had landed safely, the CMB could begin the second part of the night's work, the reconnaissance for Colonel Sarin; forty-eight hours later Agar would have to be back to pick up Peter.

First, the CMB had to creep back past the forts without being noticed. Agar then diverted towards the lighthouse at Tolbuhin, off the western shore of Kotlin Island, to look for signs of the Bolshevik Fleet. Clearly visible in the pre-dawn light were two large ships, the battleships *Petropavlovsk* and *Andrei Pervozvanni*, with a number of destroyers all anchored where they could easily bombard the rebellious fortress and still remain safely on their own side of the extensive minefields. It was the information that Colonel Sarin wanted; it was also important that Admiral Cowan should know what the Bolshevik ships were doing. Agar could then turn his CMB towards the Finnish coast at full speed back to its secret base.

Two nights later a similar operation had to be undertaken. This time Agar took Hampsheir with him in case the extra pair of hands would be useful; it also had the advantage of introducing the young officer into the route that had to be taken and the procedures used. The boat carried a machine gun with which to give the passengers covering fire should they be chased while embarking. Agar took the CMB on the same course as before and glided between the same pair of forts as on the earlier journey. The same stomach-churning tensions were present as they feared discovery at that crucial point of their mission. It seems incredible that the double trip was without incident; remarkably, Peter was at the rendezvous at exactly the right time and made contact with the boat without any trouble.

Back at Terrioki his despatches were handed over to ST30, who would telegraph the contents to 'C' in London; the actual papers would follow by courier. Unexpectedly, Dukes himself had decided to remain in Petrograd for another month, dangerous though this would be for him. Agar had sent him three dates on which he would have a boat at the rendezvous to collect him. Once the important business was concluded, Peter regaled them with horrific stories of the conditions in Petrograd at that time and also of how he had met with Dukes in full daylight in a public park[4].

The naval party had done one part of the task that 'C' had assigned them; contact had been made with Dukes and arrangements had been made to bring him out of Petrograd in a month's time. Meanwhile, the situation at Krasnaya Gorka could prove to be immensely important. The fact that the garrison in the fortress had defected was linked to a possible mutiny of the Red sailors at Kronstadt, where there was increasing dissatisfaction with the commissars and local fleet committees. Agar realised that the continued bombardment of the fort by the Bolshevik battleships could only have one ending, unless the ships could be persuaded to retire. The CMBs had one torpedo each but Agar's orders from 'C' were quite specific, limiting his activities to intelligence work only. A message was sent to London explaining the circumstances at Krasnaya Gorka and seeking permission to attack. The answer, when it came, was disappointing: 'Boats to be used for intelligence purposes only. Take no action unless specifically directed by the SNO Baltic' (Admiral Cowan). The second sentence gave Agar the loophole he required. There was no time to reach Cowan, but Agar was quite sure that the admiral would agree with his plan and would support his actions. He decided to attack that night.

The boats were ready and the torpedoes loaded; once they reached the open sea the crews would put on their naval uniforms and the boats would fly a White Ensign. Agar would command CMB4 with Hampsheir and Beeley, while Sub-Lieutenant Sindall commanded the other, CMB7. Shortly after 10.30 p.m. the two boats left the harbour at Terrioki and set course for the lighthouse at Tolbuhin, from where they could approach their targets. They had not been under way for very long when Sindall's boat hit an obstruction; it was later thought to have been a floating mine, which fortunately had not exploded. In any case, the CMB was incapable of going any further as the propeller shaft had broken; the night's mission had to be aborted as Agar towed the crippled boat back to Terrioki.

Agar resolved to try again the following night, accepting the fact that there would only be one boat and one torpedo. During the day he noticed that the two battleships had returned to Krondstadt and had been replaced by the armoured cruiser *Oleg*. Rightly or wrongly, he assumed that the battleships had run out of ammunition or else that Krasnaya Gorka was about to surrender, in which case the big ships were no longer needed. Late in the afternoon the *Oleg* was seen to fire a few salvos at the fortress, so it was still holding out.

That night the one remaining CMB slipped out of the harbour at Terrioki. The crew donned their uniforms and hoisted the White Ensign before setting off to where the *Oleg* was lying. The weather, which had been a flat calm the previous night, had changed for the worse by the time they sailed; the temperature had dropped and a nasty southerly wind had sprung up, causing a short choppy sea to run in the Gulf. Approaching the target, Agar had to slow down to creep through a screen of destroyers in much the same way as he had navigated through the line of forts on his way to and from Petrograd. Suddenly the whole boat shook and Agar slowed right down and then stopped, fearing that they too had hit something. The mystery was solved when Hampsheir appeared and reported that the torpedo-firing cylinder had prematurely discharged.

In the CMBs the torpedo was fired by ejecting it over the stern by means of a small cordite charge creating a pressure in the firing ram. Somehow Hampsheir had accidentally fired it while checking the firing cylinder. However, there were two strong safety catches, which prevented the torpedo from leaving its firing trough in the stern of the boat until the Commanding Officer was actually ready to attack; these had fortunately held the torpedo and stopped it running. It was this that had produced the severe shock waves which had rippled through the small boat. Before Agar could attack the *Oleg* the old cartridge had to be extracted and a new charge fitted.

For the next twenty minutes the CMB lay wallowing in the swell while Hampsheir and Beeley struggled to remove the spent cartridge and load a new one; it was usually a task performed with the boat lying quietly in harbour. Russian destroyers patrolled nearby, seemingly oblivious of the potential danger only a few cables away. Agar had to stand and wait, and while he waited he had to judge the movements of the destroyers, ready to send his craft roaring towards safety at full speed if he thought the CMB had been spotted or was likely to be run down. Such an action would probably spell the end of his plans for that night. The time passed slowly, the wait seemed interminable.

Eventually, Hampsheir reported that they had reloaded. Agar opened the throttle and headed at full speed towards his target. At about 500 yards range he fired the precious torpedo and then turned the boat to a reciprocal course, not only to head away from the Russian force but also to give the torpedo a clear run at the Russian cruiser. At the same time he was spotted and the guns of the *Oleg* and some of the destroyers opened up. The CMB was a small target and its fast speed and the uncertain pre-dawn light confused the Russian gunlayers; shells fell near but none hit and the boat was soon clear of the enemy. Looking astern, all three men were excited to see a large flash from abreast the cruiser's forward funnel, followed by a column of black smoke reaching into the sky, higher than the foremast. The *Oleg* sank in twelve minutes, with the surprisingly light casualty list of only five men killed.

Initially, Agar set a course for Biorko Sound to confuse any Bolsheviks who might be watching, though he suspected that most eyes would be on the *Oleg*. Only when he was out of sight of any of the Kronstadt forts did he alter course for Terrioki. They arrived back at their base elated, but soaked through, very cold and not quite unscathed, as Hampsheir was suffering badly from shock after the firing mechanism had gone off accidentally right in front of him. He had to be sent to recuperate at a Finnish hospital, but never fully recovered and needed to be sent home.

The follow-up was frenetic. Colonel Sarin was quick to suspect that the British team were the cause of the action and was very worried that they had compromised both themselves and him by committing an act of war while in plain clothes. He was eventually reassured. Thanks to the good will of the colonel, Agar was flown over the scene in an aircraft of the Finnish Air Force – still with the German markings of its original owners. He was able to see the wreck of the Russian cruiser lying on its side with just a few feet of its hull visible above the waves. He arranged to visit Admiral Cowan who was, of course, delighted when he was told the result of the night's operation. Unfortunately, the fortress of Krasnaya Gorka was by then flying the Red Flag; Agar's efforts had been too late to delay its surrender and the massacre of most of its defenders.

The news of the successful attack was less well received by the British Government, though there was little they could say in public. Admiral Wemyss, the First Sea Lord, took the opportunity to press the Cabinet to lift the restrictions on attacks by the British forces in the Baltic on the Bolshevik Fleet. Indeed, he urged that Cowan be allowed to take any action he needed to suppress the threat that this force presented to the British ships. The Cabinet eventually – and reluctantly – accepted this view[5] and reinforcements were sent to the Baltic[6] to join Cowan's squadron.

Agar was awarded a Victoria Cross for the action. The citation for the award noted his conspicuous gallantry, coolness and skill in penetrating a destroyer screen, remaining in close proximity to the enemy for twenty minutes while the torpedo firing mechanism was repaired, and then completing an exceptionally difficult operation in far from ideal weather conditions. The citation concluded by referring to the escape of the CMB, notwithstanding heavy fire from warships. Hampsheir received the Distinguished Service Order and Beeley the Conspicuous Gallantry Medal for their part in this daring attack.

Agar took both boats to Biorko Sound while Sindall's boat was repaired. There was a month to pass before either of the boats would be required to make another trip to Petrograd. Under the circumstances Agar felt that it would be wiser not to stay at Terrioki for all this time, as it would increase the risk of their presence there being discovered and reported to the Bolsheviks.

When both CMBs had been repaired and fully overhauled they were given trial runs before they returned to Terrioki, secretly by night. Agar used the maintenance period to recruit a second courier, known as Gefter, who had once been a midshipman in the Tsarist Navy. A third Russian was added to the team shortly before making the next courier run to Petrograd. He was known as Vlad and had served during the war against Germany with distinction in a Russian Guards regiment.

The next mission was planned for 18 July. The smuggler pilot turned up shortly before sailing and told Agar that he had heard that the Bolsheviks had increased patrols watching the approaches to Petrograd following the sinking of the *Oleg*. By 10.00 p.m. it was dark and the boat sailed quietly from the harbour, increasing speed once they were clear of the coast. Hampsheir was still unfit and Agar brought Marshall into the boat, along with Beeley, the smuggler and Peter. It was not long before they were approaching the barrier of forts and although Agar had already passed between them four times without trouble it did not lessen the tension. There were anxious moments for all five men as they waited for the challenge, the searchlights and the burst of gunfire which might well spell the end of their mission. To their immense relief they went through unnoticed once again and headed for the same place that they had used in their previous missions to land Peter at the mouth of the River Neva. Five minutes after Peter had left the boat, they sighted the flashed signal that all was well and the CMB was able to return to Terrioki, yet again passing safely between the forts and with no sign of the patrols reported by the smuggler.

Two nights later Sub-Lieutenant Sindall took CMB4 to make the rendezvous with Peter and land Gefter. This time the boat was sighted and fired on by one of the forts, probably the largest one near the northern shore of Kronstadt. Although the boat was not hit Sindall wisely decided to return and not try to force a passage through, which would have left him vulnerable on his return.

Before Agar could mount another mission to attempt the rendezvous he was surprised to find Peter had made an adventurous and dangerous return overland. After flashing the signal to Agar that he had landed safely he had been surprised and challenged by a patrol. He managed to elude them in the darkness but he felt sure that they would have discovered the dinghy he used to get ashore; as a result it would have been extremely hazardous to use that rendezvous again. Unbelievably, he had again met Dukes openly in one of the city's parks, and, after handing over the papers he had brought with him, Peter was persuaded by Dukes that he must return immediately to Agar. Peter's luck had held, and, despite the odds stacked against him, he had managed to evade all the border patrols – Bolshevik and Finnish – before arriving exhausted at Terrioki.

Dukes had suggested a different rendezvous and Agar looked at an alternative route to pass the forts nearer to the coast, avoiding the area where Sindall had been sighted and fired upon. They all realised how fortunate Sindall had been in returning immediately to Terrioki, rather than trying to reach the point where Peter was waiting. He would almost certainly have been trapped by the patrols waiting there after Peter's earlier near capture.

On 28 July Sindall again left to take Gefter to Petrograd. Agar knew that Cowan was planning a big attack on Kronstadt for the middle of August[7] so Gefter was told to impress on Dukes how important it was that he leave. Not only was he urgently required in London but also for his own safety, since after Cowan's proposed operation took place it would be September before Agar could try again to reach him and it was highly likely that the *Cheka* was steadily becoming closer to arresting him. Gefter was successfully landed and Sindall returned to base without any further problems.

On 8 August Agar made what he hoped would be a final trip to bring Dukes out from Petrograd. The boat passed safely over the breakwater between the forts and reached the rendezvous. There was no sign of a dinghy or the pre-arranged signal indicating that Dukes and Gefter were waiting to be picked up. Agar waited for half an hour and then had to return to Terrioki. He was very worried that the *Cheka* had at last caught Dukes; what he did not know was the sheer frustration undergone by the two men on shore. Dukes and Gefter could see the CMB waiting for them and they set out to reach it. Unfortunately the small boat they used began to sink and they had to abandon it and swim back to the land. They lay exhausted in the reeds and had to watch the CMB leave without them.

Agar made another trip the following night to land Peter with details of a new arrangement to take Dukes out of Russia. Peter was put ashore without difficulty but then the troubles began. The bottle of compressed air used to start the engine had leaked while they were waiting for the signal from Peter to say that he had landed. They had to change this for one that had already been used once but that hopefully had enough air left to start the engine. It did, but only just. The night's troubles were not over, for when they were approaching the breakwater off Terrioki the steering wheel jammed, causing the boat to make a sharp turn, hitting a rock as it did so. The blades on the propeller sheared and the shaft was fractured. They had to be towed ignominiously into harbour.

After the naval attack on Kronstadt planned by Cowan there was still one trip to be made; to get to Petrograd to bring Dukes out of the city. By then Agar was seriously worried that their base at Terrioki might have become known to the Bolsheviks. This was borne out when two aircraft flew over the village and dropped seven bombs which, although they caused no damage, certainly succeeded in making the British party less popular with the refugee inhabitants. There was also increased activity from the searchlights around Kronstadt every night; this additional defence would have to be penetrated if Agar was to reach the agreed rendezvous.

There were three days of waiting before the next agreed pick-up date, days in which the Bolsheviks could easily be strengthening their defences by positioning barriers of logs or wire cables between the forts, making it even harder for the boats to pass through. On 23 August Agar set off. With the searchlights constantly sweeping the waters he considered it hopeless to attempt to creep through unobserved as they had done previously; their best chance lay in making a high-speed dash and trusting in the fact that at 40 knots they made a very difficult target. The weather was kind to them; the night was calm and there was no moon. Initially, all went well. As they approached the forts the searchlights were passing over them seemingly without the operators becoming aware of their presence. Suddenly, from right ahead, two searchlight beams came on and immediately focused on the boat. Agar was blinded by the lights and tried to concentrate only on the compass. With the roar of the engine they were unaware of being fired at. Very soon either the rudder itself was hit or one of the tiller lines was struck by a bullet; whichever, the consequence was the same – Agar lost all control. The boat swerved off course before coming to a grinding halt as they hit an obstruction. Agar and his companions were all thrown forward, the force of the impact was enough to knock some of them temporarily unconscious.

When they were able to assess the situation they realised that they had come to a stop not far from the northern shore of Kotlin Island. The searchlights which had been ahead of them had gone out, leaving just one, which swept backwards and forwards over their heads without actually seeing them. They were 15 miles from a friendly shore and there were only four hours of darkness left. They pushed the boat off the obstruction which had so violently brought them to a halt but then found that there were two holes in the hull, which they managed to plug with spare clothing. The engine was found to be damaged beyond repair.

Agar observed that they were slowly drifting in a north-westerly direction towards the Finnish coast. However, they calculated that the drift – only about a knot and a half – was not really fast enough to take them near enough to safety before dawn. Using some boathooks and canvas torn from the foredeck they managed to rig a small sail, which added slightly to their speed. They then had a lucky break as with the dawn came a low mist, which hid them for another hour.

When the mist lifted they found themselves close to two fishing boats, manned by soldiers from one of the forts who were trying to add to their rations. Curiosity led them to approach the British boat, and one was ordered alongside with the threat from a machine gun. The Russians said that they had believed the boat to be a British aircraft which had crashed; instead, they found themselves ordered to tow the wrecked CMB back to Terrioki. The two fishing boats were then allowed to leave.

The crews of the fishing boats would be bound to report to the Bolsheviks what had happened and where they had been, rendering Terrioki's position as a base untenable. Agar's mission was over. One boat still had to be repaired[8], the other was irreparable. Agar was deeply concerned that as a consequence he was now unable to collect Dukes and Peter from Petrograd.

While Agar was busy winding up the whole operation before returning to Britain news eventually reached him that Dukes had escaped over the Estonian border and was on his way back to London. The escape had not been without problems, as Dukes at one stage was arrested by White Russian guards and narrowly missed summary execution as a Red spy. Agar himself returned to London on 16 September; he eventually met with Dukes in 'C's' office!

At Buckingham Palace Agar had a private audience with the King, who wished to hear about his exploits. He was then presented with his Victoria Cross.

TEN

THE KRONSTADT RAID
AND AFTER

At the end of April 1919 Captain Juhan Pitka, the Commander-in-Chief of the Estonian Navy, arrived in Libau on board the destroyer *Lennuk* (the ex-Russian *Avtroil*) with the news that Kronstadt was free of ice, permitting the Bolshevik ships to commence operations in the Gulf of Finland against the Estonians. Rear Admiral Cowan considered this to be a greater threat to his forces and more important in terms of his responsibilities than all the scheming by General von der Goltz. He immediately set sail for Revel in his flagship, the cruiser *Caledon*, accompanied by the two destroyers *Seafire* and *Sepoy*. He signalled the *Cleopatra* and the destroyers at Copenhagen to join him with all despatch.

Cowan had suggested that the various forces fighting against the Bolsheviks in the Baltic States should be placed under the overall command of a British general. The proposal had the support of Cabinet in London, but whether or not it had similar support in the Baltic States themselves is not known. Nevertheless, it took a whole month before the Baltic Commission, meeting in Paris, made a decision. It did not agree to the idea of a unified commander for the area, but did propose the setting up of strong Diplomatic and Military Missions, and to that end Lieutenant General Sir Hubert Gough, the one-time Commander of the British Fifth Army in France, was named as the head of the Military Mission.

General Gough established his headquarters in Helsingfors, with subordinate missions in the other capitals. The cruiser HMS *Galatea* had been placed at his disposal for use when travelling from one state to another. His terms of reference were unusually strongly worded and detailed; primarily, he was required to report how best the Allies could assist the Baltic States to defend themselves either against a Bolshevik invasion or German domination.

During the winter months of 1918/19 the Estonian land forces had been able to withstand any attempts by the Red Army to advance. With the availability of the Red Fleet to take an active part in operations there was a danger that Estonians could be outflanked by an amphibious landing. Pitka's small force of two destroyers and a single gunboat would be unable to do anything other than inflict a few pinpricks on any Red maritime excursion. The Bolshevik force was thought to consist of two battleships, one or possibly three cruisers, up to twelve destroyers, a minelayer, perhaps as many as seven submarines and a number of minesweepers and patrol craft. The assessment may have been over-generous but in any event Cowan's force of two cruisers and six destroyers was, at least on paper, heavily outnumbered.

On 30 April, having received news of a possible landing by Bolshevik troops, Cowan took his force along the Estonian coast but found no sign of the Russian Fleet. The *Curacoa* arrived in early May to relieve the *Caledon* as Cowan's flagship, the latter being due to return to England. On the 13th the *Curacoa* struck a mine while steaming at 20 knots about 70 miles west of

Revel. The damage was confined to a number of compartments aft in the ship and casualties were light. The ship was still able to steam at 9 knots and managed to return to Revel, where temporary repairs were made to enable the ship to return to England. The *Cleopatra* became Cowan's new flagship.

Despite the reduction in the size of his force, Cowan took his ships east into the Gulf of Finland to support an operation by Estonian troops on the coast opposite Seskar Island. At first there was no opposition from the Russian ships but on 18 May four minesweepers escorted by the destroyer *Gavriil*[1] left Kronstadt. The purpose of this movement is unclear, unless it was for a routine task of sweeping, as the force was unlikely to be able to cause much hindrance to General Laidoner's amphibious landing and was certainly not strong enough to take on Cowan's ships. The Russian battleship *Petropavlovsk* and the cruiser *Oleg* were sighted under way later in the morning and it may have been hoped that the smaller ships would lure the British cruiser and destroyers into a trap.

As soon as the British ships were seen to be closing on the Russians, the *Gavriil* ordered the minesweepers back to harbour while the destroyer fought a protective rearguard action. The range was too great for the *Gavriil's* guns and her shots constantly fell short of the British ships, while in turn the Russian was frequently straddled and suffered some damage and casualties from splinters, but was never hit. The action was broken off when the British ships came under fire from the 6in guns of two of the forts as they approached to within half a mile of the Russian minefields. The British ships were reinforced the following day when they were joined by the cruiser *Dragon*[2]; they then remained in the area for several days.

On 23 May Cowan was present in Revel to meet the first of the new reinforcements sent out to join his command. They were led by the submarine depot ship *Lucia* (Captain Martin Nasmith) with six submarines of the 7th Flotilla[3]. Captain Nasmith had commanded the submarine E11 during the war and had been part of the first group of submarines to try and enter the Baltic in 1915. However, he had been delayed by engine trouble and heavy German patrols caused him to abandon the attempt[4]. He later won a Victoria Cross commanding the same submarine in the Sea of Marmara. Two other officers had had wartime experience in the Baltic: Lieutenant R. Blacklock, now commanding the L12, had been the first lieutenant of the E1 in 1915, while Lieutenant C. Chapman, Commanding Officer of the L55, had been the first lieutenant of the E9.

The role of the submarine force, as the Admiralty informed Cowan, was 'to act as a menace to the Bolshevik Fleet, to operate against any Bolshevik ships attempting to bombard the Estonian coast and to protect Cowan's base at Revel from any attack'. In fact, should the Bolshevik Fleet have put to sea in strength the submarines would have been the main line of defence. It was without doubt the strongest and most unequivocal terms of reference issued by the Admiralty to any force at that time.

Within twenty-four hours of their arrival two submarines were ordered to sea to patrol a line between Seskar Island and the Estonian coast, keeping to the west of the Russian minefields protecting Kronstadt; they would be only 40 miles from the base itself. For the submariners it was a very different sort of war to the one they had been conducting in the North Sea and Heligoland Bight against the Germans a mere six months previously. To provide a proper deterrent it was considered that the submarines could spend their time on the surface until the enemy appeared and threatened them. Instead of the open sea they had small, almost landlocked, patrol areas. In the still air those on the bridge could sometimes hear dogs barking and the occasional sound of gunfire. One boat even sent the hands to bathe; a foolish decision in the light of later events.

The L16 (Lieutenant Commander Alfred Hine) made contact with the Russians on 29 May, when the destroyer *Azard* was sighted escorting six minesweepers and with the distant support of the battleship *Petropavlovsk*. Hine's attack on the destroyer was unsuccessful. The following day Hine made another attack on the same destroyer and once again missed. The tracks of the torpedoes were sighted in the calm waters of the Gulf and the *Azard* manoeuvred frantically to comb them. A second attack, by the E27 (Lieutenant Alec Carrie), had the same result.

On 4 June there was a brief and inconclusive engagement between destroyers of both sides, with none of the ships obtaining any hits before the Russians began to withdraw. As soon as the destroyers ceased fire, Chapman, in the L55, began a torpedo attack on one of the Russian ships – either the *Azard* or the *Gavriil*. To what must have been his utter consternation the submarine broke surface on firing, revealing the boat's presence to what should have been an unsuspecting target, and enabling the destroyer to evade the torpedoes. The tables were turned; the hunter became the prey. Before Chapman could get the submarine submerged again the Russian gunners were startlingly quick to open fire on this tempting target. One shell from the *Azard* hit and holed the pressure hull of the L55. The submarine sank with the loss of the entire crew of forty-two officers and ratings[5]. It was hardly an auspicious start for the submarines of the new Baltic Flotilla.

Cowan decided that the base at Revel was too distant from Kronstadt to allow him to respond quickly enough to any movement by the Russian Fleet. He had to move further east and this would only be possible with the help of the Finns. He sought their agreement to use Biorko Sound, a large anchorage only about 20 miles off the outermost limits of the Russian minefields. The Finns gave their consent and Cowan moved without delay, arriving on 5 June and leaving only the submarines to operate from Revel.

On 9 June the British ships were surprised by the *Azard* and the *Gavriil*, which made a night attack on the anchorage. Three British destroyers immediately slipped their cables and returned fire. The Russians broke off the action and retired behind their minefields, having fired about eighty rounds without effect. Nevertheless, this aggressive action was a wake-up call which could have had far more serious consequences. It inspired a letter from Cowan to the Admiralty pointing out the difficulties that he faced and his lack of resources in trying to overcome them.

The Admiralty's reply is interesting:

> The difficult position in which you are placed is thoroughly realised but cannot be avoided so long as the present policy of the Government remains in force. This precludes offensive action against Kronstadt by monitors, coastal motor boats or bombing aeroplanes. Torpedo carrying aeroplanes cannot be used against ships in Kronstadt as the torpedoes cannot be dropped in less than ten fathoms. It is hoped that the mines now being sent will render the situation more favourable[6]. In the meantime it must be realised that any departure from the policy laid down may seriously embarrass the Government. The unsound nature of the situation is again being placed before the Cabinet.[7]

More ships joined Cowan's force during the summer. The Gulf of Finland, like the rest of the Baltic, was strewn with numerous minefields and the threat from these insidious weapons was a constant source of worry. They had already caused the loss of the cruiser *Cassandra* and in addition the *Curacoa* had been forced to return to England for extensive repairs. The problem was partially eased by the arrival of the First Fleet Minesweeping Flotilla in early July.

The hazardous nature of their task was graphically demonstrated within days of their arrival. Four ships were sweeping in pairs off the island of Ösel, the *Myrtle*[8] (Lieutenant Commander Richard Scott) being paired with the *Gentian*[9] (Lieutenant Cecil Hallett), while the *Lupin* worked with the *Lilac*. During the afternoon of 15 July the latter pair swept a number of mines to the surface and the other two ships were ordered to sink them with gunfire. As they approached the floating mines the *Gentian* hit an unseen mine and her consort did the same as she closed to give assistance. The other two sweepers recovered their sweeps and also closed the two stricken vessels to give what assistance they could and to rescue survivors. The *Myrtle* sank that evening. The following morning the destroyer *Wrestler* and the Estonian tug *Ebba* arrived to assist with rescue operations and to tow the damaged ship to safety. However, during the afternoon of the 17th the *Gentian* rolled over to port and sank. Twelve ratings were killed in these two ships.

HMS *Vindictive*[10] (Captain 'Dasher' Grace[11]) arrived to join Cowan's force on 6 July and immediately went aground in the approaches to Revel. The ship had to be lightened by some 2,000 tons and even then required the efforts of two cruisers and three tugs to tow her clear after eight days of hard work. Fortunately the ship suffered no major damage and was soon available for operations and able to proceed to the new anchorage in Biorko Sound. One of the first tasks for the *Vindictive* was to return to Copenhagen and pick up more aircraft and stores, which had been brought to the Danish capital by the aircraft carrier *Argus*.

A landing strip was built on Biorko Island on a narrow peninsular that was cleared of forest and rocks to give a runway 300 yards long. Even after the clearance and a degree of levelling was complete the landing strip was far from ideal; it consisted mainly of loose sand with some projecting rocks and tree stumps. Moorings were laid off a sandy beach about a mile distant for the seaplanes. Servicing facilities were basic and provided little cover for the mechanics. Nevertheless, the first reconnaissance flight was carried out on 26 July. This became a regular feature for the RAF aircrew, the Bolshevik anti-aircraft gunners giving them an increasingly hostile reception. No aircraft were lost and no Bolshevik aircraft were seen.

To Cowan's delight the Admiralty reacted positively as a result of his letter to them in June. In July he was told that the Government had agreed that a flotilla of CMBs was being sent to the Baltic. Lieutenant Agar's sinking of the Russian cruiser *Oleg*[12] had evidently made an impression and had convinced both the Government and the Admiralty of the usefulness of these tiny boats. It was thought that the small craft could perhaps operate effectively against the Bolshevik ships without a serious escalation in hostilities. Eight of the 55ft boats were sent and although one, CMB67, foundered in bad weather in the North Sea while in tow of HMS *Venturous* and the tows of the others broke a total of eighteen times, the remaining seven reached Biorko Sound in early August. The flotilla was commanded by Commander C.C. Dobson, an ex-submariner. Once the CMBs had arrived, Admiral Cowan decided to mount an operation against the Russian ships berthed in the harbour at Kronstadt.

In the meantime, Cowan's ships had to deal with the unexpected reappearance of the Russian submarines. The *Volk*[13] left Kronstadt on 10 July, but was forced to return only twenty-four hours later with engine trouble. The *Pantera* (A.N. Bakhtin[14]) sailed two weeks later to patrol off the Estonian coast. The next morning two British submarines were sighted on the surface and Bakhtin began an attack. One submarine got under way and proceeded clear of the Russian boat but Bakhtin was able to close to four cables (800 yards) of the other – later found to be the E40 – and fired two torpedoes. They passed either side of the target, which by then was also under way, and the *Pantera* in turn had to evade a torpedo. The destroyer *Watchman* attempted a retaliatory depth charge attack, which caused no damage but persuaded the Russian boat to return to Kronstadt. Two days later the submarine *Vyepr* had a brush with the destroyers *Valorous* and *Vancouver* before returning to Kronstadt with water leaking through the forward hatch and in danger of reaching the batteries. The effect was that further sorties by Russian submarines were halted for more than a month.

Planning for the attack on Kronstadt – dubbed Operation 'RK' – proceeded at a hectic pace once the CMBs had arrived at Biorko Sound. Time was short, as the state of the moon in August would be right between the 17th and 21st. All the boats were given an engine overhaul and any other repairs that were needed were completed. The plans for the actual operation had to take into account the fact that the boats had no reversing gear to aid any tight turns that would be needed in the harbour itself. The Basin was in fact relatively small – less than half a mile square – and would seem even smaller when boats were travelling fast, as they had to. Speed was essential when firing their torpedoes, which would otherwise sink to the bottom and endanger the firing boat if they exploded prematurely. An additional factor was that the attack would take place in the dark; the Commanding Officers of each boat would most likely be blinded by searchlights and the whole harbour would be alive with defensive fire from the Russian ships.

Targets were selected as the two battleships, *Andrei Pervozvanni* and *Petropavlovsk*, the submarine depot ship *Pamiat Azova* with any submarines alongside at the time, the *Rurik*, an old cruiser believed to be carrying 300 mines, and the dry dock. Lieutenant Agar volunteered his one remaining 40ft boat and he was asked to lead the others to show them the way through the line of forts that he had come to know so well when taking agents in and out of Petrograd. Of the other seven boats, four carried two torpedoes and the other three just one each.

The RAF was brought into the plan to provide a diversion as the CMBs neared their target; the eight aircraft to be used were commanded by Squadron Leader David Donald[15]. The first CMBs were to reach the line of forts at 1.30 a.m., at which time the aircraft were to begin bombing and strafing to distract the defences and to hide the noise of the naval boats with the roar of the aircraft engines. It was also believed, as a result of intelligence sources, that as soon as the first bombs were dropped the Russian sailors would leave their ships and take cover ashore! It is not often that gale-force winds can be regarded as a piece of luck, but the gale that sprang up three days before the operation was exactly that. The bad weather caused a piling up of water in the Gulf, giving an extra 2–3ft of clearance over the obstacles in between the line of forts. The weather cleared on the morning of the 17th and the operation was ordered to take place that night.

While waiting for the gale to abate, Agar decided that he would hire two local smugglers to act as pilots for the force. He had used them before on his expeditions to Petrograd and they readily agreed to do another trip – until they found out that they would be going to Kronstadt and not the capital! They were finally persuaded to go with Agar on the promise of double pay of £25 each and a double ration of rum, two quarts instead of one. It was left to the paymaster commander of HMS *Delhi*, Cowan's flagship at that time, to account for this expenditure and answer any questions from the Admiralty's civil servants!

At 10.30 p.m. on 17 August 1919 Dobson gave the signal for all the boats to leave and Operation 'RK' had begun. Lieutenant Agar led the way in CMB7, followed by Dobson's seven boats: CMB79 (Lieutenant W. Bremner), CMB31 (Lieutenant R. MacBean with Commander Dobson embarked), CMB88 (Lieutenant A. Dayrell-Reed – known as 'Mossy' because of his large black beard), CMB86 (Sub-Lieutenant F. Howard), CMB72 (Sub-Lieutenant E. Bodley), CMB62 (Lieutenant Commander J. Brade) and CMB24 (Lieutenant L. Napier). Each boat carried one other officer, whose main task was to fire the torpedoes[16], and a motor mechanic to nurse the twin engines. Most boats also embarked additional personnel who would fire the machine guns and help with any casualties. Bremner's boat carried demolition charges to deal with the protective boom which was expected to be in place covering the entrance to the main basin.

With one exception the CMBs passed through the line of forts safely, although three boats had become separated. The Russian gunners could hear the noise of their powerful engines and fired blindly into the night; no searchlights were switched on. Previous RAF night raids ensured that the majority of the defences were alert to the threat from the sky rather than the sea, and the searchlights remained unlit for fear of drawing unwanted attention to themselves. At 1.30 a.m., exactly as planned, the RAF aircraft came in over the harbour, dropped their small bombs – none weighing more than 112 pounds – and then returned to machine-gun any worthwhile targets. By modern standards it was hardly worth the title of a raid but it served its purpose well, taking the Russian gunners' attention away from the sea and towards the sky.

The first group of CMBs to attack consisted of Bremner (79), MacBean and Dobson (31) and Dayrell-Reed (88). They glided past the destroyer *Gavriil*, which was acting as the guardship in the approaches and, with no boom to bar their way, they opened the throttles and roared into the Basin. The *Pamiat Azova*, berthed at the jetty extending into the middle of the Basin, was Bremner's target; he swung round to starboard and fired his torpedo, which struck the submarine depot ship. She listed rapidly and sank. MacBean had a more difficult manoeuvre: he had to stop the port engine as he turned sharply, engage the engine again as the turn was completed, gather speed and then fire at the battleship *Petropavlovsk*. Both his torpedoes found their target. The third boat (88) had a similar manoeuvre to complete before heading for the other battleship, the *Andrei Pervozvanni*. At this stage Sub-Lieutenant Steele noticed that they were off course – and heading straight towards a hospital ship. Dayrell-Reed had collapsed; he had been shot through the head. As he successfully completed his attack Steele tried to do what he could for his captain and then steered the boat out of the Basin, narrowly avoiding a lighter in the process. Once outside they had to pass close to the *Gavriil* and Petty Officer Morley, the motor mechanic, gave the ship a burst of machine-gun fire as they sped by.

The guardship was fortunate to be afloat; Napier (24) had the embarrassment of watching his only torpedo pass underneath the destroyer. A Russian account of the raid states that this torpedo exploded harmlessly on the Basin wall. Moreover, the Russian crew were remarkably quick to take action against the attacking boats and a shell struck Napier's boat, sinking it. Napier was blown into the water and Lieutenant O. Giddy, the other officer in the boat, and the motor mechanic were left to try and free two kapok fenders to form a raft. Before they could do so CMB24, which had been split in two longitudinally by the shell, sank beneath them. Two hours later, when the raid was over and the survivors were lapsing into unconsciousness with the cold, they were picked up by some Russian sailors from the *Gavriil*.

The second wave of three boats had been reduced to just one. Howard in CMB86 had been left behind with engine trouble on the far side of the line of forts. The firing gear of Bodley's CMB72 had been hit by a small-calibre shell, rendering it inoperative. Lieutenant Commander Brade was left to enter the Basin in CMB62 on his own and attack one of the battleships. Everyone's worst fears were realised. Brade, blinded by searchlights and travelling at high speed, rammed CMB62 into Bremner's CMB79, which was leaving the harbour and also travelling at speed, cutting it almost in half. Both boats remained locked together in the entrance, a target for every Bolshevik gunner that could bring his weapon to bear. Brade kept his engines going ahead, delaying the sinking of the other boat and giving Bremner and his crew time to abandon it. The damage to CMB62 was sufficient to make it impossible to carry on his attack so Brade left the harbour, firing his two torpedoes at the *Gavriil* as they retired. As with Napier's earlier attack both weapons passed underneath the destroyer, emphasising her charmed life that night. The Russian destroyer hit the CMB with a shell in the engine room; the boat later blew up as the petrol caught fire. Brade was killed and a badly wounded Bremner was picked up from the water and became a POW.

Agar in CMB7 fired his single torpedo through the entrance of a second basin, known as the Military Harbour. His target was a group of patrol craft and tugs berthed close together opposite the entrance; there was a clearly visible explosion. The amount of destruction caused by this torpedo has never been fully assessed, but Agar considered that it must have 'caused considerable damage and commotion'.

The raid was over and the surviving boats began the return voyage back to Biorko. Agar was the last to leave the scene in a hail of gunfire. He was bravely supported by Captain Fletcher in a Short seaplane, who shot out a searchlight which was about to illuminate the fleeing CMB and then strafed nearby gun emplacements. Bodley found the broken down CMB86 and towed it back to base. Steele met up with the flagship HMS *Delhi* and was able to transfer the wounded Dayrell-Reed to the sick bay. Sadly, he died during the following day.

It was time to count the reckoning. The submarine depot ship had been sunk and two battleships were damaged. Three CMBs had been lost. Four officers had been killed and three taken prisoner. Four ratings had been killed and six taken prisoner. There were no RAF casualties. Later the awards for gallantry were promulgated. Dobson and Steele were both awarded the Victoria Cross: the former for his gallantry and superb leadership, the latter for his gallantry in CMB88 after Dayrell-Reed had been wounded and for successfully carrying out his attack. Six other officers, including Agar, received the DSO and eight received the DSC. Fifteen ratings received the DSM. Three more of those taking part were Mentioned in Despatches[17]. The RAF was not forgotten and four officers received the DFC and ten were Mentioned in Despatches. This is the highest percentage of awards ever made for any operation, being an indication not only of the great gallantry of all those involved but also of the ferocity of the battle.

When Sub-Lieutenant Norman Morley (later Commander) died in 1989, he had the distinction of being the only naval officer to have been awarded the DSC on four occasions. Three of these were given during the Second World War. However, his first DSC was for his part in the Kronstadt raid. On board CMB88, as an additional member of the crew, he took over the duties of firing the torpedoes when Sub-Lieutenant Steele assumed command after Dayrell-Reed was shot in the head.

The British War Cabinet had tacitly sanctioned this operation when they first agreed to the boats being sent to join Cowan's force. Again, when the First Sea Lord had informed them that the raid was about to be launched there had been no objections. When Admiral Wemyss went to announce the success of the attack he was greatly surprised to receive a less than enthusiastic reception. It seems that if the Cabinet had given the matter more consideration earlier, permission to attack might have been withheld. With British forces preparing to withdraw from Archangel and Murmansk, the politicians did not want the possibility of the sinking of the Russian Baltic Fleet to compromise events in the North.

The Danish Red Cross took responsibility for helping any British POWs and for negotiating their release. The officers and ratings captured at Kronstadt spent six weeks in an ordinary prison in Petrograd sharing their cells with common criminals. They were then taken to Moscow and housed in the Androniev Monastery, except for the badly wounded Bremner, who was sent to hospital. The monastery also housed other British POWs; officers captured at Onega during the mutiny of Russian troops, RAF officers who had crashed or made forced landings on the Northern Front or in the South, and several soldiers who had been captured in the North. The men all suffered cruelly during the winter when even the solitary water pump in the yard froze, there was just one wood-burning stove, food was in short supply and bedding was merely some straw on hard boards. There was a doctor but he had no drugs and little equipment. The soldiers were allowed out into the town if they wished but this privilege was not for officers. The men were all released in April 1920.

The success of the raid changed the situation entirely for Cowan's force in the Gulf of Finland. No longer did they face the possibility of being confronted with a superior Russian Fleet; only destroyers and submarines were available to Admiral Zelenoy. The submarines proved that the Russians could not be discounted altogether.

After six weeks of inactivity the submarine *Pantera* left Kronstadt for a patrol off the Estonian coast and shortly after 6.00 p.m. on 1 September sank the destroyer HMS *Vittoria* (Lieutenant Commander Vernon Hammersley-Heenan), which was at anchor to the east of Seskar Island. Two torpedoes were fired, one of which missed ahead and the other struck on the starboard side in the engine room. The British ship sank in five minutes, breaking in two with the bow and stern sections rising vertically before quickly disappearing. Eight men were killed, the remainder being rescued by the *Abdiel* (Captain Berwick Curtis). The submarine then returned to Kronstadt. It was an action which remains to this day the largest warship to have been sunk by a Russian submarine. Hammersley-Heenan was absolved of any blame for the loss of his ship, but Captain Curtis incurred their Lordships' displeasure for having allowed the two destroyers to remain at anchor in contravention of his patrol orders.

Three days later another British destroyer, the *Verulam* (Lieutenant Commander Guy Warren), was sunk with the loss of twenty-nine men after hitting a mine while on patrol off the Estonian coast. At about 10.00 p.m. the destroyer had reached the southern limit of the patrol and was reversing course when she struck a mine on the starboard side, abreast the mainmast. The explosion was followed by several others, believed to be the ship's after magazine detonating. The position of the sinking was established to be just inside the boundary of a British minefield. Survivors were picked up by the *Walpole,* which was carrying out a patrol in an adjacent area. A Court of Enquiry found that Warren was to blame for the loss of the ship as he had failed to fix the turning point of his patrol line further from the minefield. In mitigation it was stated that it had been a very dark night and no lights were visible from on shore making navigation very difficult. Nonetheless, he too incurred their Lordships' displeasure.

There is a very moving addition to this story, one which is to be found deep in sailors' lore rather than in any dusty files containing official records. The crew of the *Verulam* had a pet dog called Lummy, a bulldog bitch. The night before the destroyer sailed for patrol the officers visited another ship of the flotilla, the *Westcott*, and took Lummy with them. All went well until the officers began to leave to return to their ship. On no account would Lummy go with them and indeed became unusually aggressive when urged down into the boat. Not knowing what was wrong the *Westcott*'s officers offered to look after the dog until the *Verulam* returned from patrol. The following morning Lummy went ashore with the canteen manager, but on return the dog sat on the upper deck near the torpedo tubes, not moving and staring wistfully out to sea. Nothing would persuade her to eat – a most unusual trait. The explosion of the mine which struck the *Verulam* was clearly heard and the night sky was lit by a bright flash. Lummy sat up and whimpered and, as the ship rapidly prepared for sea, allowed herself to be led down to one of the messdecks.

The RAF continued to harass the Russians in Kronstadt, though with little actual success; both day and night bombing was a very inaccurate science at that time, and in any case the bombs dropped were too small to do much damage even if they should hit the target. In all, some sixty raids were made. On 14 October the destroyer *Svoboda* and the surfaced submarine *Tigr* were attacked while at sea on exercises; the destroyer suffered some minor damage and casualties. Bolshevik aircraft made some sorties in an attempt to discover and attack the British airfield, but their effect was described as 'generally insignificant'.

The Swedish merchant ship *Eskstuna III* managed to elude Cowan's patrols and reached Petrograd with a cargo of handsaws. The ship was not so fortunate on her return, being intercepted to the south-west of Kronstadt with a cargo of flax. However, Cowan's orders were only to intercept vessels approaching Russian waters from the west, he had no orders concerning ships leaving. The problem was solved by handing over the vessel to the Finns, who eventually returned the ship to the Swedes! It was a very unsatisfactory way of dealing with the situation and the Admiralty pressed the Foreign Office for a clear ruling to cover future exigencies. As a result the Supreme Allied War Council in Paris announced a full blockade of Petrograd. Despite the hostilities which had taken place at sea over the summer months, there was no formal declaration of war between Great Britain and the Bolshevik Government in Russia, so technically the declaration of a blockade was of questionable legality. However, it was a positive ruling which gave Cowan a firm basis on which to make his plans and orders.

Captain Nasmith took the submarine depot ship *Lucia* with the flotilla of submarines back to England in September. Before leaving they landed the 12-pounder guns which were fitted to the 'E' class boats; these were given to the Estonians. A large quantity of ammunition for the guns came from England in a supply ship and this too was handed over. Commander Max Horton in the depot ship *Maidstone* with the small 'H' class submarines of the 3rd Flotilla arrived in Revel as replacements. Horton was well acquainted with the problems of submarine operations in the Baltic, having risen to fame in 1915 when in command of the E9. The flotilla were to continue the monotonous patrols until the winter ice ensured that the Bolshevik Fleet would not be able to make any sudden sortie from Kronstadt. They sailed for home on 2 January 1920.

In September Lieutenant Agar in CMB4, which had been repaired, led Lieutenant MacBean in CMB31 to the south side of Kronstadt and laid a cluster of mines in the main channel leading in and out of the Russian base. The mines were carried in the troughs which normally held the torpedoes. They lay deadly but dormant until 21 October, when they fulfilled their purpose. On that day four Russian destroyers sailed from Kronstadt with the purpose of laying a minefield which would prevent British ships approaching and bombarding the Russian positions that were facing the Estonian army. Three ships, the *Gavriil*, *Konstantin* and *Svoboda*, blew up and sank with the loss of all hands, except for twenty-five men who managed to reach shore. The *Azard* succeeded in manoeuvring clear and returned safely to Kronstadt. Seven of the survivors came ashore behind Estonian lines and were made POWs. Fortuitously, they were from the *Gavriil* and were able to give British officers information about the failed attacks on their ship in August and details of the survivors who had been picked up from the water. These destroyers were four ships of a fleet, already badly reduced in size, which Admiral Zelonoy could ill-afford to lose.

This was at a time when General Denikin's southern army had captured the town of Orel in its drive to reach Moscow while, more importantly, General Yudenitch's White Russian Army in Estonia had advanced to within 8 miles of Petrograd. Despite the Red Fleet's recent losses in Kronstadt, it was able to assist the Red Army in defence of the city. The battleship *Sevastopol*, immobilised in Petrograd for lack of fuel, used her 12in guns to bombard the White Russian lines. Yudenitch's men were so close to the city that even the 4in guns on the destroyers *Vsadnik* and *Gaidamak* could be brought into action. Commissar Martinov led 11,000 seamen from the fleet at Kronstadt into the battle and Yudenitch's advance was halted and then turned back. Petrograd was saved. The battle represented a high-water mark for the White Russian Army; never again would they be in a position to capture Petrograd. The Bolshevik Government had surmounted the gravest danger to its existence that it had ever met.

The Estonians still continued their endeavours to capture the fortress of Krasnaya Gorka. Earlier, Cowan had asked for two monitors to be sent to join his force so that they could be used to batter the defences of this bastion. The Admiralty's reply at the time showed their unwillingness to accede to this request and quoted the experience of the Dardanelles, where battleships had failed to reduce the Turkish forts. Following another request from Cowan the *Erebus*, which had been homeward bound from Murmansk, was diverted to the Baltic. The arrival at the end of October of the ungainly looking ship, with its single vast turret and two 15in guns, was certainly good for morale among the Estonian troops. Despite two days of bombardment, the fort remained in Russian hands; Admiralty misgivings about the value of the effect of the naval gunfire had proved correct.

In Latvia, Commodore Duff continued to have to contend with General von der Goltz's unhelpful attitude, designed to keep German troops as long as possible in that country and in Lithuania. In mid-June this led Duff temporarily having to withdraw the destroyers *Waterhen* and *Vancouver* from Riga, as it was feared that they might be seized by German troops. In early July the *Vancouver*, by then back in Riga, reported that a German merchant ship, the *Hannover*, escorted by two German torpedo boats, had arrived in the port. This was against the terms of the Armistice as no German warships were allowed to be at sea, except for minesweepers. Duff sent the cruiser *Danae* to Riga to ensure that the warships returned immediately to Germany.

In a report to the Admiralty in July, Duff wrote:

All reports tend to show that the German command has halted its preparations for evacuating Latvia. Troops are returning again from Prussia. It is believed that Goltz considers the situation so unstable that it is worth waiting to see if it might be possible to avoid complying with the order to evacuate the Baltic States.

The receipt of Duff's report led the Secretary of the Admiralty to request the Foreign Office to draw the attention of the Supreme Allied War Council in Paris to the urgency of the recall of the German general. On 1 August the German Government was instructed to order von der Goltz to withdraw by the end of the month. When Berlin passed the message on to the Germans in Latvia, von der Goltz was instructed not to co-operate with General Gough or members of his mission.

Needless to say, the situation in Latvia did not change as a result. Duff's chief weapon in the diplomatic tussle with the intransigent German general was his strict control of German shipping arriving in any of the Latvian ports with supplies for the German troops. A refusal to permit the landing of any supplies was inconvenient for the Germans, but little else. More important was the commodore's tact and determination not to allow any of the petty manoeuvrings to stand in the way of the ultimate German withdrawal, however long that might take. In the final resolution of any argument or dispute, he was backed by the guns of the British and French warships.

For the remainder of the year the cruisers *Delhi*, *Dragon* and *Dunedin* carried out bombardments of Red Army positions to relieve the pressure on Estonian troops holding the frontier. The *Princess Margaret* laid several minefields in the Gulf of Finland to the west of the Russian mine barrage to thwart possible sorties by any of the Russian ships; this was particularly important following rumours that the *Sevastopol* was being made ready to leave Petrograd. The rumours were in fact false, but the British remained concerned. Destroyers and submarines maintained their dreary patrols with little or no action to relieve the tedium. There were several reports of the presence of Russian submarines, some as far west as Revel, but no firm contact was made. Winter weather conditions did little to help the crews of the British ships, especially those men required to stand watches on the upper deck. The nights were long, there was fog, snow or driving rain coupled with increasingly low temperatures. It is a measure of Cowan's leadership, together with the discipline and the professionalism of the crews, that enabled them to continue with this apparently endless task.

In September the Soviet Government (as Lenin's Government by then was known) offered to end hostilities with the Provisional Governments in both Estonia and Latvia and to recognise their independence. The Allies still had done no more than 'recognise the autonomous existence' of the Baltic States for fear that anything more might lead to demands for full-scale military support against the Red Army. On 23 September the British Government agreed that the States themselves should negotiate with the Russians in any way to preserve their national existence[18]. Churchill, with his strong anti-Bolshevik views, wrote to the Prime Minister urging that the States be given immediate recognition. Lloyd George replied equally strongly that he was not prepared to do this at that time; he feared having to send a full-scale military expedition to defend any independence as 'whoever won in Russia, the Government would promptly recover the old Russian Baltic ports'. Before matters could be concluded General Yudenitch's offensive by White troops towards Petrograd frustrated further moves.

On 8 October troops of what came to be called the West Russian Army attacked Riga; they were commanded by the Tsarist Russian Colonel Pavel Bermondt-Avalov (self-promoted and usually referred to as General Bermondt), a puppet of von der Goltz. This army was formed from Russian ex-POWs and some German volunteers, armed and equipped by von der Goltz. After fierce fighting, the Lettish Army, loyal to the Prime Minister, were ousted from the city. British ships were fired on during the battle and Bermondt's troops occupied the fort commanding the entrance to the harbour, from where they could threaten all shipping using it. On 15 October, after an ultimatum had failed to enforce the fort's evacuation, it was bombarded by British and French warships. Bermondt's men abandoned their positions and order was restored in Riga. During this action the cruiser *Dragon* was hit by a shell from the fort and suffered nine fatal casualties. Cowan believed that this attempted coup by Bermondt was one of the causes of the failure of Yudenitch's offensive on Petrograd[19]. The possibility of any success by Bermondt had worried the Estonians and they diverted their own troops to prevent a northward advance from Riga towards Revel. Yudenitch himself was furious with his fellow Russian and called him a traitor.

What in fact turned out to be the final battle for Riga began on 3 November, when Lettish troops advanced through the city against Bermondt's division. The Letts were supported by gunfire from the cruiser HMS *Dragon*, four British destroyers and some of the French ships, which were anchored near the mouth of the Dvina. The battle lasted for eight days before Bermondt admitted defeat and his troops retired from the city and its environs. The withdrawal of the German puppet force was not before time; the Allied ships were running out of ammunition.

A similar situation developed at Libau, where more of Bermondt's troops started to threaten the city. A small British force of two cruisers and three destroyers supported the small garrison. Captain L. Dundas, commanding the cruiser *Phaeton*, reported the impending attack to Cowan. The admiral instructed him that he was to evacuate all civilians from the vicinity of the Naval

Harbour so that he could bombard the area without worrying about the effects on a friendly. He added that Dundas should avoid destroying the church.

The attack began on 4 November and the Allied ships were heavily engaged all day, the fighting dying away as night fell. The battle resumed the following morning and continued intermittently for the next ten days. The Allied ships were reinforced on the 9th by the arrival of the monitor HMS *Erebus* (Captain J.A. Moreton), armed with two 15in guns. On the 14th the enemy made a determined assault on the town and initially made some progress, before being driven back by a fierce counter-attack, supported by the fire of the British ships and the French sloop *Ancre*. Although the Letts continued to advance the situation remained serious; the destroyer *Valorous* had expended all her ammunition and the other ships were only in a slightly better state. There were no reserves available to replenish them.

A similar attack on the port of Windau was also repulsed with the help of gunfire from the British ships berthed there. Again, the expenditure of ammunition was prodigious and after the fighting had ceased the ships were left with near-empty magazines until Cowan could arrange for an ammunition ship to be sent to them.

It is singularly unfortunate that at this time a series of cases of failure of discipline and mutiny should occur in Cowan's ships. It marred the record of the men of the Royal Navy who had achieved so much to enable the politicians to reach a position where the navy's task in the Baltic was almost at an end. On 11 October about 100 men of a destroyer flotilla, who had recently returned from the Baltic, walked off their ships in Rosyth when they learnt that they were to return. The destroyers eventually sailed for the Baltic with their crews made up to strength by men taken from the battleships. In November there was a mutiny among a small number of men of the *Vindictive*. A number of 'Hostilities Only' ratings in the minesweeping flotilla also refused duty. In December there was trouble on board Cowan's own flagship, HMS *Delhi*.

The mutinies themselves were soon resolved and were followed by a number of courts-martial. All the prison sentences awarded were greatly reduced on review. It is the many causes of these incidents that are so important. Cowan felt that the hazardous nature of their duty in waters where the threat of mines was always a menace, the severe weather conditions for much of the year, poor pay[20] and poor food all played their part. The Admiralty and the Treasury were worried about the cost of any improvements! The problems of fighting 'a war that was not a war', coupled with poor planning regarding the reduction of the strength of the navy to peacetime requirements, meant that some ships were required to make frequent returns to the Baltic. In addition there were the consequent delays in demobilisation, which affected the men's chances of finding new jobs. Behind almost every mutiny in any era there can usually be found the effects of poor 'man management', both in the Admiralty and in the fleet itself. The Baltic in 1919 was no exception.

By the end of November Latvia had been cleared of all Germans. Bermondt's men were either dead or had fled; Bermondt himself went into exile. By the end of the year Lithuania had also been cleared.

There were indications on all fronts that the fighting was coming to a cessation. The Baltic States were clear of German and Red Army troops and the national armies were maintaining a wary status quo, while the diplomats and politicians were working out their own peaceful solutions with the Government in Moscow. The corresponding need for the presence of Allied warships was such that the majority could be sent home. Cowan in his flagship sailed from Biorko Sound at the last possible moment before the ship became iced in for the winter. He made a brief call at Copenhagen and sailed for Plymouth on 1 January 1920.

Commodore Duff was left behind to keep a watchful eye on events over the winter in HMS *Caledon* with the *Dunedin* and the 4th Destroyer Flotilla in company, along with three French ships. Diplomatic negotiations continued before the Soviet Government eventually granted each country an end to hostilities and its independence. The actual wording used was that Soviet Russia 'voluntarily and forever' renounced its rights over the peoples of the Baltic States, words which rang hollow in June 1940 when the tanks rolled over the borders.

The blockade on Petrograd was relaxed, although until the Gulf became free of ice in the spring of 1920 this made little difference as no shipping could reach Petrograd. In May 1920 two battlecruisers, the *Hood* and *Tiger*, and a flotilla of destroyers were sent as reinforcements for the ships in the Baltic for the summer of 1920. However, they were called home after reaching Copenhagen – a sign that there was a greatly reduced likelihood that hostilities would continue. At the same time Commodore Duff was told by the Admiralty that offensive action against Russian ships was not to be taken. Throughout 1920 a decreasing number of light cruisers and destroyers maintained a presence in the area. In 1921 the strength of the force had been reduced to one light cruiser and two destroyers. The Royal Navy was completely withdrawn at the end of the summer.

The undeclared naval war was over. In the words of Admiral of the Fleet Sir David Beatty, then First Sea Lord, Admiral Cowan and the men of his Baltic Force had added 'lustre to the great Service of which you are such a distinguished member'.

ELEVEN

IN RETROSPECT

Intervention in Russia began on 6 March 1918 with the credible objective that the European Allies, with the reluctant support of the United States, wished to keep Russia in the war against Germany. They also needed to ensure that the vast stockpiles of military stores and equipment, which lay unused in the Russian ports where they had been unloaded, were not allowed to reach enemy hands. All this changed on 11 November 1918 when the Armistice with Germany came into effect. It should perhaps have ended there and then. It didn't.

Many reasons were put forward for maintaining an Allied presence in Russia; indeed, the frequently changing policy allowed for passive – and at times active – intervention in the Civil War which ravaged Russia for the next three years. Even with the benefit of hindsight there were few incidents which proved the politicians to be right, though as usual the armed forces carried out their role with quiet efficiency and gallantry, marred only by a small number of sporadic and deeply regrettable incidents of ill-discipline.

Except in the Baltic, where the Royal Navy performed a task that was totally different from that in any other theatre of intervention, the Allied forces were unable to affect the outcome of the Civil War. Both Winston Churchill and Bruce Lockhart had argued that the Allies needed to intervene on a massive scale to achieve any long-term effect on the situation. After the four years of slaughter on the Western Front, the idea of sending huge numbers of men to start a new war in Russia was politically impossible. The White Russians had some successes but lacked any unity, and, because they had no viable political agenda as an alternative to Bolshevism to put to the people, their troops were unreliable and their cause unpopular. The rank and file soldiers would not fight to restore the old regime and way of life that many of the Russian officers loyally continued to support. In these circumstances the half measures employed by the Allies were futile and ultimately the policy of intervention failed.

From November 1918 the Allied armies in France and Belgium had to follow the retreating Germans at a time when thousands of men were looking forward to their demobilisation. Similar activities took place on all the other fronts. Except in Russia. For the Allied forces there, the war was not over and they faced an implacable foe, as Leon Trotsky energetically reorganised the rabble of revolutionaries into an effective fighting force – the Red Army. It was, therefore, most unfortunate that in his 1918 Christmas message to the armed forces, King George V began with the words: 'At last there is no longer fighting.'

On the British side, history will forever note the way in which the country's servicemen conducted themselves in this totally pointless war. In addition to the military achievements of the army and the RAF, the Royal Navy's operations by the flotilla on the River Dvina, the Royal Marines at Murmansk and the CMBs on Lake Onega stand out amidst political vacillation. The actions of the Caspian Sea force, with their odd collection of converted merchant ships and a flotilla of CMBs, together with the armoured train and converted gunboats in the depths of Siberia, are unique in the navy's history. In the Black Sea area, the navy can be proud that many thousands of unfortunate refugees were evacuated and enabled to start a new life in safety.

Apart from a handful of submarines the Baltic Sea had been closed to the Royal Navy, until the Armistice in November 1918 had allowed Rear Admiral Alexander-Sinclair to lead his small force into the area. He was relieved in January 1919 by Rear Admiral Cowan. The task of the two admirals had been to protect the newly gained freedom of Finland, Estonia, Latvia and Lithuania, each of which was seeking independence, while the Bolsheviks were determined to bring them back into their domain. At the same time German ambitions in the new Republics had to be thwarted. In addition, the British task force, later aided by units from the French Navy, was to ensure that the German troops remaining in these countries obeyed the terms of the Armistice and then to supervise their eventual evacuation. Finally, like the British commanders in other parts of Russia, Cowan had to deal with a number of Russian generals, each of whom had their own agenda and viewed their compatriots with jealous suspicion. It was no easy task, and it is to his credit that he led his men to a successful conclusion. It was no coincidence that, as Cowan's flagship passed the breakwater into Plymouth Sound in January 1920, he received a signal congratulating him and his men on their work:

> The Board of Admiralty desire to convey to Rear Admiral Sir Walter Cowan and to the officers and men of the Baltic Force now returning to England their marked approbation of the manner in which the work of the Force has been performed. The Baltic Force has during the past year cheerfully endured trying conditions, and when the occasion has offered has attacked the enemy with the utmost gallantry. It has prevented the destruction of States which had upheld the Allied cause, has supported the forces of civilisation when menaced by anarchy, and has worthily upheld the honour of the British Navy. This record is the more praiseworthy because it comes after the long previous strain of war, at a time when the forces of the Crown have for the most part been enjoying a relaxation of effort. The Board's gratification is to be made known to all concerned.

Success in the Baltic had not come without a price. It had required a massive effort by the Royal Navy, which at the same time had been adjusting from war to peace, with its attendant problems of shortages of personnel and ships as men were demobilised and vessels paid off into reserve. From November 1918 to the end of 1919, a total of 238 British warships and auxiliaries were deployed to the Baltic at various times, including twenty-three cruisers and eighty-five destroyers. Seventeen ships were lost, a further sixty-one were damaged. Casualties – killed, wounded and POW – amounted to thirty-three officers and 164 ratings. Overall, the financial cost to the nation, already reeling from the massive expenditure of the Great War, was so immense that it hindered post-war recovery.

The work of the Royal Navy has not been forgotten in Estonia. On the outside of 'Fat Margaret', a large round medieval tower on the edge of Tallinn (as Revel is now known) which houses the Maritime Museum, there is a plaque commemorating the four British admirals involved in Estonian independence, who were each awarded the Estonian Cross of Liberty. Named are: Admirals Sir Edwyn Alexander-Sinclair and Sir Walter Cowan, who commanded the ships in the Baltic; Admiral Sir Sydney Fremantle, who had been Deputy Chief of Naval Staff in the Admiralty; and Admiral Sir Bertram Thesiger who, as the captain of HMS *Calypso*, had been involved in the first skirmishes off Revel in 1918. The inscription is in both Estonian and English. The plaque, which is in black marble topped with the silhouette of a destroyer, has only recently been replaced; the original disappeared during the Russian occupation from 1940. In the Church of the Holy Saviour there is a plaque naming all those men of the Baltic Force killed in action[1]. This too has replaced the original, which was also removed by the Russians. A similar plaque has been placed in Portsmouth Cathedral.

The respect in which Admiral Cowan is still held by the Estonians is reflected by the honour accorded him in 2007. The Estonian Navy bought three minehunters from the Royal Navy; one was renamed the *Admiral Cowan*.

Despite the intervention of the many Allied forces in various parts of Russia and regardless of the efforts of the various White armies, the Bolsheviks were victorious on all fronts when the Civil War was over in 1922. Lenin and his successors were to rule what had become the Soviet Union for over sixty years. They were destined to fight another bitter war with Germany: the Great Patriotic War of 1941–45. When that war was over the Soviet Union climbed the ladder of nations to become the second most powerful in the world. Then, almost as quickly as Tsarist Russia had succumbed to the Bolsheviks to become the Soviet Union, so Soviet Russia in turn disintegrated to become increasingly democratic independent states in the 1990s.

There are many lessons to be learned from this sad episode of British and Russian history, lessons which are just as potent in the twenty-first century as they were in 1920. Any civil war is terrible in its concept, and its aftermath affects the nation for years to come. Intervention by a third party is inexcusable – unless, perhaps, it's on the winning side. The whole War of Intervention in Russia was a political disaster for Britain and her Allies, and, like the American war in Vietnam, those valuable lessons have become lost in a desire to forget. The German philosopher Georg Hegel (1770–1831) perhaps best summarised such stubborn refusals to learn from failed endeavours:

'What experience and history teach is this – that people and governments have never learned anything from history, or acted on principles deduced from it.'

END NOTES

CHAPTER ONE

1. The cruiser *Askold*.
2. One of these was the cruiser *Oleg*.
3. The city's name was changed to Petrograd shortly after the outbreak of war in 1914. It became Leningrad in 1924 and St Petersburg again in 1991. It was the capital of Russia until 1917.
4. At this time the Russians were using the old Julian Calendar and dates in the Russian style were thirteen days behind the rest of Europe. The change to the Gregorian Calendar was made after the Bolshevik Revolution when it was decreed that the day after 31 January 1918 would become 14 February.
5. Completed in Nickolaiev in 1903, the ship displaced 12,800 tons and had a main armament of four 12in guns.

CHAPTER TWO

1. See *Baltic Assignment* by Michael Wilson, Leo Cooper, 1985.
2. See *The Tsar's British Squadron* by Bryan Perrett and Anthony Lord, William Kimber 1981.
3. Count Keller left Russia during the Civil War from Sevastopol.
4. *Baltic Assignment*.
5. Ibid.
6. Kornilov fought as a junior officer in Manchuria during the war with Japan, 1904–05. In 1914 he was commanding a brigade in Galicia. By May 1915 he was commanding a division during the Austrian offensive; he was taken prisoner when his division was surrounded after the divisions on his flanks withdrew prematurely. He escaped a year later and on his return to Russia was given command of a corps. After the Revolution Kerensky made him Commander-in-Chief of the Russian Army with instructions to restore discipline. He soon clashed with Kerensky, which led to his downfall.
7. The October dates are by the Julian Calendar, which was still in use in Russia, hence 'The October Revolution'. By the Western-style Gregorian Calendar the dates would be 7-8 November.
8. *From Dreadnought to Scapa Flow Volume V* by Arthur Marder.
9. The Extraordinary Commission for the Suppression of Counter-Revolution, which in Russian is *Chrezvitchainaya Kommissia*, abbreviated to the '*Cheka*'. The notorious Felix Dzerzhinsky subsequently took over as the head of the *Cheka*.
10. Mary Britneiva, a young army nurse from an Anglo-Russian family, left an account of events in her book *One Woman's Story*, published by Arthur Baker in 1934.
11. See Appendix 1.

CHAPTER THREE

1. Launched in 1895, 14,820 tons displacement.
2. Q-ships, or Special Service Ships, were elderly merchant ships with guns hidden within dummy deckhouses or behind parts of the superstructure. The intention was to lure U-boats into close

range when a White Ensign would be hoisted, the guns would be exposed and the U-boat would be attacked. Fourteen U-boats were sunk by Q-ships during the war and a further sixty damaged.

3.   The Leitsergyeev, Bezshumni, Kaptyurasovski and Bezstrashni.

4.   The cruiser was armed with twelve 5.9in guns in single mountings, together with twelve 3in guns. She had been launched in March 1900.

5.   Launched May 1905, 13,550 tons. Main armament of six 9.2in guns and four 7.5in.

6.   Launched 1902, 9,350 tons. Main armament of two 7.6in guns and eight 6.4in.

7.   Launched 1892, 5,860 tons. Main armament of four 8in guns and four 7.5in. The *Olympia* had been the flagship of Commodore Dewey at the Battle of Manila Bay against the Spaniards in 1898 and as such is now preserved at Philadelphia as a museum ship

8.   See Chapter 2 for General Poole's previous duties in Russia and his time at the Astoria Hotel in Petrograd at the outbreak of the Revolution.

9.   The *Alexander* (8,000 tons) had been built in England for the Russian Government, but was taken over early in 1918. She was manned by a naval crew and had reached Murmansk in March 1918. The ship's armament consisted of one 4in gun, two 12-pounders and a single 2-pounder pompom.

10. Lenin had moved the capital from Petrograd to foil any German plans to try and capture that city.

11. One was the *Sviatogor*, which had been involved in the incident with HMS *Alexander*. The ship was subsequently raised, repaired locally and then commissioned with a British crew. The other ship scuttled in the river was the *Mikula Selianovitch*. After being salvaged she was taken to England by a Russian crew, refitted, manned by a French crew and returned to the White Sea.

12. The ship was subsequently recommissioned with a British crew as HMS *Josephine*. Seventeen trawlers were also captured, of which fourteen were given British crews and commissioned under the White Ensign with names ending in 'axe'. The *Woodaxe* was later handed over to the French.

13. The *Advokat*, *Razlyff*, *Opyt* and *Tolstoi*. Each ship was armed with a single 100mm gun.

14. The ship's name should have been *Cicada*, but a spelling mistake at the time of launch gave rise to this corruption; the name was never changed.

15. He was actually serving as a brigadier-general and not promoted to major general until a few days after his arrival in Russia.

16. See *The Ignorant Armies* by E.M. Halliday for a full description of this battle.

CHAPTER FOUR

1.   An armoured cruiser of 9,500 tons, launched in 1899.

2.   The force was to include the old cruiser HMS *Fox*, the seaplane carrier *Pegasus*, and the repair ship *Cyclops*. Among the additional monitors was HMS *Humber*, armed with two 6in guns and had a draught of only 5ft 7½in. Six fast 55ft CMBs were included in the force, their top speed was 42 knots.

3.   A cruiser of 4,360 tons, launched in 1893. The cruiser had served in East Indies and Middle East during the war, returning to Chatham to pay off in 1919. The ship was then specially fitted out and recommissioned for service in North Russia.

4.   The 60-pounder guns were first introduced into service in 1904. The total weight of the gun and carriage was 4 tons 8 hundredweight. The maximum range was 12,300 yards.

5.   The papers are held in The National Archives (TNA) under reference WO95/5430.

6.   The 'Dance' class minesweepers were 130ft long and had a draught of 3ft 9in. They were adaptations of tugs being built for the army for use in Mesopotamia. Their shallow draught enabled them to sweep inshore for mines at low tide, their propellers being protected in tunnels. Apart from the four sent to Russia two additional ships were prepared for service but did not leave the UK.

7.   Six CMBs had arrived in Archangel in June on board a transport ship; they formed part of the reinforcements for the River Flotilla authorised in February. The boats did valuable work on the river but did not have the success that might have been expected due to the shallowness of the water. The boats were commanded by Lieutenant ('Stormy') Dickinson in CMB77.

8. Rudolf Gajda had a remarkable military career. A pharmacist by trade, he was conscripted into the Austrian Army and captured by the Russians in 1917. He became one of the leaders of the Czech Legion in Siberia after the Revolution, and was promoted to Lieutenant General by Kolchak. Kolchak dismissed him from his command a few weeks after this defeat by the Bolsheviks. He returned to his native country in 1920 and became Chief of the General Staff in 1926 but was later cashiered for taking part in an attempted fascist coup. During the Second World War he collaborated with the Germans and was executed in 1945.

9. It is interesting to note that Rawlinson's ADC was Captain Colin Gubbins, who in 1940, as a major general, was responsible for building the embryo SOE from scratch. In 1943 he became its Executive Director.

10. Karelia is an area to the south of the Kola Peninsular, partly in Russia and partly in Finland. The inhabitants hoped to be able to set up their own state, independent of both other countries. Their dream has never materialised.

11. The *Chester* had been launched in 1907 and the *Galveston* in 1903.

12. The Russian air ace Major Kazakov's death occurred in a flying accident a few days after he had heard of the British withdrawal. The news had deeply affected him. He started a low-level loop when his engine stalled and his aircraft nose-dived into the ground.

13. Despite having a badly disabled arm, the result of a wound at Gallipoli, the officer was given a suit of civilian clothes and sent home on board a collier. He later joined an undercover unit working in Ireland – hardly the act of a coward.

CHAPTER FIVE

1. A 9,800-ton armoured cruiser built in Portsmouth and completed in May 1904. She carried ten 6in guns, including a twin electrically powered turret fore and aft. With a speed of 23½ knots, the *Suffolk* had been the flagship of the China Station since August 1917.

2. Launched in 1899, a pre-dreadnought-type battleship of 15,200 tons displacement and armed with four 12in guns.

3. Launched in 1896 for the Russian Navy as the *Orel*, captured by the Japanese in 1905 and refitted.

4. The 9,215-ton heavy cruiser *Brooklyn* was first commissioned in December 1906. She was armed with eight 8in and twelve 5in guns and was fitted with five 18in torpedo tubes. The three-funnelled cruiser had been the flagship of the American Asiatic Fleet since 1916.

5. *Nurse at the Russian Front 1914-18* by Florence Farmborough.

6. Semenov escaped into Manchuria at the end of the Civil War where he remained until 1945. He was caught by the Red Army when they invaded after declaring war on Japan. He was executed.

7. Kolchak was a noted Polar explorer and had served with distinction during the war with Japan in 1904–05. He commanded a destroyer flotilla in the Gulf of Riga in 1916. Promoted to rear admiral, he commanded the Baltic Fleet destroyers before taking command of the Black Sea Fleet as a vice admiral in July 1916. He was one of Russia's most effective commanders during the war but was unable to halt the advance of revolutionary ideas in the Black Sea Fleet. He was sent to Washington in 1917 by the Provisional Government and was returning to Russia by way of Japan when the Bolshevik revolution occurred.

8. After Jameson returned to Vladivostok Ewing served first with Major General Knox and then with Admiral Kolchak. He was captured by the Bolsheviks in November 1920 and shot.

9. The *Carlisle* was a light cruiser of 4,290 tons displacement and armed with 5 x 6in guns. The ship was completed in November 1918.

10. HMS *Cairo* was the guardship in Vladivostok when this evacuation took place. The Captain's Report of Proceedings dated 24 February 1920 may be found at The National Archives (TNA) under reference ADM 1/8581.

11. The Captain's Report of Proceedings may be found at TNA under reference ADM1/8642.

CHAPTER SIX

1. Sixteen gunboats of this class were built by Yarrow on the Clyde and transported in sections to be re-erected for use on the River Tigris. Each ship displaced 98 tons, was 126ft in length and had a speed of 9½ knots. The armament varied but usually included a 4in gun. Their shallow draft and flat bottoms would have made them unsuitable for use in the Caspian Sea.

2. Both these gunboats returned to the UK after the end of the war and were then fitted out for service in North Russia. See Chapters 3 and 4.

3. Armed transports.

4. The cruiser sailed to return to Chatham immediately after the war was over in 1918. In 1919 the ship was specially fitted out for duties in North Russia. See Chapter 4.

5. The debate is given in great detail in *Britain and the Russian Civil War, Volume 2* by Richard Ullman, Oxford University Press, 1968.

6. An oil tanker armed with three 6in and one 4.7in gun.

7. Armed with two 4.7in guns.

8. Armed with one 12-pounder. Later renamed *Edinburgh Castle*.

9. In April 1915 Lieutenant Robinson commanded one of two picket boats which were specially armed with torpedoes to enter the Dardanelles and sink the submarine HMS E15, which had been swept ashore by the current while attempting to pass up into the Sea of Marmara. The submarine had been hit by Turkish shell fire but it was essential to destroy the boat in case it could be salvaged to use against the British Fleet. Under intense fire from Turkish guns the two picket boats achieved their objective.

10. Bowhill was one of the RNAS' early flyers, having done flight training in 1912 as an officer in the Royal Naval Reserve. He had been awarded the DSO. During the Second World War he was Commander-in-Chief of Coastal Command from 1937–41. He retired in 1945 as an Air Chief Marshal.

11. HMS *Theseus* was an old cruiser (launched 1892) which had served briefly in the White Sea in 1916. In 1918 she was acting as a depot ship for trawlers in the Aegean and formed part of the fleet sent to the Black Sea. Two of the ship's casement 6in guns were sent to Baku in 1919 and mounted ashore to form part of the defences of the port. That, and the fact that the ship had acted as a depot ship, probably accounts for the name *Theseus II* being given to the shore establishment at Baku. The ship returned to England in 1920 to pay off and was then scrapped.

12. The submarines *Okun*, *Makrel* and *Katsaka* were in the Caspian at the time. These three boats posed little threat as by 1919 they were obsolete and were comparable with the British 'A' class. The *Minoga*, which was transferred from the Baltic to the Caspian in 1918 or 1919, was slightly larger and had an increased performance over the other three, but was still of little threat to the British forces despite their total lack of any anti-submarine equipment.

13. The ship was known to the British sailors as the *Venture*.

14. The *Moskvityanin* was a ship of the Emir Bukharski class, built in 1905. The name ship of the class and the *Finn* were also in the Caspian. The other Bolshevik destroyers were six ships of the Storozevoi class, which had transferred from the Baltic to the Caspian Sea in 1918.

15. The plan collapsed when there was a change of Government in Italy.

16. Interestingly, during the Second World War, Fraser was personally awarded the Order of Suvorov by Marshal Stalin.

CHAPTER SEVEN

1. Commander Bond was a Royal Navy officer on loan to the Royal Australian Navy.

2. *The Official History of Australia in the War of 1914-18*, Volume XI, A.W. Jose.

3. *Intervention in Russia* by M. Hudson, Leo Cooper, 2004.

4. See Chapter 6.

5. Admiral Seymour was second in command of the Mediterranean Fleet and the commander of the British ships in the Black Sea.

6. Andre Marty was paroled after serving only two years of a lengthy goal sentence. In 1936–37 he was the Commissar in charge of the International Brigades during the Civil War in Spain and earned himself the nickname of the 'Butcher of Albacete' for his indiscriminate use of terror against friend or foe alike. He later became the leader of the French Communist Party.

7. Later Admiral Sir William Fisher and Commander-in-Chief of the Mediterranean Fleet.

8. Collishaw was born in British Columbia and served with the merchant navy before joining the Royal Naval Air Service at the start of the war in 1914. As an air vice marshal he commanded the RAF in the Western Desert in 1941–42.

9. See *The Day We Almost Bombed Moscow* by Dobson and Miller.

10. See Chapter 4.

11. Admiral McCully was particularly keen to ensure that families of those fighting at the front should be evacuated.

CHAPTER EIGHT

1. The Admiralty papers on this subject may be found at The National Archives (TNA) under reference ADM 1379/1949.

2. See Chapter 3.

3. All the 'C' class cruisers were completed in 1917; they were of just over 4,000 tons and carried an armament of five 6in guns and had a maximum speed of 29 knots.

4. Both minelayers were converted merchant ships. The *Princess Margaret* was 5,900 tons and could carry 500 mines, the *Angora* was 4,300 tons and could carry 320 mines.

5. Papers concerning this exchange of prisoners are held at TNA under reference FO 371/3941.

6. Not to be confused with the Dvina, which flowed south from Archangel.

7. Foreign Office Telegram of 14 February 1919 held in TNA under reference ADM 137/1664.

8. The 'V&W' class destroyers were ships of 1,300 tons displacement and capable of 31 knots. Most ships of the class had an armament of four 4in guns and six 21in torpedo tubes, a few ships mounted 4.7in guns.

9. As Admiral of the Fleet Sir Dudley Pound he was the First Sea Lord from June 1939 until March 1942.

10. The 'S' class destroyers were smaller than the 'V&W' class ships and displaced 1,070 tons. They mounted four 4in guns and four 21in torpedo tubes. All ships of the class were laid down during the war years and most were completed in 1918.

11. Later Admiral of the Fleet Viscount Cunningham and Commander-in-Chief of the British Mediterranean Fleet during the Second World War.

12. Later Admiral of the Fleet Lord Tovey and Commander-in-Chief of the Home Fleet during part of the Second World War.

13. *A Sailor's Odyssey* by Viscount Cunningham, Hutchinson & Co., 1951.

14. The only other Allied ships in the Baltic at this time were fourteen American destroyers, but these ships were not part of Cowan's force. Their duties were only concerned with safeguarding the American food shipments organised by the Hoover Relief Organisation.

15. See Chapter 7.

16. Copies supplied by the Naval Historical Branch of the Ministry of Defence.

17. Letter to the author by Stato Maggiore della Marina.

18. Letter to the author by Danish Naval Library.

CHAPTER NINE

1. A date in February is suggested in Agar's *Baltic Episode*, which was not published until 1963, but he stated that it was May in his lecture to the Royal United Services Institute in 1928. This latter date is used here, as it would fit in with the ice conditions in the Baltic, which would not have allowed a small steamer to reach Helsingfors (Helsinki) or Hango in February.

2. Subsequent heads of the service have also been known by this single initial.
3. Later Sir Paul Dukes.
4. See *The Story of ST25* by Sir Paul Dukes.
5. The papers are held at TNA under reference CAB23/5
6. See Chapter 10.
7. See Chapter 10.
8. One boat was destroyed with explosives at Terrioki, the other was towed to England and is now part of the Imperial War Museum exhibition at Duxford.

CHAPTER TEN

1. One of a class of destroyers completed during the war. These ships were of 1,260 tons displacement and were nominally capable of 32 knots. They were armed with four 4in guns and were able to carry fifty mines.
2. The light cruisers of the 'D' class were slightly larger and more heavily armed than their contemporaries of the 'C' class and had all been completed in 1918–19. Armed with six 6in guns, they had been designed for a maximum speed of 29 knots.
3. Initially the L12, L16, L55, E27 and E40, followed by the L11.
4. *Baltic Assignment* by Michael Wilson.
5. The L55 was salvaged by the Soviet Navy in 1928. In an unexpected gesture the bodies of the British crew were returned to England for burial in the Royal Navy cemetery in Gosport. The submarine was refitted and commissioned into the Soviet Navy under her old name. The boat saw service in the 1941–45 war and was scrapped in 1960.
6. The minelayer *Princess Margaret* returned to the Baltic at the end of June, accompanied by the *Abdiel* and the 20th Destroyer Flotilla, which was also equipped for minelaying.
7. This document, and many other interesting papers for the first half of 1919, may be found at The National Archives (TNA) under the heading ADM 137/1666.
8. The minesweepers of the 'Flower' class were single-screw coal-fired ships displacing 1,200 tons. They had a maximum speed of 17 knots and carried two 4in guns. See in TNA reference ADM 137/1667.
9. One of the Arabis class; similar in size and armament to the 'Flower' class. See in TNA reference ADM 137/1667.
10. Not to be confused with the old cruiser of the same name which was expended as a blockship at Ostend following its famous role in the raid on Zebrugge. The new *Vindictive* was a heavy cruiser of the Hawkins class armed with four 7.5in guns. It had been partially converted during building as a mini aircraft carrier carrying twelve aircraft.
11. Son of the famous cricketer Dr W.G. Grace.
12. See Chapter 9.
13. The *Volk, Tigr, Tur, Vyepr* and *Pantera* were completed in 1916–17, displaced 500/840 tons and were capable of 10 knots on the surface and a claimed 9 knots submerged. They were armed with four 18in torpedo tubes, had dropping gear for eight more torpedoes and had a gun armament of two 6-pounders.
14. The Russian account of the action does not give any ranks for personnel, as was usual at the time.
15. David G. Donald joined the Royal Navy Volunteer Reserve in 1914 with the rank of probationary surgeon. He transferred to the RNAS and learnt to fly in 1915. He continued his flying career in the RAF after that service was formed on 1 April 1918 and retired in 1947 with the rank of air marshal.
16. Three boats, numbers 24, 72 and 79, carried only one torpedo, the others two each.
17. Until the 1970s only the VC (and later the GC when instituted) and Mentioned in Despatches could be awarded posthumously. In itself a Mention in Despatches was a minor award, but could sometimes hide a high degree of gallantry in which the recipient did not survive the action.

18. A Foreign Office telegram to this effect can be found in TNA under reference ADM 137/1667.
19. TNA reference ADM 137/1668.
20. The basic pay of an able seaman had been set at 1s 6d per day in 1852 and had only risen by 1d by 1912 when they were awarded a further 1d per day. Despite the high rise in prices caused by inflation during the war, naval pay was not again increased until 1917 when there was rise of 10 per cent across the board.

CHAPTER ELEVEN

1. Letter from Rodney Bennett to the author.

APPENDIX

EXTRACT OF THE TERMS OF THE ARMISTICE BETWEEN THE ALLIES AND GERMANY, 11 NOVEMBER 1918

Article XII. All German troops at present in the territories which before belonged to Austria-Hungary, Rumania, Turkey, shall withdraw immediately within the frontiers of Germany as they existed on August First, Nineteen Fourteen. All German troops at present in the territories which before the war belonged to Russia shall likewise withdraw within the frontiers of Germany, defined as above, as soon as the Allies, taking into account the internal situation of these territories, shall decide that the time for this has come.

Article XIV. German troops to cease at once all requisitions and seizures and any other undertaking with a view to obtaining supplies intended for Germany in Rumania and Russia (as defined on 1 August 1914).

Article XV. Renunciation of the treaties of Bucharest and Brest-Litovsk and of the supplementary treaties.

Article XXV. Freedom of access to and from the Baltic to be given to the naval and mercantile marines of the allied and associated powers. To secure this the Allies and the United States of America shall be empowered to occupy all German forts, fortifications, batteries, and defence works of all kinds in all the entrances from the Kattegat into the Baltic, and to sweep up all mines and obstructions within and without German territorial waters, without any question of neutrality being raised, and the positions of all such mines and obstructions are to be indicated.

Article XXVI. The existing blockade conditions set up by the allied and associated powers are to remain unchanged, and all German merchant ships found at sea are to remain liable to capture. The Allies and the United States should give consideration to the provisioning of Germany during the armistice to the extent recognised as necessary.

Article XXIX. All Black Sea ports are to be evacuated by Germany; all Russian war vessels of all descriptions seized by Germany in the Black Sea are to be handed over to the Allies and the United States of America; all neutral merchant vessels seized are to be released; all warlike and other materials of all kinds seized in those ports are to be returned and German materials as specified in Clause Twenty-eight are to be abandoned.

Article XXX. All merchant vessels in German hands belonging to the allied and associated powers are to be restored in ports to be specified by the Allies and the United States of America without reciprocity.

Article XXXIV. The duration of the armistice is to be thirty days, with option to extend. During this period if its clauses are not carried into execution the armistice may be denounced by one of the contracting parties, which must give warning forty-eight hours in advance.

BIBLIOGRAPHY

Agar, A., *Baltic Episode*, Conway Maritime Press, 1985

Arthur, M., *The True Glory, The Royal Navy 1914-1939*, Hodder & Stoughton, 1996

Ashmore, L.H., *Forgotten Flotilla*, Manuscript Press & RN Submarine Museum, 2001

Bennett, G., *Cowan's War*, Collins, 1964 (republished by Birlinn Ltd in 2002 as *Freeing the Baltic*)

Churchill, W., *The World Crisis: the Aftermath*, Thornton Butterworth, 1929

Cornish Nik, *The Russian Army and the First World War*, Spellmount, 2006

Darriens, H. and Quéguiner, J., *Historique de la Marine Française (1815-1918)*, L'Ancre de Marine, 1997

Farmborough, F., *A Nurse at the Russian Front*, Constable, 1974

Halliday, E.M., *The Ignorant Armies*, Weidenfeld and Nicolson, 1961

Hosking, G., *A History of the Soviet Union 1917-1991*, Fontana Press, 1985

Hudson, M., *Intervention in Russia 1918-1920*, Leo Cooper, 2004

Humble, R., *Fraser of North Cape*, Routledge & Kegan Paul, 1983

Kinvig, Clifford, *Churchill's Crusade*, Hambledon Continuum, 2006

Meister, J., *Soviet Warships of the Second World War*, Macdonald & Jane's, 1977

Morrow, Ann, *Cousins Divided*, Sutton Publishing, 2006

Pares, B., *The Fall of the Russian Monarchy*, Jonathan Cape, 1939 (Paperback Ed. Phoenix, 2001)

Perrett, B. and Lord, A., *The Czar's British Squadron*, William Kimber, 1981

Roskill S., *Naval Policy between the Wars, Volume I*, Collins, 1968

Summers A. and Mangold, T., *The File on the Tsar*, Victor Gollancz Ltd, 1976, updated in 2002 by Orion Books

Weeks, C.J., *An American Diplomat in Revolutionary Russia*, US Naval Institute Press, 1993

Wilson, M., *Baltic Assignment*, Leo Cooper, 1985

PUBLIC DOCUMENTS

Cmd 8, Cmd 307, Cmd 395 and Cmd 772 – Statements on expenditure on naval and military operations in Russia over various periods from 11 November 1918 to 31 March 1920.

Cmd 818 – The Evacuation of North Russia, 1919.

INDEX

Ranks given are those in use on the first occasion of mention.

Visit our website and discover thousands of other History Press books.

www.thehistorypress.co.uk